Invisible Country

Invisible Country
Four Polish Plays

Edited & Translated by Teresa Murjas

intellect Bristol, UK / Chicago, USA

First published in the UK in 2012 by
Intellect, The Mill, Parnall Road, Fishponds, Bristol, BS16 3JG, UK

First published in the USA in 2012 by
Intellect, The University of Chicago Press, 1427 E. 60th Street,
Chicago, IL 60637, USA

Performance permissions: Anyone wishing to perform any of the
plays should contact Teresa Murjas for her permission at the following
address: Department of Film, Theatre & Television, University of
Reading, Minghella Building, Shinfield Road, Reading, Berkshire,
RG6 6BT

Copyright © 2012 Intellect Ltd

All rights reserved. No part of this publication may be reproduced,
stored in a retrieval system, or transmitted, in any form or by
any means, electronic, mechanical, photocopying, recording, or
otherwise, without written permission.

A catalogue record for this book is available from the
British Library.

Series: Playtext Series
Series editor: Roberta Mock
Series ISSN: 1754-0933

Cover designer: Holly Rose
Copy-editor: MPS Technologies
Production manager: Jessica Mitchell
Typesetting: Planman Technologies

ISBN 978-1-84150-414-8

For Mike Stevenson

With special thanks to Simon Bedford-Roberts
Irena, Jola and Mała Murjas
Doug Pye

Contents

Introduction	1
Ashanti (1906)	37
In a Small House (1904)	129
Snow (1902)	187
All the Same (1912)	229

Introduction

Polish Naturalism: A duel with the self

This introduction to *Invisible Country: Four Polish Plays* is presented in five short sections. In *Section A: The Translation Project*, I explain the rationale for creating the collection and outline the research methodologies employed. *Section B: Partitioned Poland* provides an overview of the Polish historical contexts within which these plays can be read and understood, indicating further research routes for the reader. *Section C: Play Synopses* contains plot summaries of all four texts, on account of the plays' relative obscurity, and is provided in order to ground *Section D: Polish Naturalism*, which in turn offers analyses of the playwrights' various approaches to questions of theatrical form. *Section E: Biographies* contains more specific information about each playwright, and this can most usefully be read in light of preceding sections. The second part of the book contains my four play translations. These are organized in the order in which they were translated, rather than chronologically, as the plays were originally written. The rationale for this choice rests in the fact that the first play text in the collection, *Ashanti*, incorporates additional material that has evolved as a result of my practice-led research methodology, which is outlined in *Section A: The Translation Project*. My work on *Ashanti* subsequently informed my decisions about which of a broad selection of un-translated fin-de-siècle naturalistic Polish plays to include in the book. Accordingly, the book's structure reflects the evolution of that decision-making process.

Section A: The translation project

Invisible Country is the latest book to emerge as part of a long-term practice-led translation project focusing on late nineteenth-/early twentieth-century Polish naturalistic drama. The book builds on two existent volumes, *The Morality of Mrs. Dulska* (Bristol/Chicago: Intellect, 2006) and *Zapolska's Women* (Bristol/Chicago: Intellect, 2009).[1]

As editor of these two volumes, I developed and drew together new English translations of four plays by Gabriela Zapolska, who was a contemporary of Stanisław Przybyszewski, Tadeusz Rittner, Włodzimierz Perzyński and Leopold Staff. Three of the four plays had not previously existed in published translated form. Similarly, the plays I have included in *Invisible Country* do not have Anglophone translation histories. *Śnieg* (*Snow*, 1902) was translated for an early twentieth-century American audience and is printed on demand by

BiblioLife (2011) as a pre-1923 historical reproduction.[2] However, *W małym domku* (*In a Small House*, 1903),[3] *Aszantka* (*Ashanti*, 1906)[4] and *To Samo* (*All the Same*, 1912)[5] have no prior published English versions. This situation remains entirely characteristic of Polish dramatic writing of this period, largely irrespective of whether the playwrights are regarded as canonical in their original national context.

The starting point for this particular collection was a research performance that was staged using my draft translation of Perzyński's *Ashanti*, which I directed and designed in 2009–10. I was motivated to realize this work theatrically by my growing curiosity about how, comparatively, Zapolska's professional peers approached naturalism as a theatrical form and how their plays relate to arguably more familiar European counterparts, created by Ibsen, Strindberg and Chekhov. In terms of my research methodology, both the rehearsal process and performances facilitated the development of the text of *Ashanti* included in this volume, in which both that process and those performances have inevitably been encrypted. Additionally, the research questions raised through the production have informed subsequent choices about which plays to group together in this book. Essentially, I have arranged the four texts around a series of congruent themes and corresponding formal approaches.

Evidently, theatre research is based on the analysis of live performance and its histories, as well as written texts. Some aspects of theatre research are most effectively undertaken through practice. For a theatre translator, conceptualizing research within a practical framework that enables live theatrical embodiment can be an extremely useful, investigative strategy. As an empirical research method, it allows for the gathering of experiences, corporeal reflection and embodied knowledge. However, within an academic context, it can impose its own particular demands in relation to time and resources and, in my own case, needs to be used selectively. In terms of the Research Excellence Framework (REF), which is relevant specifically to lecturers and postgraduate students working in the arts and humanities in a UK academic context, practice as research is defined as a versatile methodology that can lead to stand-alone, performance-based research outputs (for example, a film, a performance, an exhibition), as long as their theoretical and critical parameters are carefully and systematically defined. Practice-as-research outputs can also be supported by – or indeed support – other kinds of outputs (for example, journal articles, books etc.). In these terms, and within the framework of my longer-term project exploring Polish Naturalism, translation can therefore productively be framed as constituting both a research outcome – or series of related outcomes (e.g. a book and/or performance) – and a research methodology (that is, an intercultural and dynamic scholarly practice). As such, it must also be inextricably combined with methodologies of textual and performance analysis, historical analysis and archival research, all of which are necessary for both the enhancement of my own understanding of relevant translational and historical contexts (particularly complex given Poland's fin-de-siècle political circumstances) and for the effective critical framing of the published texts as they are introduced to an Anglophone reader. Extensive archival research into fin-de-siècle Polish theatre – particularly with regards to performance – can be a problematic task, especially in relation to these playwrights. Materials have been destroyed and given Poland's complex and often violent history, coherent archives do not exist in each case. The notion of documenting performance has not in any case always framed the collection of material that is in existence. Importantly, it is not the purpose of this book to explore in great depth and detail a Polish performance history of the plays translated here; this would entail a lengthy, involved process for which I would require significant additional time and resources. This approach has featured more extensively in my books on Zapolska's work. Nevertheless, an *overview* of some aspects of performance history has been possible within the parameters of *Invisible Country*.

Since 2002, the practice-as-research strand of my wider research, which incorporates both translation and performance, has focused on critically analysing the under-investigated area of naturalism as a theatrical form in Polish theatre, during a period when Poland did not exist on the map of Europe: before the First World War it remained partitioned for 123 years by Russia, Prussia and Austro-Hungary. My research in this area has been driven by a number of related objectives: to formulate key research questions about performance history and context in relation to such a complex national and geographical status quo; to engage with concepts of 'liveness' in relation to theories of translation and interculturalism; to make the work of key European playwrights 'visible' in Anglophone contexts and, finally, to develop translations as scripts, for publication and, potentially, for further use.

My practical emphasis in this specific area of my work (which more broadly takes as its subject East Central European theatre and film, including Holocaust representation)[6] has been on producing and contextualizing ten new translations; nine of which have now been published, and six of which I have directed. As already mentioned, realistically, it is not always possible, given constraints on time and resources, to combine translation and performance in application to every chosen play text intended for publication. However, my documentation of the performance practice where it does occur remains integral to the critical writing that finally accompanies the published material in book form. For example, in this particular book, my reflective writing about the research production of *Ashanti* interleaves my translation of that play, and this is also complemented by illustrative images from the performances, which I have selected for their particular critical bearing on my analysis of the original Polish text. These interleaving images and words form an archive of the performance. By including them, I aim to expose some of the aesthetic and practical choices that informed the evolution of the translation, and consequently, the evolution of the collection, as well as the development of a tone, idiom and register, in which ultimately, the plays as a group have been situated. The purpose of the practice is therefore not to engage with methodologies of reconstruction; my aim is not to re-enact an 'original' performance. Rather, my research performances have a dramaturgical function; the choices I make as a director, as they develop, involve ideological, conceptual and practical negotiations, which aid the materialization of the text within a new linguistic, cultural and historical context.

Typically, the re-drafting of the translation continues prior to rehearsals, during rehearsals and long after the performances have taken place.

I have not yet staged *Snow*, *In a Small House* or *All the Same*. These translations came about in what might be regarded as a more conventional way, sometimes informed by group readings at various stages in the drafting process but – largely – achieved through focused solitary endeavour. This contrasted with my spatially dynamic, relational, collectively embodied engagement with an ensemble of actors and theatre technicians when working on the development of my English language version of *Ashanti*.[7] As a translator, these contrasting approaches have in some ways rendered the process of producing *Invisible Country* more problematic. I believe that my own perception of how the un-staged translations might function theatrically – particularly how theatrical space might be conceptualized in response to the Polish source texts – remains far less clearly defined. This is especially the case since only one translation of one of these plays exists. I regard this perception, gained empirically in the case of *Ashanti*, as significant because it can directly affect my own linguistic and stylistic choices in the target language. My attitude towards those translations that were produced without live performance having acted as a 'mediating lens' is that they have a different status to *Ashanti* – I regard them as less developed 'drafts'. This does not mean that I consider my translation of *Ashanti* to be definitive and complete. Indeed, the process of theatrical translation has a tendency to encapsulate notions of incompleteness at every level – dissatisfaction, perhaps – and discourses informing it as a cultural practice ought arguably to remain strongly focused on questions of choice, ideology and on enhancing the translator's visibility. This notion becomes particularly significant when one is involved in culturally reframing texts that were written over a century ago so that they can potentially interlock with the conditions for liveness produced and re-produced within one's own very specific socio-historical contexts. Any closure – if that is what one seeks – implied by the publication process is, for these reasons, specifically chimerical in relation to theatrical translation. As part of my subjective experience of translation, the conviction persists that the texts I produce are less stable, in an ethical sense, than the texts that they aim to encapsulate. Their semantic slipperiness appears so strong because I remember the choices I have had to make in the lead up to a publication deadline that is largely defined by the constraints of my professional working context. I have within my repertoire of translational 'attitudes' one that involves a somewhat reverential engagement with the source texts. This is tempered by another that is founded on the understanding that they too inevitably underwent a series of sometimes haphazard developmental theatrical and publication processes, particularly if the playwrights who created them wrote in more than one language and were translators themselves. Nevertheless, the fact that the texts have reached me with some form of intactness, especially their materiality as books, inspires me to perform linguistic and semantic mediations, which connect overtly to my own relationship with Polish histories and cultures. In short, in each case, the translation process reflects a deeply personal, politically motivated attempt to 'reach back in time' and engage with notions of origin. However chimerical and mutable these turn out to be, I feel that this process sometimes requires source material around which to temporarily 'coalesce'. As the bilingual daughter of post-war refugee immigrants to the UK, it constitutes for me one dynamic strand of an attempt to dialectically reinvigorate and deconstruct my sense – and understanding – of my political identity. I work imaginatively through a prism of family trauma, which has defined my personal orientation – and my family's linguistic reorientation – within a specific ('new') cultural context. In this sense, theatre's liveness offers endless regenerative possibilities. Through efforts of will and speech acts, these can perpetually replay the conceptual and literal tensions between ephemerality and embodiment, mutable and concrete material heritage. However, the pleasures of translation can sometimes, for me, be difficult to access.

Significantly, practice-as-research is an inherently phenomenological activity and provides a framework for foregrounding the pathic aspects of research – those that are situated, relational, embodied and enactive. In a project such as this, it can thus facilitate critical and experiential investigation into concepts of national culture and ethnic identity, heritage and immigration, bilingualism and self-identification, ethno-national and translational discourses, historiography, community spaces and their politics. All my research performances have taken place in Reading, where I work as a lecturer, and at the Polish Cultural Centre (POSK) in Hammersmith, London. Since 1974, this has been one centre for the UK diasporic Polish community, of which I am a member, and houses a purpose-built theatre, which operates as a charging venue and hosts a programme of local and visiting artists. Through these performances, non-academic/diasporic communities have become both the subject of my research, and one of its intended audiences.

Over the past ten years, the hoped-for effect of my research has been to enrich and engage reciprocally with this established and – post-1989 – growing UK community group, many of whose cultural and educational activities are centred on this specific London-based venue. I believe I have contributed innovatively to its cultural programme, changing behaviours in intercultural terms, by making new translations and producing performances. I have aimed to develop the community's representation in a variety of performance-based forums and in the media by, for example, publishing material about its cultural practices. I have brought the community into contact with a series of academic and student audiences, facilitating clearly definable, ongoing relationships and increasing educational opportunities for all parties. As such, for me, this practice-led translation project constitutes a direct engagement in the politics of UK multiculturalism. My understanding is that its cumulative effect has led to an enrichment of diasporic community and cultural resources/self-representation – including my own, as a member of that community. My hope is that it has resulted – through live performance and publication – in the increased visibility of a highly significant and, in certain contexts, previously inaccessible area of Polish and European cultural history, to a wider audience of both specialists and non-specialists. Importantly, late nineteenth-/early twentieth-century Polish Naturalism is a relatively unknown quantity in Anglophone translational, scholarly and theatrical contexts. Nor has it been a prime focus for theatre scholarship in Poland.

Section B: Partitioned Poland

When I lived at home, in our country, this girl fell in love with me. Know what she did, when I left? Go on, guess ... poisoned herself. Honestly.[8]

Why might someone choose to commit suicide? There are many possibilities, as evidenced by methodologically diverse research, ranging from the psychopathic to the political.[9] In addition to being shaped by the fact that they share certain formal characteristics, this collection of dramatic texts has also been established around the theme of suicide. The four plays included here are essentially naturalistic and their narrative structures involve engagement with the causes and, to a lesser extent, the effects of suicidal acts. Each playwright deploys and experiments with theatrical form in contrasting ways. However, ideologically, they all emphasize psychological and socio-political viewpoints, highlighting, in a manner characteristic of naturalistic drama of this period, intersections between heredity and environment as determinants of motivation. Indeed, it is precisely the theme of suicide that allows the playwrights to engage dialectically with these concepts. The plays share a narrative focus on gender and family relationships, played out primarily in a variety of domestic – or pseudo-domestic – settings. Also, they explore a variety of possible scenarios leading to a suicide, and express their relationship to the aforementioned contexts as integral. In each play, the domestic, private sphere is presented as a 'highly charged' and politicized environment, shaped by a variety of constraints. These constraints gradually create a pressure-cooker effect, in which personal boundaries and privacy become difficult to maintain, protect and re-establish. In addition, the precise methods of suicide that are chosen by individual characters (shooting, drowning or self-defenestration) further a debate about the politics of the act, even if that act – in terms of plotting – can be framed in performance as unexpected or even anti-climactic.

Consequently, the plays may be read historically in relation to a range of influential European predecessors of the same dramatic form, and with shared thematic preoccupations, which include the practical and philosophical problems of suicide: for example, plays by Ibsen (*The Wild Duck*, 1884; *Rosmersholm*, 1886; *Hedda Gabler*, 1890), Strindberg (*Miss Julie*, 1888) and Chekhov (*The Seagull*, 1896). Additionally, however, their naturalistic approach to representation invariably roots them firmly within a related series of Polish socio-historical contexts and environments that need to be taken into account. Within the Polish-language literary and dramatic tradition their position, as naturalistic works, has been somewhat decentred, particularly by retrospective scholarship, which has largely tended to concentrate on the analysis of theatrical symbolism and early expressionism. Indeed, these forms were frequently utilized by those Polish fin-de-siècle writers who had an interest in positivism and nationalism, and were favoured as vehicles for state-of-the-nation plays that, ideologically, both evaded and challenged state censorship – for example, Stanisław Wyspiański's *Wesele* (*The Wedding*, 1901).

Introduction

Ashanti, *Snow*, *In a Small House* and *All the Same* were created by men with divergent political interests, who were highly significant and prominent literary figures. All four earned their living fully or partly through writing – predominantly in Polish and German – though none of them wrote exclusively for the theatre. The playwrights' lives – which are explored later in this introduction – and their dramatic writing engaged with the complex political circumstances that Poles experienced in the decades leading up to the Second World War (1939–1945): the final years of over a century's partition by Russia, Austria and Prussia (1795–1918); the Great War (1914–1918); the Polish-Soviet War (1919–1921); and a period of politically fraught inter-war national independence (1918–1939).

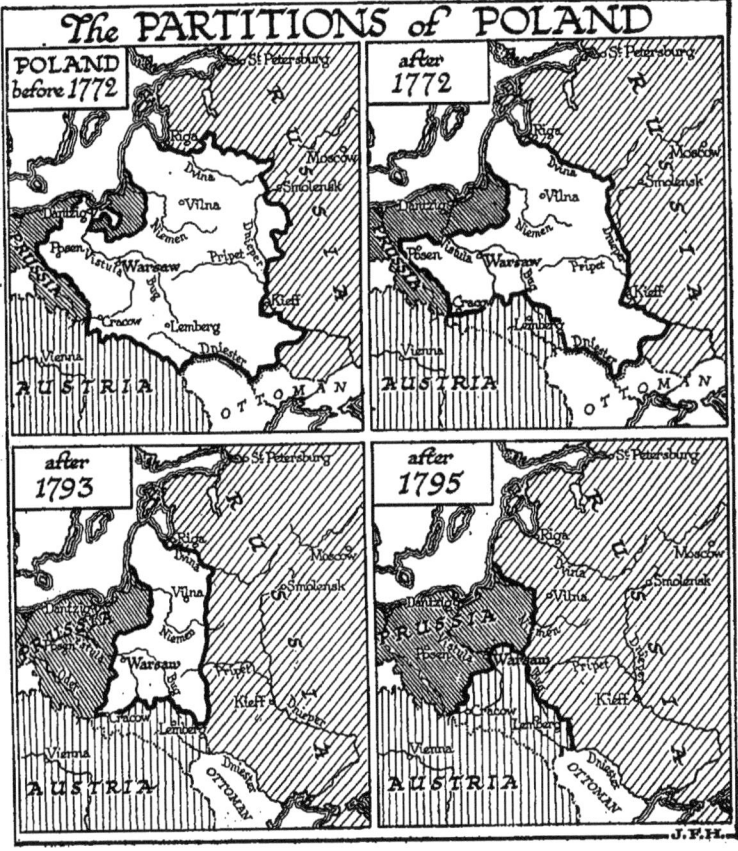

Figure 1: A map showing the partitioning of Poland between 1772 and 1795. The map shows Poland before 1772, and the three territorial annexations by Prussia, Russia, and Austria in 1772, 1793, and 1795. Source: http://outline-of-history. mindvessel.net/350-princes-parliaments-and-powers/357-crowned-republic-of-poland-and-its-fate.html.

The period encompassed by both the creation of these plays and their setting is 1902 and 1912. During this time, Poland remained uneasily divided among the empires into three separate geographically defined governmental, legislative and administrative systems. This affected the material conditions and the ways in which theatre and other forms of representation were – and could be – practised, as well as the subject matter chosen by writers and artists. This was a period of political unrest, cultural repression, mass emigration, large-scale industrialization and modernization. Poland did not exist on the map of Europe. However, as a former 'place' and nation state, with associated languages, cultural practices, evolving discourses of nationhood and organized modes of political resistance, it was indeed an 'invisible country'.

In his comparative regional history of East Central Europe, Piotr S. Wandycz underlines the challenges of writing about partitioned Poland, in a section dedicated to discussing how the Industrial Revolution functioned in different geographical contexts:

> For what was Poland in the nineteenth century? It was not an economic reality, its lands being part of the partitioning powers' economies. There was no Polish market, and the adjoining parts of the former Commonwealth were separated by customs barriers. The Congress Kingdom [in the Russian partition] had to import coal from the Donets basin rather than from the neighboring Silesia. The Poles themselves could be said to be a governing nation (to some extent) only in the autonomous Galicia. After 1864 the Kingdom was reduced to the status of an occupied province. Hence their ability to shape economic developments was severely restricted.

In a commentary that is equally applicable to the analysis of the early years of the twentieth century, Wandycz also underlines how pronounced the cultural and material differences were between the three regions. He asserts that:

> Galicia was clearly a neglected and underdeveloped province, little affected by industrialization … The building of strategic railroads by Austria stimulated the province's economy to some extent as did subsidies for agriculture and the creation of the first provincial credit bank.

However, it should be noted that any investment in infrastructure could not adequately respond to rapid demographic growth – 85 per cent in the second half of the nineteenth century – and Galician oil production 'brought profits mostly to foreign capitalists'.[10] *In a Small House* and *All the Same* reflect these conditions, both in their evocation of geographical location, and provincial and urban Galician social conventions. For example, Rittner's evocation of the Doctor's small house as situated close to the railway, at the start of the play, and his wife's constant reference to the possibilities of going on a lengthy journey or greeting new visitors compound the atmosphere of isolation and stagnation.

The role of the railroads in Polish developments was distorted by the fact of the Partitions. The railroads were built to connect Prussian Poland to Prussia and Germany, the Congress Kingdom to Russia, and Galicia, except for the strategic east-west line, to Austria. In that sense they promoted the integration of the economy of the individual Polish lands into the economic fabric of the partitioning powers. The density of the inter-Polish network was low [and] adjacent regions were frequently unconnected by rail.[11]

Focusing on the Russian partition, and restricting his analysis to the former Congress Kingdom (which, following the January Uprising of 1864, was renamed Vistula Land), Wandycz identifies this as 'the only area of the old Commonwealth that experienced the Industrial Revolution',[12] with textile production at the forefront, followed by coal. In the early 1850s the technical revolution had begun and the customs barrier with Russia was abolished, resulting in a higher demand for products and materials. This in turn impacted on the scale of investment in steam transport infrastructure, as well as the scale of the urban population, which doubled between 1879 and 1910. Consequently, the growth of factories also increased (particularly in Łódź, often referred to as the Polish Manchester), as did the size of the labour force. These conditions are reflected and critiqued in *Ashanti*, which is partly set in Warsaw. Industrial development combined with political disempowerment is shown by Perzyński as producing a profoundly socially and psychologically destabilizing effect, realigning class hierarchies and exacerbating poverty.

In the Prussian partition, often referred to as taking a more Westernized developmental route, the technical modernization of agriculture and light industries was most in evidence and was reliant on 'local credit, cooperatives and self-aid associations'.[13] Poles had to compete with local Germans, whose capital was greater and who were backed by the state. As a result of these factors, this area of the former Commonwealth saw the largest growth of a Polish middle class. None of the plays in this collection is set definitively within the Prussian partition. Przybyszewski's *Snow* has not yet been mentioned in this section and this is partly because the fact of its indefinite setting – compounded by the blizzard of the title – is essential to the play's thematic and narrative structures; the notions of invisibility and obfuscation are central. However, a reading of this play as dealing overtly with the notion of a defunct, politically disempowered and dysfunctional Polish aristocracy, vampiric and torn ideologically between dreams of revolution and imperialist conquest, is entirely possible.

A key date in late nineteenth- and early twentieth-century Polish history is 1863 – the date of the failed January Uprising, which began a period of increased repression by the partitioning powers. In addition, the so-called Polish Question, relating to national independence, gradually faded from political discourses at the international level. The result was an 'internal' ideological crisis concerning the possibility of revolution, a crisis that bore within it political viewpoints espousing compromise with the partitioning powers, expressed particularly in ostensibly conservative Galicia. In reading the plays in this collection, it is crucial to bear in mind the extent of the frequently violent repressive measures exercised by the occupying powers on a mass scale, particularly in Russian and Prussian Poland, which aimed at no less than the Russification and Germanization of the Polish population, including the elimination of the Polish language. In addition, the Polish gentry, for example, were prevented from following career paths in politics or administration, which further problematized the prospect of national self-determination. Broadly speaking, these repressive measures might now be regarded as unsuccessful, in that they came to contribute directly to the development of political and national movements that enabled the breakdown of the partition-based stranglehold. Indeed, the first decade of the twentieth century – which the plays included in this collection encompass – was one of radical political mobilization and consciousness raising in East Central Europe, and it saw the demise of 123 years of that particular form of imperialist domination. It was a period when social and national change appeared increasingly possible to those both on the socialist left and on the national democratic right, and the concept of a border-defying, unified Polish culture strengthened following the 1905 Revolution in the Russian Empire. This idea of a unified Polish culture was ideologically appropriated in different forms, some of which – like right-wing Roman Dmowski's – were exclusive and tended to define 'otherness' along ethnic lines, espousing opposition against non-Polish nationalities, with a strongly anti-Semitic inflection. Along with other political ideologues – including Józef Piłsudski and Rosa Luxemburg on the left – Dmowski was preoccupied with the question of what shape his currently invisible country would take, once partition borders were dissolved.

> Although the partition borders had deepened division among Poles and even affected their mentality, Polish culture continued to be the surest and strongest national link.[14]

As a medium for cultural expression, theatre became an important centre for engaging debates around the themes of national identity and sociopolitical change. In his book on the history of Polish theatre, Kazimierz Braun traces the influence of the fin-de-siècle Great Reform of Theatre on dramatic and theatrical practice, as directors, playwrights and actors in all the major cities – in Galicia initially, where there were greater freedoms of expression, and then in Russian Poland – responded to the ideas of Edward Gordon Craig, Adolphe Appia, André Antoine, Max Reinhardt and Konstantin Stanislavsky.[15] The playwrights whose work features in *Invisible Country* might all be considered responsive to the Reform. Any analysis of Polish theatre practice of this period, however, must also take into account questions of censorship and how this operated within each partition – particularly given the fact that in the Russian partition, for example, the theatre was for a significant period of time the only forum where the Polish language could be publicly spoken. Much work remains to be done by contemporary scholars of this period on the operation of theatre censorship in partitioned Poland – it is no easy task to gather relevant material together and the scope of the project is great. Braun devotes much of his section on early twentieth-century theatre to the work of Stanisław Wyspiański, the highly significant, groundbreaking Galician writer and artist, who practised predominantly in Kraków.[16] However, there is still little focused scholarship on how censorship functioned in relation to naturalism specifically – indeed, this situation is in itself partly a legacy of the complexities (often highly bureaucratic and operating at the level of written text, rehearsal and live performance) of evolving and often highly repressive systems of censorship put in place by the partitioning powers.

Section C: Play synopses

Śnieg (*Snow*, 1902) by Stanisław Przybyszewski

A sensitive young woman, married to a landowner who once had military aspirations, struggles to understand the origins of her fear of abandonment. This has been triggered by her wealthy husband's obsession with their extremely rich female friend, whom she also desires. In the depths of a blinding winter blizzard, on a country estate, their triangular relationship is complicated by the presence of her husband's brother, whose love for her is entirely dependent on her lack of reciprocity. As these relationships evolve, the young woman is compelled to bravely confront her early traumatic experiences. She gradually becomes fully conscious of the fact that, during their childhood, her sister drowned herself on a seemingly ordinary day in their father's mere. This process of remembering is facilitated by the arrival of the young woman's aged former nursemaid, who brought her up. As her confused, over-powered husband and vampiric former school friend draw closer together, she orders that the mere on her country estate be cleared of snow and ice-holes be cut for carp fishing. She then proposes a double suicide by drowning, to her compliant brother-in-law, who cheerfully accepts her offer.

W Małym Domku (*In a Small House*, 1903) by Tadeusz Rittner

An aspiring young doctor studying in Kraków gets his landlady's daughter pregnant. They marry – reportedly, this is not regarded as the essential outcome for a man in his predicament – and he sets up a private practice in a small provincial town to run alongside his surgical work at the local hospital. The town is located very close to a railway line, which is visible from his house. There, to his extreme, poorly concealed delight – as expressed by his perceptive sister, also his ward – he becomes mayor. Shortly after his victory, his neglected wife betrays him with an apparently experienced cad – an engineer overseeing a local bridge-building project – to whom the doctor has offered to rent a room. This dashing 'European' pays her far more attention – and compliments – than her husband. Following a disastrous soirée at which local luminaries – including a judge and his wife – are present, the doctor shoots his wife dead. To the surprise of the politically idealistic local schoolteacher, who is in love with the doctor's sister, he is subsequently acquitted by the local court. Upon returning from a prolonged trip, he fails to re-integrate into the local community and blows his brains

Figure 2: Celina Niedźwiecka as Bronka in a scene from a production of *Snow* by Stanisław Przybyszewski. This was staged in December 1927 at the Juliusz Słowacki Theatre in Kraków. Copyright: Narodowe Archiwum Cyfrowe.

Figure 3: A scene from the March 1938 production of Tadeusz Rittner's *In a Small House*, staged at the Juliusz Słowacki Theatre in Kraków. From the left, seated: Zygmunt Modzelewski as the Engineer; Romana Pawłowska as Maria, the Doctor's Wife; Janina Wernicz as the Judge's Wife; Kazimierz Szubert as the Pharmacist's Assistant; Józef Karbowski as the Doctor; Maria Bednarska as Wanda. Copyright: Narodowe Archiwum Cyfrowe.

out, potentially dashing any hope that his two children, his sister and the enamoured schoolteacher have for a 'happy life'.

Aszantka (*Ashanti, 1906*) by Włodzimierz Perzyński

A rich young landowner 'keeps' a poor young woman in Warsaw, 'procured' for him by his closest friend, an older man who knows the city and its underbelly very well. The 'couple' moves to Florence in order to avoid offending the landowner's disapproving family, including his rather moralistic and pompous – though ultimately practically minded – uncle. There, the woman betrays him with a well-travelled hotel waiter, who has fled Poland in order to avoid conscription and will never be able to return to his country. When the landowner learns of the affair, he takes out his gun and shoots in the woman's direction. Luckily for her, he misfires. The relationship, however, dies a death, and they return to Warsaw, where she becomes a high-class prostitute and is courted as a potential mistress by a wealthy factory owner. Unable to come to terms with the course events have taken, and having squandered his own fortune, the formerly rich young landowner reportedly blows out his brains and is taken to hospital, where the prognosis is death. He does so having recently tried to borrow money from his former lover and having failed to seduce her professional female associate.

Figure 4: A scene from the 2009/2010 production of *Ashanti*, which I staged at the University of Reading and POSK Theatre, London. Magdalena Kwiatkowska as Władka. Copyright: Matt Ager.

Introduction

***To Samo (All the Same, 1912)* by Leopold Staff**

An elderly man who has come down in the world ekes out a meagre existence through forgery and gambling in Polish Galicia. He lives with his wife, who has withdrawn from society and enjoys a good grumble, a poor young man inducted into his line of work, who could well be his son by another woman, and his young daughter, who offers private English tuition all over town. One of her pupils, a rich young landowner, falls in love with her, but his inability to obtain a divorce from his estranged wife prevents them from marrying. Her self-confident father, deducing the man's affection, engages in a cheque-based financial transaction with him, in which he appears to sell him his daughter, apparently partly motivated by a desire to return to his former way of life. He does so without knowing that the couple have already begun an affair, and this blurs the terms and discourse around the transaction. When the paper trail resulting from it is uncovered by the daughter, she suggests that prostitution might be a more fitting profession for her. She leaves the room with the apparent intention of going out into the street, and throws herself out of the tenement hallway window.

Section D: Polish naturalism

Two gunshots – rather excessive, perhaps, for one play.

Thus writes the literary scholar Artur Hutnikiewicz in his assessment of Tadeusz Rittner's drama *In a Small House* (1903), one of the plays included in this collection of translations from the Polish.[17] Hutnikiewicz is not entirely accurate. In fact, there are three gunshots in the play. With the first two gunshots, a Doctor kills his wife (onstage) and with the third, later on in the play, himself (offstage). It seems, however, that Hutnikiewicz collates the two first gunshots and refers in his comments to the suicide as the second gunshot.

Hutnikiewicz's comments are incorporated in his comprehensive monographic survey of the fin-de-siècle modernist literary and artistic Young Poland movement. In exploring Rittner's approach to realism, as part of a vast biographically structured overview of work by a range of practitioners, he touches only very briefly, with an emphasis on plot summary, on two important points. Firstly, he alludes in the somewhat wry statement translated and quoted above to the formal interplay between naturalism and melodrama in this particular play text, which, he appears to imply, sometimes borders on *grande guignol*. By this, he implies a question about whether it is dramatically necessary to thus underline the Doctor's suicide. Secondly, he comments on the fact that Rittner's fundamentally naturalistic characterization – achieved through his local, colloquial dialogue and realistic approach to establishing and developing dramatic situation – has the potential to render the play 'strongly engaging' in live performance.

Figure 5: Józef Karbowski as the Doctor in the March 1938 production of Tadeusz Rittner's *In a Small House*. This was staged at the Juliusz Słowacki Theatre in Kraków. Copyright: Narodowe Archiwum Cyfrowe.

Hutnikiewicz directly connects this second point with the high level of textual detail offered to actors for effective role development and the dramatic productiveness of its progressive narrative build-up. The detail is couched in a dynamic interplay between dialogue, which drives the plot, and stage directions, which facilitate the visualization of live performance and spatial configuration. This interplay arguably results in a structural clarity that proposes definable through-lines of theatrical action and apparently logical strands of dramatic interpretation. This would be particularly useful for actors taking a systematic Stanislavskian approach to developing their performance. Indeed, Hutnikiewicz suggests that the potential theatrical effectiveness of Rittner's play specifically relates to the playwright's interest in the concept of individual character psychology – an interest shared by many contemporary European Naturalist playwrights and also theatre directors such as Konstantin Stanislavski and André Antoine, who were involved in exploring methods for staging their work.

Additionally, however, whilst emphasizing Rittner's realist theatrical strategies, Hutnikiewicz indirectly and accurately acknowledges, through his descriptions, the playwright's reliance – to the point of formal tension described above – on melodramatic stock character types (e.g. 'that pathetic, tuppence-ha'penny Don Juan'). He also alludes to the location of these vividly drawn characters on a behavioural spectrum that is inclusive of extreme mental states, intense emotional responses and psycho-pathology, leading one to question what kind of performance style might be best suited to – and was originally deployed for – the play's live realization.

Against this backdrop, Hutnikiewicz appears to argue that Rittner lacks the kind of writerly restraint that allows an audience room for speculative narrative intervention and comes close to saying that the 'second' gunshot in the play – arguably motivated by trauma – amounts to a dramatic over-exposition of motivation that has already been sufficiently revealed through the dialogue. To the viewer, the Doctor's suicide is likely to be read in the context of the contrasting perspectives offered throughout the play, by its full range of characters. These encompass a range of interconnected subjects, including idealistic notions of social justice, social mores and behavioural conventions, as well as the mechanisms of the current official legal system. From the actor's perspective, a key focal point for expressing the Doctor's motivation prior to his final exit into the offstage room where he takes his own life must surely be his emotionally and politically charged conversation with the Judge. This focuses on the nature of his own punishment following the murder of his wife – arguably a 'crime of passion' provoked by her infidelity, but also framed by the Doctor's apparent inability to fulfill his professional ambitions, on account of family responsibilities. Here, the Judge's 'smoke and mirrors' deployment of subtext as an implicational mode of persuasion reaches a highly performative level. The Doctor's words regarding the fact that he feels insufficiently chastised by the mechanisms of the local legal system and the Judge's ambiguous – though, on the face of it, logical – comments about taking justice into one's own hands should be considered particularly significant in this regard. Systemic corruption within the Galician legal system is implied – the Doctor sees that he now 'belongs' to the Judge – as does the rest of the town – in ways that he may not have fully anticipated. He sees that he will neither be forgiven, nor get away with murder even though the official sentence implied a kind of absolution.

One might indeed argue that Hutnikiewicz's pre-emptive assessment of the potential effect of the aural presence of the 'second' gunshot, emanating from a room offstage, is by no means a foregone conclusion, given that *In a Small House* is a text written for the purpose of live performance and therefore, by its nature, is subject to theatrical interpretations that will always be essentially dependent on a complex range of material contexts, ideologies and conventions. Indeed, the 'second' (in fact, third) gunshot may be constructed in performance as both expected and intentionally banal, in order to engage a rather nihilistic philosophical tone: the Doctor must be heard acting as his own executioner in order for Rittner's political conundrum and social critique of the sinister implications of Polish Galician parochialism to be fully expressed. Indeed, the Galicia of that period might be regarded as the only partition in which the Poles were involved in any form of self-government, however limited this was in its scope and possibilities. Additionally, Sielski, the teacher, and the Doctor's sister, Wanda, who have just proclaimed their love for each other, must arguably be seen witnessing the aftermath of his act – a potentially cathartic moment for the spectator, given the Doctor's bitter control over his family – in the space where the Doctor murdered his wife. This allows an inflection of the action that suggests the Doctor's continued, somewhat pathological, exertion of control over his sister, as well as posing an ethical challenge to Sielski, who loves her, and whose left-wing political idealism has always been beneath the Doctor's contempt.

Both in spite and because of their (by necessity) generalized quality, Hutnikiewicz's comments can be applied to some degree to all the modernist play texts included in this collection. As a starting point, all four focus on representing 'everyday' behaviours and environments – expressed and reflected in colloquial dialogue, with stylistic variations – and they are set predominantly within domestic spaces that are rooted more or less precisely within a defined time period and geographical place. Przybyszewski's *Snow* is the least clearly located in this sense, for thematic reasons, though its evocation of class relationships and treatment of characterization and language produces a particular type of naturalistic locational and spatial anchorage. *In a Small House* and *Ashanti* provide the most unequivocal indicators of geographical and local detail. *All the Same* creates a sense of spatial and class-based ideological orientation through its binary opposition – within the narrative rather than the setting – of urban and rural environments, implied in Stefan's journey from his country estate to the tenement block in town. In addition, however, all four texts propose the idea that, within the domestic – or pseudo-domestic – spaces represented, 'naturalized' familial and gender interactions will eventually, in one guise or another, yield up the uncanny; this is frequently signaled through language, which is more imagistic and rhythmic in tone and formal in its register. The plays share a tendency to explore the concept of cognitive dissonance (associated with psychoanalytic theories of the uncanny) as part of their causally structured approach to character development. In each case, this results in the clear prioritization of subtext as a key strategy for dramatically encapsulating and engaging the notion of complex yet linearly readable psychological motivation.

However, the varying approach to subtext within these plays also accounts for significant contrasts in the formal 'territories' within which they can be read, including – particularly with Przybyszewski's *Snow* (1902) – a type of proto-expressionism. A similar approach is identifiable in August Strindberg's early twentieth-century dramas – which the Anglophone reader may recognize more readily on account of their relatively frequent performance and re-translation – for example, *Easter* (1901). In these plays, characters initially established according to the conventions of naturalistic dramatic practice gradually attain a more symbolic function. This occurs as their subjective perception of and relationship to their environment – and each other – is shown to alter in response to relational and social stress factors within the narrative. Makryna, the old nursemaid in *Snow*, can be read as having such a function, specifically in relation to Bronka's state of consciousness, as can Szymon, the railwayman in *In a Small House*. Theatrically, this may potentially result in significant shifts in how the stage environment, the spatial boundaries of a represented place and its related or defining objects – in the form of stage properties – operate. Accordingly, this is likely to affect the audience's reading, in any given production, of these elements' thematic and visual significance, given the initially established contrasting illusionistic approach. An emphasis on the dramatic representation of subjective experience or a plot-defining irreconcilable clash of subjective viewpoints leading to a crisis in which material and emotional determinants intertwine – as in Leopold Staff's *All the Same* (1912) – is in fact a key structural aspect of each of the texts in this collection.

In addition, the destabilization of the realism of domestic locations themselves is in each case achieved via a somewhat palimpsestic approach to their dramatic and consequently potential live theatrical signification. Importantly, each set of stage directions implies performance on a proscenium arch stage. In Przybyszewski's *Snow* the fashionably furnished room is an almost identical replica of another in a different house that is not represented in the play, but is described, hinting at a character's previous relationship and its codependent nature. In Rittner's *In a Small House* the room on stage has a number of competing domestic and professional functions, which are alluded to by its physical arrangement and the placement of various significant objects within the space. In Perzyński's *Ashanti* the initial setting of a well-to-do bachelor apartment in Warsaw, 'Poland', is gradually deconstructed; the action shifts away from that place (relatively atypical in terms of naturalistic theatre practice), is viewed from a different national vantage point – Florence – then returns again to an obverse though related space. This happens to be a conventionally feminized apartment inhabited only by women, which echoes the initial bachelor setting but belongs to his former lover, a high-class prostitute who, financially and emotionally, now has the upper hand. In addition, this spatial destabilization is prefigured and reinforced by the doomed imperialist fantasy played out by the aristocratic male characters Loński and Kręcki. This is also reminiscent of the thematic framework in which Tadek and Ewa conduct their sexually charged negotiations in Przybyszewski's *Snow*: indeed, Tadek speaks about travelling to Africa and hunting tigers. As politically impotent, 'colonized' Polish men themselves, living in the repressive Russian partition yet still adhering to old class conventions and relying on old money, Loński and Kręcki are shown by the playwright at the start of *Ashanti* as literally and imaginatively colonizing Władka's body and identity through a process of sexual engagement, barter and dispossessive renaming. This is expressed through a meta-discourse employed by Loński, which he articulates in the narrative style of an oral fairytale. He uses this fairytale to facilitate and justify his initial interactions with Władka, which are shown as the 'breaking-in' and procurement of a prostitute-cum-mistress, who is arguably compliant in the process through a complex set of motivations, including economic necessity, sexual naïveté, attraction to Loński and fear of Kręcki. The latter, it seems, has found her in the street, possibly during her first attempt at soliciting. Loński chooses to romanticize his sexual bargaining with Władka, which is overseen by Kręcki, by relating to her a tale of the apparently willing subjection of an African woman of the Ashanti tribe to a so-called white man, who comes to take her into captivity. He overlays this narrative with Cinderella-derived motifs in order to both sweeten and obfuscate her transition into sexual slavery. The extent, to which either character consciously engages with the implications of this tale, or its subtext, is to be decided by the director of the play. However, this process of displacement of the men's intertwined sociopolitical and psycho-sexual frustrations onto an apparently vulnerable – though not necessarily ignorant – woman is expressed by the playwright through the dialogue in their racist 'colouring' and 'othering' of the economically impoverished Władka as 'dark', both on the basis of her lower class and dirty appearance.

WŁADKA:	And then?
ŁOŃSKI:	Then? A white man comes and takes the Ashanti girl into captivity.
WŁADKA:	I wouldn't let him.
ŁOŃSKI:	Suppose you liked him?
WŁADKA:	If I liked him … What do you do in captivity?
ŁOŃSKI:	Listen carefully. Once upon a time, there was an Ashanti girl, just like you, who lived on the banks of the Vistula River. She worked at the factory. Every day she got out of bed and rushed to the other side of town in the rain, the mud or the snow, just to sew, sew and sew. Until her poor head ached.
WŁADKA:	Just like me … But I don't work at the factory any more. (*ŁOŃSKI laughs*) Alright, what happened next …?
ŁOŃSKI:	A white man came and captured her. He shipped her out to a country where no rain falls. There is no mud, or snow; it's always warm, the sun shines, like here in June or July. And there the Ashanti girl lived with him in a little marble palace, with a scented garden and she had lots of lovely frocks, pearls and gems, and many servants, and she did nothing for days on end, but play, and laugh and dance …

Perzyński shows Łoński conflating locations within his story, and consciously or unconsciously engaging in reflection on imperialism. The banks of the Vistula River and the Gold Coast seem to become one 'place'. Given their extremes of climate – probably a familiar fact to both readers and spectators – the conflation is an extremely uneasy one, at least in literal terms, if not conceptually. As a result, when Łoński begins to speak of shipping Władka away to a hot country, the resultant effect is arguably her symbolic relocation to the Gold Coast and therefore – by implication – back in Warsaw, because they are 'the same'! Metaphorically, no-one moves. This 'semantic overload' has a disorientating effect which, in performance, can be usefully deployed as part of Łoński's method of persuasion. In narrative terms, Łoński may actually, of course, be thinking of Italy, where he does later take Władka. Importantly, the variety of locations discussed by characters in the play – including Egypt and France – provides a sustained engagement with concepts of identity, displacement, belonging and the ability to 'escape'.

Introduction

In addition, in the scene from which the above quotation is taken, Władka is shown dancing to the cakewalk, accompanied on the piano by Kręcki. The men's verbal projection, on to these actions and on to her appearance, of ideas about her wildness and savagery (in other words, her potential for sexual voracity), arguably allows them to vent their own sense of political dispossession. This dispossession is expressed as acute in spite of their wealth and social status, and it frames and drives their power-relationship up until the point when Władka chooses to engage in negotiations of a sexual nature with the Director of a Warsaw factory. This follows Łoński's failed attempt to shoot her in Florence, after she admits to having had an affair with Franek, a Polish hotel waiter. The Director is representative of a rising class with new money, the implication being that he is compliant with fiscal and ideological systems imposed by the Russian imperial occupier, who would in reality have been driving the development of trade and industry during this period in that part of East Central Europe, when the industrial revolution in that area was reaching its peak. At this point in the play, Władka is notorious in Warsaw – practically a legend – and says that she is more or less universally addressed as Ashanti, even by schoolboys in the street. Perzyński's deployment of this colonialist meta-narrative furthers the geopolitical debates of the play and, in addition, intensifies his palimpsestic approach to spatial definition, in both material theatrical and symbolic terms. Indeed, Władka's appropriation of the name Łoński gave her – Ashanti – which parallels her increasingly business-like approach to sexual relationships, signals his demise, the breakdown of his relationship with Kręcki, and his apparent suicide. Indeed, one might also relate Perzyński's approach in this regard to Staff's evocation of space in *All the Same*, since in this play the tiny tenement living room rented by a family that has 'come down in the world' is ghosted by memories of spaces associated with their previously affluent way of life. Additionally, the window in the downstage room is echoed visually by another located in the upstage hallway, which is visible only when an exit door is ajar.

In each of the four plays, windows constitute important theatrical signs – as walls of glass, interfaces, pervious boundaries and sites of communication. They are used to highlight themes of constraint and memory; reflection and perspicacity; travel and nostalgia; distance and longing; presence and absence; voyeurism and vulnerability; visibility and invisibility. Characters are frequently depicted opening and closing them, lingering close to them, looking through them. They provide the playwrights with a means of creating partitions between interior and exterior spaces that can simultaneously encapsulate a range of symbolic functions. Any gaze through a window – inquisitive or otherwise – is framed theatrically by it. The foregrounding of acts of looking and perception through the incorporation of windows into the plays' architecture has a reflexive function that tests the parameters of illusionism, facilitating an exploration of shifting relations between inside and out, public and private. Thus, the bodies on stage can simultaneously be expressed as located within their physical environment and in a state of disjunction from it. When the two windows in *All the Same* are flung open in quick succession at the end of the play, it seems inevitable that a self-defenestration will ensue. Julja (*pron.* Yoo-lya), the daughter of the household, unable to

Figure 6: Władysław Krasnowiecki as Kazimierz (Kazio) in a scene from a production of *Snow* by Stanisław Przybyszewski. This was staged in December 1927 at the Juliusz Słowacki Theatre in Kraków. Copyright: Narodowe Archiwum Cyfrowe.

contain her rage at the level of domestic control exerted upon her by the men in her life, which, she believes, has practically rendered her a prostitute, seeks to regain that control through the act of suicide. That act can be read as a bold assertion of independence, an ironic comment on 'going onto the street', and a tragic turning in on herself of the incapacitating limitations of her environment. The audience watches her through the 'fourth wall' characteristic of naturalism (given the staging conventions implied) and, in leaping, she removes herself from their gaze. Like Rittner's third gunshot, Perzyński's second gunshot and Przybyszewski's double suicide by drowning, Staff's self-defenestration indicates, and then underlines, microcosmically, the notion of Polish society in crisis and increasingly unable to resist the impulse to attempt a breach of partition. However, for all these playwrights, the notion of a breach of boundary or partition, on a number of semantic levels, is primarily conceptualized in fatalistic terms. No strong sense of a 'destination' is evoked. Indeed, the notion of destination remains problematic and frustratingly chimerical – rather like the notion of an 'invisible country'.

Section E: Biographies

Stanisław Przybyszewski (1868–1927)

Snow (1902)

Przybyszewski's plays are rarely encountered in the twenty-first-century Polish theatrical repertoire, though a particularly noteworthy production of his political, Nietzschean drama, Matka (The Mother) was staged in 1979 by the internationally significant Polish director Krystian Lupa. During the decade prior to Lupa's production, Przybyszewski's plays were frequently performed, specifically in relation to the fiftieth anniversary of his death and in association with two international conferences that took place in Poland, focusing on his oeuvre. Nevertheless, Przybyszewski's influence on the development of Polish and European theatre is clearly evident and he has been regarded in his own country as an important conduit for, and interpreter of, modernist theories and practices.

Stanisław Przybyszewski was born in Łojewo, in the Prussian partition. He was a key figure in the modernist Young Poland movement, and had a reputation in Europe as a writer of influence and provocation, who challenged sexual and social mores and taboos. He wrote in both Polish and German, worked as a translator and his prose work was itself translated into numerous languages, including English and Yiddish. His psychologically based analyses of Nietzsche, Chopin and Ola Hansson were particularly influential texts.

Przybyszewski's career as a writer ranged widely; he was a journalist, poet, prose and manifesto writer and playwright. Additionally, throughout his life he was closely involved in politics. In 1889 he moved to Berlin to study architecture and medicine. From 1892 he edited the *Gazeta Robotnicza* (*Workers Newspaper*), which was the official organ of the

Figure 7: A portrait photo of Stanisław Przybyszewski. Date unknown. Copyright: Narodowe Archiwum Cyfrowe.

Polish socialist party in Berlin. There, he also frequented *Zum schwarzen Ferkel*, a tavern patronized by many contemporary modernist writers. His association with the artist Edvard Munch, who painted his portrait, and the playwright August Strindberg (both of whom are associated with expressionistic forms of artistic practice) has been well documented, as has been his marriage to the Norwegian writer Dagny Juel (who also had romantic relationships with Munch and Strindberg). Przybyszewski's interest in Satanism, occultism and socialist politics was also shared in particular by Strindberg. In theatrical terms, the fact that Przybyszewski edited a number of key journals throughout his career, including *Życie* (*Life*), is significant, as his position enabled him to disseminate his views on contemporary theatrical practice.

Przybyszewski's plays include *Złote Runo* (*The Golden Fleece*, 1901); *Śnieg* (*Snow*, 1903); *Matka* (*Mother*, 1903); *Śluby* (*Vows*, 1906); *Topiel* (*Deep Water*, 1912) and *Miasto* (*The Town*, 1914). The early staging of his dramas, including *Snow*, is associated with the Russian practitioner Vsevolod Meyerhold, who, having left the Moscow Art Theatre, set up his own company with Alexander Koscheverov ('Comrades of the New Drama') and experimented with work by the Symbolist writer Maurice Maeterlinck and with Przybyszewski's particular – though related – brand of psychological naturalism. Meyerhold directed three of Przybyszewski's plays between 1902 and 1906, including *Snow*. The realization of Przybyszewski's most significant roles in Russia is credited to the prominent Russian actress Vera F. Komissarzhevskaia, who produced his plays on four occasions in the early 1900s. Meyerhold also later based a film – no longer in existence – on Przybyszewski's novel *Mocny Człowiek* (*The Strong Man*, 1929).

Przybyszewski was well-travelled and lived in numerous locations, including Norway. However, during the inter-war period he returned to Poland, where he took up a number of key administrative positions in local government, particularly in Poznań and Gdańsk, and became strongly associated with Polish nationalism and the cause of the new Polish state. His complex and tragic personal life, including his relationship with drugs and alcohol, has always been of interest to biographers, particularly given the fact that he was the father of the communist playwright Stanisława Przybyszewska. Przybyszewska wrote the key play *Sprawa Dantona* (*The Danton Affair*, 1929), on which Andrzej Wajda based his 1983 film *Danton*, and throughout her short life devoted herself exclusively to dramatizing the French Revolution. Her obsessive relationship with her father, whom she met only in her late teens, following the death of her mother, has been the subject of biographical analysis.

One of the most fascinating aspects of translating *Snow* into English has been trying to capture the intersection of psychological motivation and theatrical symbolism expressed through Przybyszewski's dialogue and approach to characterization. The main focus of the play is clearly the way in which Bronka's childhood trauma affects her behaviour as an adult. As such, Przybyszewski's dialogue-driven proto-expressionist text deploys psychoanalytic tropes in order to develop ideas around 'interiority' or 'inner life'. Significantly, these are placed in particular tension with his use of the word 'dusza' or 'soul', which has religious connotations. However, Przybyszewski's theories on the 'naked soul' – a primarily artistic inner essence existing outside and beyond convention – are not specifically religious, although they do engage with religious discourses in a manner that is not uncommon in fin-de-siècle dramatic literature. Deciding on how to situate these concepts within an Anglophone context has been of primary concern and my decision to translate the word 'dusza' in a variety of ways – almost always deviating from the literal – has been reached with some difficulty. This has particularly been the case because my chosen terms of reference frame Bronka and Kazio's suicide pact both linguistically and conceptually and, as such, inflect my interpretation of its psychological and political significance.

Tadeusz Rittner (1873–1921)

In a Small House (1903)

The full range of Rittner's plays still features within the contemporary Polish repertoire, to a greater extent than Przybyszewski's. The formal correspondences of Rittner's plays with those of his contemporary Gabriela Zapolska – which are frequently revived – arguably create a point of interest and comparison for theatre goers. Stanisław Ignacy Witkiewicz parodied W małym domku (In a Small House) *in his anti-realist play of 1921* W małym dworku, *the title of which has been translated by Daniel Gerould as* Country House. *Gerould describes Witkiewicz's play as a 'wicked subversion of all those realistic psychological dramas of jealousy, adultery, murder and suicide that ask to be taken seriously'.*[18] W małym domku (In a Small House) *was also directed for Polish television by Andrzej Łapicki in 1992.*

Tadeusz Rittner was born in Lviv (then Galician Lemberg, or Polish Lwów). He was, through his grandparents, of German extraction. From the age of eleven, he lived and was educated in Vienna. He was bilingual and wrote plays in Polish, which was his first language, and in German. After the First World War, during the onset of Polish independence, he chose to have Polish citizenship, though he spent most of his short life, suffering chronic ill health, in Vienna. He often used the pseudonym Tomasz Czaszka, literally 'Thomas the Skull'. Rittner was involved in the theatre profession in a number of guises; he worked as a critic and theoretician, as well as a playwright and translator. He was also a successful prose writer, producing novels in both languages, and a journalist.

Writing was not, however, Rittner's sole profession. Interestingly, his father had held a number of nationally significant positions within Galicia. This included being a high-ranking government official, professor of church law and rector of the University of Lwów. Rittner himself read law and similarly took up a position as government administrator, attaining a high level of seniority.

Rittner's most significant works for the theatre are *W małym domku* (In a Small House), which premiered in Poland in 1904 and in Germany in 1908; *Głupi Jakub* (Foolish Jacob),

Figure 8: A portrait photo of Tadeusz Rittner. Date unknown. Copyright: Picture Archives and Graphics Department of the Austrian National Library. Copyright: ÖNB/Wien, 204.229-D.

whose Polish premiere was in 1910, and the German, in a slightly different version, in 1910; *Don Juan,* which premiered in Germany in 1909 and in Poland in 1913; *Lato* (*Summer*), whose Polish and German premieres were in 1913; *Człowiek z budki suflera* (*The Man from the Prompter's Box*), which premiered in Poland and Germany in 1913; *Wilki w nocy* (*Wolves in the Night*), Polish and German premieres in 1916; and *Dzieci ziemi* (*Children of the Earth*), with the German premiere in 1915, and the Polish in 1922.

Rittner's dramas, many of which focus on Galician domestic life and are influenced by the work of Anton Chekhov, Frank Wedekind and Hugo Hofmannsthal, were frequently staged in Poland, particularly during the inter-war period, and were extremely popular in Germany and Austria prior to the First World War. They were staged in important main houses in capital cities, such as the Burgtheater and Deutsches Volkstheater in Vienna. For a short while he ran his own theatre in Vienna, where he produced, among other performances, Shakespeare's *Hamlet*, with a woman in the lead role, and comedies by the Polish naturalist playwright Gabriela Zapolska.

Most notably, his play *In a Small House* is titled 'a comedy'. This is particularly significant given the fact that, in 1911, Rittner outlined his theatrical manifesto in an article titled 'Comedy'. In it he concluded that tragedy as a theatrical form had no place within contemporary society and attributed this to shifts in understanding and convention associated with varied new perspectives on social behaviour, opened up by the development of the psychological sciences. This information is of significance to a twenty-first-century translator of Rittner's work, particularly in terms of locating tone. The challenge here is in capturing the comedic aspects of characterization and stage business in the translated dialogue. At the same time, it is important, through the process of linguistic transference, to provide actors with sufficiently robust character-related and culturally recognizable psychological material for them to be able to fully stress Rittner's ideological approach through performance. Additionally, there is the challenge of providing the director of a production, through translation, with opportunities to allow movement between an emotional disengagement *and* a critical engagement with the Doctor's suicide.

Włodzimierz Perzyński (1877–1930)

Ashanti (1906)

Perzyński's dramas have consistently formed a staple of the Polish theatrical repertoire into the twenty-first century. Perzyński's success as a playwright, all the more notable given that he died at the early age of fifty three, led directly to his interest in film. Not only were his plays rapidly picked up by early Polish film-makers, but he himself was one of the first Polish writers to tackle film criticism. Aszantka (Ashanti) was adapted for film – as Wykolejeni (Derailed) *– in 1913 by Kazimierz Kamiński and* Uśmiech Losu (The Smile of Fate) *by Ryszard Ordyński in 1927.*

Figure 9: A portrait photo of Włodzimierz Perzyński taken in 1927. Copyright: Narodowe Archiwum Cyfrowe.

The 1991 production of Lekkomyślna Siostra (The Foolish Sister), *staged by the Teatr Polski in Warsaw, was subsequently directed for television by Andrzej Ziębiński. This play was also staged by the Teatr Narodowy (National Theatre) in Warsaw in 2009 and subsequently directed for television in 2011 by Agnieszka Glińska.*

Perzyński was born in the Opoczno region, near Radom, which fell within the Russian partition prior to the First World War. He attended school in Warsaw and Petersburg, where his interest in Russian theatre and literature was cultivated; he came into contact with the theories of Konstantin Stanislavsky and Nemirovich-Danchenko, and practices at the Moscow Art Theatre. Perzyński worked as a journalist and registered as a student of Polish Literature at the Jagellonian University in Kraków, a course that he never completed, participating rather in the bohemian artistic life of the city. In 1899 he left Poland and spent an extended period of time travelling in Italy, France and Egypt. He studied the Italian language and literature in Florence and in Paris, French literature and theatre. He came into contact with the theatrical practice of André Antoine and the Grande Guignol Theatre. Perzyński's ability to operate fluently in a range of European languages created professional and artistic possibilities throughout his life, particularly in terms of his obtaining work as a journalist and translator. His European connections also eventually led him to establish friendships with important contemporary Polish theatrical figures, including Tadeusz Boy-Żeleński, the writer and critic and the playwrights Stanisław Przybyszewski, Jan August Kisielewski and Adolf Nowaczyński.

The writer returned to Poland in 1901, where he resided, excepting a series of trips abroad prior to the First World War, until his death. He took up a number of permanent editorial positions for key journals, including *Głos Narodu* (*Voice of the Nation*) in Kraków and *Tygodnik Ilustrowany* (*Illustrated Weekly*), in Warsaw, where he settled permanently. He debuted as a poet in 1902 and a few years later, in 1906, as a novelist. During this early period, he had little direct connection with the Polish theatre until he experienced cash-flow problems. At this point, some of his sketches for a comedy, created at the suggestion of a friend, were passed to an eminent theatre director in Lwów, Tadeusz Pawlikowski, who commissioned the work, and backed this up with an advance. The successful 1904 production of *Lekkomyślna siostra* (*The Foolish Sister*) was the foundation for Perzyński's prolific dramatic output, which was translated into many languages, and included: *Aszantka* (*Ashanti*, 1906); *Szczęście Frania* (*Frank's Luck*, 1906); *Majowe słońce* (*May Sunshine*, 1906); *Konkurs* (*The Competition*, 1911); *Dzieje Józefa* (*What Joseph Did*, 1913); *Strach na wróble* (*The Scarecrow*, 1916); *Polityka* (*Politics*, 1919); *Uśmiech losu* (*The Smile of Fate*, 1926); and *Lekarz miłości* (*Doctor Love*, 1927).

On first reading – and in contrast with Przybyszewki's and Rittner's work – what is most notable about *Ashanti* from a translator's perspective is the sparseness and incisiveness of Perzyński's dialogue. This is likely to impact in a number of ways, in performance, on character development and consequently performance style. In *Snow* Przybyszewski is acutely focused on achieving a sense of 'psychological layering' through the dialogue, on experimentation with the possibilities of the naturalistic monologue and on the functioning of language in the arenas of gender and domestic politics. Rittner's dialogue for *In a Small House* implies a faster-paced delivery. Its relationship to the stage action is more fluid and is focused on the ways in which everyday domestic business can evoke – but not directly expose – motivation; Rittner's characters appear far less self-involved, and perhaps self-aware, than Przybyszewski's. For Perzyński, however, in *Ashanti*, words act as frequently brutal surface indicators of an existential struggle for survival that is firmly rooted in economic imperatives. In this play, the dialogue is bound inextricably to establishing the characters' acute sense of their own social performativity. From thence emerges the playwright's satirical viewpoint on fin-de-siècle Polish life as a decadent theatre of instability and corruption, and an unregulated market for fleshly transactions. As a translator of Perzyński's dialogue, one is conscious of its potential for transference, in a strikingly contemporary way, into a twenty-first-century linguistic idiom. However, this translational approach arguably needs to be tempered by attention to the possibilities of historicization, which can be deployed in order to convey a viable ideological context for the play's action and may, consequently, effectively express (as far as possible) its now essentially anachronistic naturalistic form.

Leopold Staff (1878–1957)

All the Same (1912)

Staff's work is an unusual addition to this collection. To Samo (All the Same, 1912) *is the only play he wrote that employs naturalistic dialogue and it has no currently identifiable performance history. Staff is chiefly known in Poland as a Nobel Prize nominated poet – a member of the experimental 1920s Skamander group – who wrote only a handful of predominantly verse dramas. Staff attained a number of highly significant literary roles in Poland. During the period 1924–1931, he was the president of the Society of Polish Writers and Journalists and from 1934 till 1939 – the vice-president of the Polish Academy of Literature. During the Second World War he lived in Nazi-occupied Warsaw, lectured in the underground University and participated in the Warsaw Uprising.*

Staff was born in Lemberg (Galician Lwów) in the Austro-Hungarian partition, where his father worked as a confectioner. His family was of German-Czechoslovakian extraction. Staff studied law and philosophy in Lwów, followed by Romance languages. His first volume of poetry, *Sny o potędze* (*Dreams of Power*), which focused on Nietzschean themes, was published in 1901 and established him as a significant new literary voice. As a poet, in spite of formal variations throughout his extensive career, he maintained a strong interest in contemporary classicism and was an exponent of work that explored the notion of the 'everyday', particularly in the context of war, several of which he witnessed during his lifetime. Throughout this extensive career, Staff also worked as an editor-contributor with a

Figure 10: A portrait photo of Leopold Staff. Date unknown. Copyright: Narodowe Archiwum Cyfrowe.

variety of periodicals. He was a prolific translator of literature, transposing texts from the Greek, Latin, German, Italian, Chinese and French, including the work of Thomas Mann and Johann von Goethe.

During the First World War, Staff lived in Kharkov, which was then part of the Russian Empire and in 1918 moved to Warsaw, where he remained throughout the Second World War, until the city was razed to the ground following the failed Warsaw Uprising. He left the city with nothing except for a handful of poems – his house was plundered, and then blown to smithereens. Following a stint in a transitional camp in Pruszków and having been taken off a German transportation vehicle in Starachowice, he sought refuge there with a local vicar. He returned to Warsaw, where he continued his successful career as a writer, only in 1949.

Staff wrote six plays that did not meet with notable critical acclaim. These were *Skarb* (*The Treasure*, 1904); *Godiwa* (*Godiva*, 1906); *Igrzysko* (*The Playground*, 1909); *To Samo* (*All the Same*, 1912); and *Wawrzyny* (the name of a Polish village, 1912); *Południca* (*Lady Midday*, 1920). *The Treasure* is recognized within Polish scholarship as Staff's most significant dramatic work. This may be partly because it falls identifiably within a strong tradition of symbolist drama, whose chief Polish exponent was the highly influential artist, theatre designer and playwright Stanisław Wyspiański. In line with his other symbolist poetic dramas, Staff drew in this play on classical themes and legends as a basis for the narrative.

On discovering a never previously borrowed, early twentieth-century edition of Staff's play *All the Same* in a London library, I was immediately struck by its use of colloquial Polish Galician dialogue and the vividness of its characterization. Locating a tone and register for my translation of this work – given its local specificity – has been challenging, particularly due to Staff's interest in evoking comic verbal misunderstandings, for which he often employs the dramatic strategies of repetition and long-windedness. I was also struck by the play's negotiation of comedic situations and tragic outcomes, particularly the way in which the build-up to the ending and Julja's apparent suicide (by leaping from a tenement block window) is theatrically envisioned. Staff's interest in feminist politics resounds in this work. The clarity of Julja's political intentions in choosing to carry out her rebellious act – albeit resolved in the white heat of passion – is more clearly marked within the dialogue and plot of this play than similar choices in other texts included in this collection.

Notes

1 See http://www.intellectbooks.co.uk/books/view-Book,id=4578/ and http://www.intellectbooks.co.uk/books/view-Book,id=4625/ for further information.
2 See http://www.archive.org/details/snowaplayinfour00przygoog.
3 I referred to several versions of this play during the translation process. A key Polish edition, however, was T. Rittner, *W małym domku* (Kraków: Universitas, 2003).
4 I referred to several versions of this play during the translation process. A key Polish edition, however, was W. Perzyński, *Aszantka* (Kraków: Universitas, 2003).

5   I referred to several versions of this play during the translation process. A key Polish edition, however, was L. Staff, *To Samo* (Warszawa: Bibljoteka Polska, 1923).
6   See http://www.tandfonline.com/doi/abs/10.1080/10486801.2011.610307 for my recent article about the National Theatre production of Tadeusz Słobodzianek's play *Nasza Klasa* (*Our Class*).
7   The production was rehearsed at the University of Reading during autumn 2009. Performances took place in Reading and London, at POSK theatre, in autumn/spring 2009/10.
8   Franek in *Ashanti*, p. 81.
9   See, for example, the official publication of the International Academy of Suicide Research, entitled *Archives of Suicide Research*. It is published by Taylor & Francis. See http://iasr.mcgill.ca/
10 P. S. Wandycz, *The Price of Freedom: A History of East Central Europe from the Middle Ages to the Present* (London: Routledge, 1996), pp. 176–177.
11 Ibid., pp. 179–180.
12 Ibid., 178.
13 Ibid.
14 Ibid, p. 194.
15 K. Braun, *A Concise History of Polish Theater from the Eleventh to the Twentieth Centuries* (Lewiston: Mellen, 1993).
16 Ibid, p. 121.
17 A. Hutnikiewicz, *Młoda Polska* (Warszawa: Wydawnictwo Naukowe PWN, 2008), p. 226.
18 See http://books.google.co.uk/books/about/Country_House.html?id=4-Dyak5fmEUC&redir_esc=y.

Ashanti (1906)

Włodzimierz Perzyński

Reading *Ashanti*

Presentation of the Translation

As suggested in my Introduction to Invisible Country, *this particular translation is presented somewhat unconventionally. It is interspersed with text boxes containing documentation of my 2012 research production of the play. My intention in incorporating information about the production is not to over-determine the reader's interpretation of the play text, nor to imply a 'correct' approach to its practical realization. Rather, I aim to evoke the conditions and critical choices that informed a given theatre production – created in an academic context – which was realized specifically in order to develop the translation and contextual research published here.*

My inspiration for this mode of textual presentation can be traced to an aspect of Bertolt Brecht's practice, which he developed with the Berliner Ensemble, namely, that of creating 'model books'. These forms of performance documentation had a part-reflective, part-instructional function. The main anchoring feature of their structure was production imagery, such as photographs and designs. They were intended to present the researcher with a view of the solutions that had been developed by a group of practitioners during their realization of a given play text, written by Brecht. Simultaneously, they exposed an ideologically-driven process of choice-making and its politico-historical contexts.

The reflections and images presented here are offered in the spirit of sharing with the reader a sustained and collective process of practice-led interpretation and research.

Please note:

- *The text boxes contain my reflections on the research performance and its practical and – to some degree – linguistic evolution. Some of them incorporate imagery from the performance, generated by Matt Ager and Lib Taylor, plus related text. Others contain that imagery alone, or text alone.*
- *The text boxes intersperse the translation at relevant points in the narrative. As such, the images also function within the conventions of 'illustration'. Where written material accompanies them, it focuses on analysing theatrical channels of communication and systems of performance, which I put in place as director of a research performance. The*

written material was developed whilst working on this book, and resulted from critical reflection. This was itself based on visual documentation of the performance (including video recording and photographs), rehearsal notes and personal memory. Collectively, these varied sources form an archive of this book's evolution.
- *There are numerous possible ways of reading this section of the book. One is to read 'between' the translation and the text boxes: another, to follow them as separate strands. A given mode and 'rhythm' of reading will, I expect, be primarily informed by the intention of the reader and her/his contexts for – and purpose in – reading.*
- *I have not directed any of the other translations in this book. As such, I consider them to be less developed 'drafts', whose evolution has been directly informed by my practice-as-research work on Ashanti.*
- *The reflections do not appear in the form of micro-linguistic analyses of specific translational choices. Indeed, the translation published here is not the version of my translation that was used during the performance being documented. That translation continued its development both during and after the run of performances, over two subsequent years. It altered in tone, inflection and register, as indicated in the Introduction. It continued to be shaped by the discoveries I made as a result of directorial choices. Its most recent 'manifestation' has been included in this book.*

Performing *Ashanti*

Space and setting

Early productions of this play would have employed a box set. The locations involved (two apartments and a hotel room) would have been fully realized theatrically, to look like realistic environments. As a contemporary director, I decided to take a different approach, and used space rather more expressionistically in order to foreground themes that I regarded as critically significant.

The audience were positioned end on in a studio space, on raked seating above a performance area. Within the setting, no boundaries indicating a room, such as walls, were created. Rather, three permanently present groups of items within the theatre set were used to highlight three significant and related themes. A series of variously shaped white window frames were suspended from the rig upstage, in an overlapping pattern, in order to express a palimpsestic approach to location and encompass themes of travel, displacement, nostalgia and reflection. This photograph shows the stage manager, Phoebe Garrett, hanging the frames.

Image copyright: Matt Ager.

Ashanti (1906)

Ashanti (1906)

Włodzimierz Perzyński

Dramatis Personae

EDMUND ŁOŃSKI (MUNIEK, MUNIO), a young landowner
BRATKOWSKI, his uncle
BARON KRĘCKI, ŁOŃSKI's friend
STANISŁAW ROMKOWSKI, a painter
LUTOBORSKI, a landowner
DIRECTOR
JAN, ŁOŃSKI's servant
MESSENGER
FRANEK (FRANUŚ), a hotel waiter
MRS LUBARTOWSKA
WŁADKA LUBARTOWSKA (WŁADZIA, ASHANTI), her daughter

MAID
VIOLA, WŁADKA's friend

Act 1

A fashionably arranged room in ŁOŃSKI's bachelor apartment. On the left hand side the door to the bedroom, screened by a heavy portiere. On the right, doors to the hallway. Upstage, windows. Against the wall on the left hand side stands a piano. In the corner on an easel a picture turned away. A winter's day. Four o'clock in the afternoon. Dusk. A beam of light shines through from the bedroom.

Scene One

JAN, ŁOŃSKI, KRĘCKI

A bell rings. From ŁOŃSKI's bedroom enter JAN, he goes to the hallway, after a while returns, leading KRĘCKI with him.

KRĘCKI:	(*A balding blonde man; a small moustache and sideburns, his face is harrowed, he is dressed according to the latest fashion*) Is he awake?
JAN:	His lordship is dressing.
KRĘCKI:	(*Approaches the bedroom door*) Hello, Munio.
ŁOŃSKI:	(*Offstage*) Ah, Baron, it's you! Hello.
KRĘCKI:	Sleep well?
ŁOŃSKI:	So-so. (*He enters from the bedroom, he is half dressed, in a coloured shirt, entering he ties his cravat*) And you?
KRĘCKI:	A good night's sleep leaves me shattered … Rare event, thank God.
ŁOŃSKI:	(*Approaching the window*) Our decadent lifestyle! Ah, the lamplighters, already …
KRĘCKI:	Yes – it's still quite early.
ŁOŃSKI:	(*Looks down onto the street*) Just look at that snow!
KRĘCKI:	All day, relentless! I hoped it might ease off on my way home. (ŁOŃSKI *looks through the window at the street, starts whistling*) Shall I tell him to lower the blinds and light a lamp?
ŁOŃSKI:	What for? Let's stay like this.
KRĘCKI:	Atmospheric lighting? You're not feeling – amorous?

Ashanti (1906)

Image copyright: Matt Ager.

Secondly, the key themes of travel, displacement, nostalgia and reflection, evoked through the suspended window frames, were also extended through the use of items of furniture. That furniture was covered in dust sheets, and positioned on either side of the performance space. There were three sets of matching seating and tables that

Ashanti (1906)

varied in style, in order to evoke historical period and location. As locations shifted for each act, new elements of furniture were uncovered and brought into the centre of the performance space, to replace others, which were removed. No other significant items, such as props, were used to produce the illusion of a coherent, boundaried room. Aesthetically, this resulted in a rather sparse, streamlined effect, with the edges of the performance space melting into darkness. As is evident from the photographs, under the restrained and selective lighting scheme, which favoured the creation of shady spaces rather than bold illumination; the white frames and dust sheets picked up colour schemes. They cast angular shadows across the stage space. Lighting also picked out textures and patterns on fabric and a range of other surfaces, foregrounding a variety of forms. Sometimes this had a ghostly effect, particularly through the use of dust sheets, which was appropriate for evoking the tone of the first and third acts, which are set in Warsaw.

Image copyright: Matt Ager.

ŁOŃSKI:	Not quite sure … wait, I'll put on my jacket. *(He enters the bedroom, returns shortly)* Damnation! A daily dose of natural light – half an hour at least – that's what I need – remind me.
KRĘCKI:	As you wish. I'm your friend – and must tolerate your little quirks.
ŁOŃSKI:	You old goat!
KRĘCKI:	*(Winces)* Sometimes you're … frightfully rude.
ŁOŃSKI:	Don't be angry … I was only tea … *(Yawns)* Teasing.
KRĘCKI:	You're not tired, surely?
ŁOŃSKI:	Just bored, with everything … *(Approaches the window)* All that snow …
KRĘCKI:	Ha, you've got snow sickness!
ŁOŃSKI:	Don't you ever get bored?
KRĘCKI:	No – not bored or tired either.
ŁOŃSKI:	It's true! An iron constitution. Everyone agrees …
KRĘCKI:	That's right – even the most devout – I'm an idealist, like them.
ŁOŃSKI:	Is that so!
KRĘCKI:	Why yes … I instruct today's youth – for example, you – in how to have a jolly good time. With absolute dedication, I uncover, exclusively for you, unique sources of subtle distraction. I'm not unlike … mm …
ŁOŃSKI:	Who?

In choosing to use space and setting in the manner described, my intention – in terms of mood and tone – was to create a sense of transition and ephemerality within the black box space of the theatre studio, and evoke the idea that the characters were almost 'free-floating' or dislocated within the enveloping darkness. As already outlined, the permanently fixed window frames and flexible dust sheets reflected the play's themes of travel and absence, as well as the tension the text sets up around ideas of nostalgia and the possibility of objectively viewing one's place of origin. These elements of setting also mirrored structural features of the text that engage with the theme of changing perspectives. These are in turn rooted in the play's exploration of Polish masculinities and their relationship to concepts of national identity, colonization and imperialism (as suggested in the Introduction). The play specifically explores how these ideological issues are expressed in – and through – intimate relationships and friendships, within domestic, or pseudo-domestic settings. Its engagement of a debate around the relationship between the personal and the political is extended into a more global frame of reference by its title, Ashanti.

I should also add that, thirdly, a series of suitcases and trunks were permanently located in the downstage area. Their various contents (mostly clothing) gradually spilled out into the performance space, as actors frequently interacted with them, integrating them into the action. On another level, through the presence of these objects, I was trying to explore the idea that, wherever the characters moved to, they were still carrying the same emotional 'baggage'.

In summary, the window frames, covered furniture and suitcases acted as both a literal and symbolic frame for the action. By using this frame, I also wished to evoke the fact that I was engaging in a reflection on naturalism as a theatrical form, rather than working strictly

Ashanti (1906)

within conventions associated with illusionism. Through the idea of physical framing, I also wanted to extend the idea that I was actively framing and constructing the play's 'Polishness' in a language other than Polish.

The box positioned on top of the suitcase in this image was chosen in order to evoke ideas of the 'exotic'. These tied in with the play's title and its central character, Ashanti. The box differed in colour and style from other elements of setting – no other decorative prop was present in the space – and it was used as a receptacle for Łoński's gun and Władka's fan, which feature in Acts 2 and 3. However, there was no way for the audience to realise this until these objects were revealed at the appropriate moments in the action. As such, the box was intended to acquire somewhat mysterious attributes, given that its function may have been rather difficult to read, though its design was likely to attract attention. The box was always positioned downstage, amongst the luggage, when it was not being used as part of the action; it was therefore visible to the audience constantly. Though the playwright does not mention the use of such a box in the stage directions, it was used theatrically rather like a 'Pandora's box'; when it was opened, the sense of danger for the characters (whether emotional or literal) increased significantly.

Image copyright: Matt Ager.

KRĘCKI:	Powerful character from ancient mythology – his name escapes me – I'm not the bookish type! Do let me know when your poetic mood wears off – I'll see to the lighting and blinds.
ŁOŃSKI:	Of course.
KRĘCKI:	And guess what I was doing, while you were fast asleep?
ŁOŃSKI:	I've no idea. Sleeping as well, I expect.
KRĘCKI:	Now, now!
ŁOŃSKI:	You secured – upon your word of honour – a loan of twenty five roubles – until tomorrow.
KRĘCKI:	In Poland – these days!
ŁOŃSKI:	Then I'm stumped. Reveal all.
KRĘCKI:	The ingratitude! And mocking tone! I found something – for you … mm, hmm! *(He blows a kiss)*
ŁOŃSKI:	What, exactly?
KRĘCKI:	A pearl … No really – a veritable pearl!
ŁOŃSKI:	Oh! And has this … pearl … been pinned in many cravats?
KRĘCKI:	Nobody's actually. Not, that is, from our circle.
ŁOŃSKI:	The rest don't count?

Łoński (Matt van Niftrik) is pictured in his Warsaw bachelor apartment, where he spends the day recovering…

Image copyright: Matt Ager.

KRĘCKI:	Certainly not! The virginity baseline for tarts – lies here. The same baseline for society ladies – here. Poles apart, you see.
ŁOŃSKI:	*(Laughing)* You old goat …
KRĘCKI:	My little joker …
ŁOŃSKI:	Yes, yes, temper, temper. When will you show me?
KRĘCKI:	Today – we'll eat dinner, together. Agreed?
ŁOŃSKI:	Who is it? Tell me.
KRĘCKI:	No. I'll show you.
ŁOŃSKI:	Who is it? A seamstress? Shop girl?
KRĘCKI:	You'll see … now, now …
ŁOŃSKI:	Is she young?
KRĘCKI:	Eighteen.
ŁOŃSKI:	And pretty?

Ashanti (1906)

KRĘCKI:	Now, Munio - remember - there's not a single woman alive who's so ugly that she lacks *one* positive asset. And such are the assets sought by true connoisseurs. *(He narrows his eyes and traces a meaningful gesture in the air with his hand)* You see?
ŁOŃSKI:	Pure philosophy, dear Baron. Shame you'll die intestate …
KRĘCKI:	Tragic … but my works shall endure … fifty years from now, restaurants will still be serving filet of deer *à la baron Kręcki*.
ŁOŃSKI:	*(Holds out his hand)* Bravo!
KRĘCKI:	Why thank you. Modesty is my finest asset. Right, I'm off. I'll bring her over, and then we'll devise a plan of action. Agreed?
ŁOŃSKI:	Very well. She does at least bother to wash, this pearl?
KRĘCKI:	Oh no – that's precisely what magnifies her savage appeal. See you shortly. Ten minutes. *(KRĘCKI exits)*

Scene Two

ŁOŃSKI, BRATKOWSKI, JAN

ŁOŃSKI:	*(Lights a cigarette and paces the stage. The bell is heard. He stops and looks expectantly in the direction of the door. Enter BRATKOWSKI)*
ŁOŃSKI:	*(Rushing up to him)* Uncle! *(They kiss)*
BRATKOWSKI:	How are you, my boy?
ŁOŃSKI:	When did you arrive?
BRATKOWSKI:	Yesterday night.
ŁOŃSKI:	Why didn't you send a message?
BRATKOWSKI:	Oh, it was late. Catching you at home can be tricky, I know. Here for a few hours, that's all, on business. Must get back tonight.
ŁOŃSKI:	Tonight? A wasted journey. You could stay in Warsaw for a couple of days.
BRATKOWSKI:	Out of the question. Must leave tonight. For the wedding, day after tomorrow.
ŁOŃSKI:	What wedding?
BRATKOWSKI:	Oh, in Wojtkowice – little Zawadzka girl.
ŁOŃSKI:	Alright …
BRATKOWSKI:	You see, you've not the foggiest what's going on at home.
ŁOŃSKI:	Alright, yes that's right … *Kazio's* getting married … So glad you jogged my memory … I must send a telegram.
BRATKOWSKI:	I've a better idea. Pack your things and come with me. They'll be delighted and you'll have a good time and it's the right thing to do.
ŁOŃSKI:	Hm …

Łoński (Matt van Niftrik) spends his evenings dining out and making frequent visits to the theatre, with a variety of women and his friend the Baron Kręcki. In the stage directions, Łoński is described as emerging from his offstage bedroom into the main playing space when Kręcki arrives at the beginning of the play. In this production, he was shown sleeping on a dark red chaise longue in the main playing space, which for Act 1 represented the character's living room. He was covered by his coat (as shown in the previous image) in order to portray a somewhat decadent lifestyle that is congruent with the ideologies and conventions of stereotypical fin-de-siècle Polish (and European) bachelorhood. This image, above, of the character lounging on the floor in his fur trimmed coat, encapsulates my interpretation of him in the initial scenes – sleepy eyed, unshaven, slightly eccentric and rather unfocused. However, these opening moments of the performance also became an opportunity for the actor to express the character's lonely vulnerability and pre-figure his decision to commit suicide at the end of the play.

Image copyright: Matt Ager.

Ashanti (1906)

BRATKOWSKI:	Consider it … please … just you remember, Warsaw living, cash down the drain … Hm … hm … year, or two, it'll be goodbye Płaczków before you know it. Damned shame, if you ask me.
ŁOŃSKI:	Glass half empty, uncle, again.
BRATKOWSKI:	And after that, shared lodgings with any old Tomek, Rysiek or Bartek, or else, loitering on street corners. No fun then, is it.
ŁOŃSKI:	It won't come to that.
BRATKOWSKI:	Was Kręcki here?
ŁOŃSKI:	Yes he was.
BRATKOWSKI:	I met him downstairs, by the gate. Slithered by … pretending not to see me. Why throw your lot in with rogues like that?
ŁOŃSKI:	He's very entertaining.
BRATKOWSKI:	I bet you feed him, water him and he borrows your money as well.
ŁOŃSKI:	Oh, he's comparatively cheap, I'm sure and someone like him is always handy in the city.
BRATKOWSKI:	Handy for the devil's work. I'm here to make plans for this evening. Are you free?
ŁOŃSKI:	Absolutely! At your disposal, uncle, entirely.
BRATKOWSKI:	You're not looking so well, by the way. Life on the edge, I expect! Well, your decision? Are you leaving with me?
ŁOŃSKI:	Indeed I am.
BRATKOWSKI:	At last, a glimmer of sense. And what's this? *(He approaches the easel)*
ŁOŃSKI:	My portrait. Friend of mine, a painter.
BRATKOWSKI:	Let those artists suck you dry as well, that's right, it's all bound to end terribly well. *(He takes his hat and cane)* I'm leaving at midnight. Where shall we meet?
ŁOŃSKI:	How about the theatre?
BRATKOWSKI:	Aha, well, if there's something jolly on, I could be tempted.
ŁOŃSKI:	I'll take you to a smashing operetta.
BRATKOWSKI:	Marvellous! And we'll talk as much as we like on the train.
JAN:	*(Entering)* Pardon, sir, the messenger's brought a note. *(He hands him the letter)* He's waiting.
ŁOŃSKI:	Apologies, uncle. *(He smiles)*
BRATKOWSKI:	What's so funny?
ŁOŃSKI:	Nothing at all. *(To JAN)* Tell the messenger to hold on. *(JAN exits)*
BRATKOWSKI:	Well, goodbye for now. Wait for me …wait … just come straight to the theatre.
ŁOŃSKI:	Alright I will.
BRATKOWSKI:	Yes and be ready. As for that Baron, I'd get rid of him, if I were you. *(Exits)*

What is particularly interesting about the opening scenes of the play is that the playwright introduces a series of male characters to the audience, and uses their interactions to develop power relationships and hierarchies that drive the plot. His perception of how class systems might operate within the everyday, in an urban environment, is revealed to us. Interestingly, the power relationship between Łoński and Kręcki is expressed as somewhat complicated, given distinctions in age, title and actual (rather than implied) wealth. However, when the Messenger arrives (Dan Whateley, pictured here, left), Jan, the servant, has no compunction in making him feel his place in the pecking order, in the same way that Łoński (Matt van Niftrik, right) relates to him. For me, as a director, identifying and evoking this chain of displacement was very important, particularly in terms of echoing tone of voice and behaviour patterns within the men's interactions.

Image copyright: Matt Ager.

Scene Three

ŁOŃSKI, MESSENGER, JAN

ŁOŃSKI:	*(Goes to the bedroom, brings a small travelling bag, puts it on the armchair, then rings for JAN)* Where's that messenger?
JAN:	In the hall.
ŁOŃSKI:	Call him.
JAN:	*(Goes towards the door)* Come here, you oaf. *(The MESSENGER enters)*
ŁOŃSKI:	You know the man, who gave you this?
MESSENGER:	I do, sir. Baron Kręcki.
ŁOŃSKI:	He's at the patisserie?
MESSENGER:	Yes.
ŁOŃSKI:	You'll go to him and say one word – 'now'. Just that word! Alright?
MESSENGER:	Oh yes, if you please, sir.
ŁOŃSKI:	Hurry up then. *(Hands him some money)*
MESSENGER:	Thank you very much, sir. *(Exits)*
ŁOŃSKI:	Jan, I leave for the country, tonight. Back in about a week. Pack my things and drive them to the station by midnight. Including my tail suit.
JAN:	Very well. *(The bell rings)*
ŁOŃSKI:	That must be the Baron. Anyone else, I'm out.

Scene Four

ŁOŃSKI, KRĘCKI

ŁOŃSKI:	*(Bursts out laughing)* Poor little baron! Uncle rattled your cage.
KRĘCKI:	I saw Bratkowski in the hallway, all desire to converse left me. Hence the messenger.
ŁOŃSKI:	He did mention you'd crossed paths.
KRĘCKI:	Anything about me?
ŁOŃSKI:	No, no.
KRĘCKI:	*(Eyeing ŁOŃSKI suspiciously)* Bratkowski's taken against me, he blackens my name. He may be your uncle but he's got bad manners.
ŁOŃSKI:	Oh calm yourself, Baron. If he is gossiping, it's only because he means well.

Uncle Bratkowski (Chris Montague, left, with Matt van Niftrik) is shown disapprovingly regarding a portrait in his nephew's apartment.

Within my research production, the naturalistic form of the play was further problematized through the use of certain actors playing multiple roles. This performance system was employed in three instances. The actor playing the 'butler' Jan also played the hotel waiter Franek, who features in Act 2. Both are servant characters and Łoński interacts with both of them in not so friendly terms. In addition, one actor took on three roles: the Messenger in Act 1, Lutoborski in Act 2 and the Director in Act 3. Each of these characters is from a different social class but they fulfil a similar dramatic function. They are all rather pragmatic people, who are shown getting on with their lives on their own terms. This approach to existence contrasts with the complex entanglements and neuroticism of some of the main players in Perzyński's menagerie of types. Finally, the actor who played Uncle Bratkowski took the role of Romkowski, the artist, in Act 3. The parallel between these two characters is their connection with the countryside, as well as their rather nostalgic view of Poland and their essential conservatism. However, Bratkowski is clearly shown by the playwright as firmly rooted within his Polish context, whereas Romkowski

Ashanti (1906)

wistfully remembers his family from the context of his new (but rather unstable, given his hand-to-mouth existence) Venetian home. Within naturalism, the device of doubling is evidently not conventional. However, given my establishment of an expressionistic setting for this particular performance, within which elements of naturalistic performance were framed, it became possible to establish a system of multi-casting in order to underline both character function and the theme of performativity. The latter was key to reaching an understanding of the play. As a translator, this casting device also made me think carefully about how each of these characters, who are clearly linked within the thematic and narrative structures of the play, might actually speak. I also considered in some detail whether tonal vocal echoes, rhythmical patterns or expressive inflections could be established in order to further encrypt these connections.

Image copyright: Matt Ager.

KRĘCKI:	I know that. Otherwise, I'd have rapped his knuckles by now. *(Noticing the travelling bag)* What's this?
ŁOŃSKI:	I'm going to the country, with uncle.
KRĘCKI:	When?
ŁOŃSKI:	Tonight.
KRĘCKI:	But she'll be here any minute.
ŁOŃSKI:	Who?
KRĘCKI:	What do you mean, who? You've not forgotten?
ŁOŃSKI:	Oh, that pearl. There's time enough, not leaving 'til twelve.
KRĘCKI:	All that trouble for nothing
ŁOŃSKI:	I'll authorize a transfer.
KRĘCKI:	*(Enlivened)* Meaning?
ŁOŃSKI:	Of my rightful privileges.
KRĘCKI:	*(Bats his hand)* Your uncle's wound you up.
ŁOŃSKI:	Why didn't you bring the pearl with you?
KRĘCKI:	If that old codger had seen us together, he'd tell the world that I procure women for you! Devil take him! Such jolly evening plans and now they're completely bloody ruined … The level of control – honestly – beyond me. One minute Bratkowski appears, ta daa! You're both off to the country …
ŁOŃSKI:	I did want to go.
KRĘCKI:	You never mentioned it.
ŁOŃSKI	Oh, that's enough. I don't like arguments. Where's that pearl? *(The bell rings)*
KRĘCKI:	Aha, she's on her way. *(She runs into the hall, ŁOŃSKI exits to the bedroom)*

An important aspect of directing these initial scenes was the dramatic development of the relationship between Łoński (Matt van Niftrik) and Kręcki (George Bull). The images featured here show the younger man's rather playful approach to the relationship, which the actor expressed through his style of performance, particularly his use of facial expression. However, proxemically, the positioning of the two men in relation to each other tended to strongly evoke a complex power relationship. This was intended to be evident to the audience and to Kręcki, but not to Łoński. I attempted to achieve this through the use of levels of height, however subtle, as well as the direction of each character's gaze; the Baron was often shown looking at Łoński, who in turn looked away from him, out into the audience space. He did so without acknowledging the audience's presence, as this would have broken the idea of a 'fourth wall', which remained a convention throughout this performance. In addition, lighting is shown in these images as functioning to create a sense of mystery and potency around Kręcki's character. Conveying a sense of sexually-charged (and economically-driven) codependency and enmeshment between these two characters also became important to the actors as they worked in rehearsal and performance. For me the dynamic they established was certainly tinged with sinister connotations, given our portrayal of the Baron as particularly volatile, beneath his veneer of self-control.

Image copyright: Matt Ager.

Ashanti (1906)

Matt van Niftrik as Łoński and George Bull as Kręcki.

Image copyright: Matt Ager.

Scene Five

KRĘCKI, WŁADKA, ŁOŃSKI

KRĘCKI:	*(Enters first)* Please, come through. *(WŁADKA follows him in. She is dressed poorly, breathless, evidently overwhelmed)* Why so glum?
WŁADKA:	Mmm, I was just wondering if I should leave.
KRĘCKI:	Why's that?
WŁADKA:	Because you left me by myself.
KRĘCKI:	You've nothing to fear.
ŁOŃSKI:	I'm a silly girl, that's all. Nothing scares me second time around, but sometimes I … well … I … *(She notices ŁOŃSKI and breaks off)*

KRĘCKI:	Allow me … Mr Munio, Miss Władzia.
ŁOŃSKI:	Miss Władzia. What a delightful name.
KRĘCKI:	Utterly delightful.
ŁOŃSKI:	*(Approaches WŁADZIA, scrutinizes her)* Well …? *(To KRĘCKI)* Oh my God, she's blushing.
KRĘCKI:	Aah, well you see, Miss Władzia – terribly reserved.
ŁOŃSKI:	Is she now?
KRĘCKI:	To the point where she was scared, to come here alone.
ŁOŃSKI:	And why is that?
WŁADKA:	I don't know really. Downstairs the doorman eyed me in a funny way. I thought he wouldn't let me in.
KRĘCKI:	No!
WŁADKA:	But, when he stepped into the street, I shot through the hallway and flew up those stairs; I was nearly panting outside your door …

The relationship between the two characters (played by Matt van Niftrik and George Bull) is developed kinesically and proxemically.

Ashanti (1906)

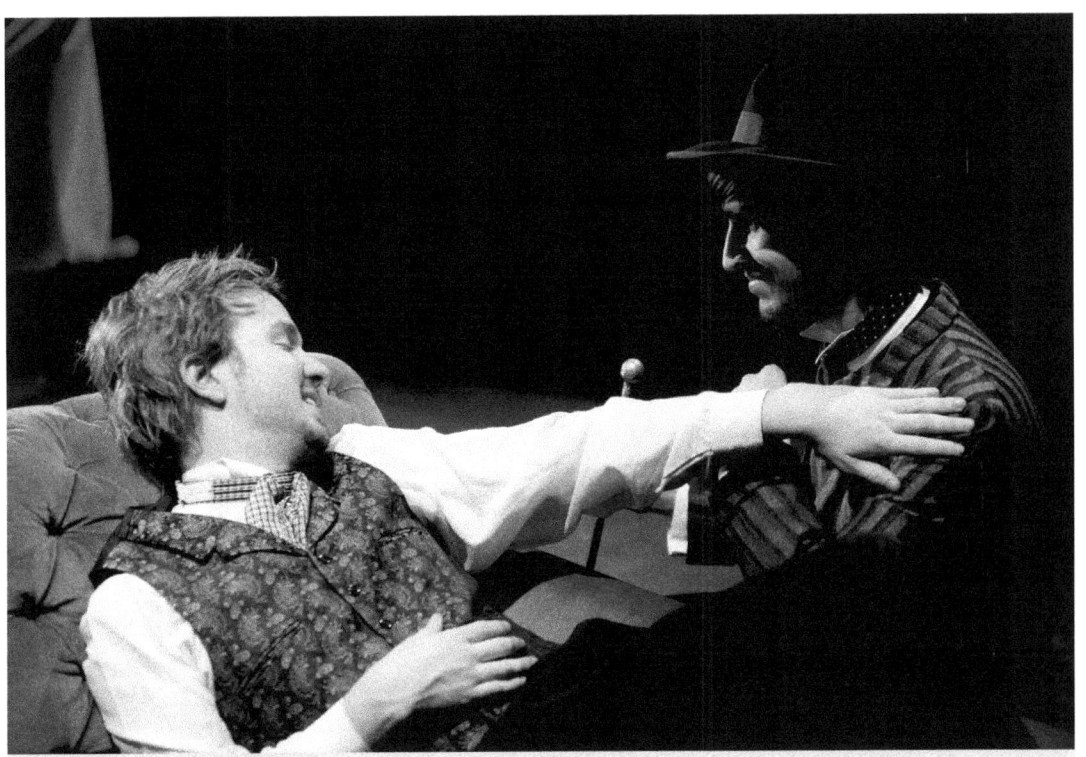

Image copyright: Matt Ager.

ŁOŃSKI:	You poor thing.
WŁADKA:	I know this house.
KRĘCKI:	You do?
WŁADKA:	A doctor lived on the ground floor. And Mother always did his laundry.
KRĘCKI:	*(To ŁOŃSKI)* Obviously she comes from a very hygienic family.
ŁOŃSKI:	Make yourself at home, I insist. Remove your hat. *(He removes her hat)* And jacket. *(He pulls off her jacket)* My goodness me, wet through.
WŁADKA:	Mm, well the snow's coming down.
ŁOŃSKI:	*(To KRĘCKI)* Be a good chap and hang this in the hall. *(KRĘCKI exits)*

Magdalena Kwiatkowska as Władka and George Bull as Kręcki.

Image copyright: Matt Ager.

Scene Six

ŁOŃSKI, WŁADKA

ŁOŃSKI: *(For a while he examines* WŁADKA *carefully. She lowers her eyes)* Now, let's sit down … Here might be best … on the couch. *(He puts his arm around her waist and leads her to the couch)* These boots are soaked.
WŁADKA: Ah, no galoshes … so much snow …
ŁOŃSKI: You should invest. You'll catch your death. *(He seats her on the couch, takes a step back, looks closely at her)* Never mind! I have it … perfect! *(He runs through to the bedroom, returns shortly, carrying a pair of women's shoes)* Please, remove your boots, try these.

Ashanti (1906)

Costume was one of the most significant channels of theatrical communication within the production. Through it, we attempted to reveal differences in economic and social status, as well as a sense of location and given circumstances. Any sense of naturalism was anchored by the costumes rather than through the setting, as has already been explained. Władka is shown in this image just after her first entrance, in a rumpled brown dress, having had her coat removed. One of the aspects of her character that the playwright problematizes, and which must be addressed through performance, on a visual level, is her level of sexual experience and whether or not, at the start of the play, she is having a relationship with Kręcki, since this idea comes up later on in the text. Our decision to keep the actor's hair short and dyed red was important in our conceptualization of this character, since red hair might conventionally, during the period in which the play is set, be associated with prostitution. Whether or not this anchored readings of Władka's sexual inexperience or experience too strongly was an issue that was raised in the research seminar that followed the production. In terms of my intentions, the choice to show Władka with red hair was related to her construction of herself as a prostitute, perhaps rather clumsily, since the dialogue does offer the possibility that she has already begun soliciting before the Baron approaches her in the street. Interestingly, there were two different actors playing the character of Władka (Magdalena Kwiatkowska, pictured above, and Joanna Lucas) on different nights throughout the production, and doubling as the Maid in Act 3 respectively. The other actor did not have red hair, nor did we choose to portray her appearance in the same way as for the actor pictured here. As a translator, this strategy assisted my thinking about Władka's possible circumstances and back-story, and consequently affected how I approached her tone of voice and choice of words. Much of what she says might be considered self-consciously seductive and there is a question about whether she is performing a role, at the Baron's behest, and when exactly she is doing so. Using red hair as a stereotypical signifier of prostitution in some performances was a provocative way in which to critically engage with some of the problems the text unfolds in this regard.

Image copyright: Matt Ager.

WŁADKA:	No … no … no …
ŁOŃSKI:	I insist.
WŁADKA:	Huh, take off my boots? Not likely.
ŁOŃSKI:	It's bad for you. You'll catch your death …
WŁADKA:	*(Laughing)* No.
ŁOŃSKI:	I'll do it myself then. *(Sits next to her)*
WŁADKA:	*(She picks up the shoes and starts to laugh heartily)* How did you get these? They're not yours.
ŁOŃSKI:	A … lady friend - left them behind.
WŁADKA:	What was on her feet when she left?
ŁOŃSKI:	She had spares … Well, off they come.

Ashanti (1906)

WŁADKA:	No.
ŁOŃSKI:	Mm ... tricky .... nothing for it ... *(He kneels before her and wants to unlace them)*
WŁADKA:	Oh, really ... *(Laughing she begins to wave her legs around)*
ŁOŃSKI:	Surrender is the only option.
WŁADKA:	Well ... well ...! He'll come back and laugh.
ŁOŃSKI:	*(He pulls off one boot)* There's a little hole in your stocking.
WŁADKA:	Is there now! *(She extricates herself)*

Scene Seven

ŁOŃSKI, WŁADKA, KRĘCKI

KRĘCKI:	*(Enters the room. Seeing ŁOŃSKI kneeling before WŁADKA, he turns on the spot, sits by the piano and begins to play and sing)* Es war einmal ein bonvivant /Und eine dame de Coeur /Er war ein bisschen amusant ...
ŁOŃSKI:	Enough of that, really ... I'd prefer you to watch not sing, lesser of two evils.
KRĘCKI:	Pardon me! My voice is rather distinctive. *(With emphasis)* Don't waste time, do you.
ŁOŃSKI:	Actually I was just persuading Miss Władzia to remove her boots and try the shoes.
KRĘCKI:	Inherited from Nina ...
WŁADKA:	Oh, I'm so embarrassed ...
KRĘCKI:	You simply must put them on.
WŁADKA:	In that case, no peeking, sir.
ŁOŃSKI:	What about me?
WŁADKA	You ... well, alright. *(She bends over quickly)*
ŁOŃSKI:	She keeps on blushing.
KRĘCKI:	And I avert my eyes. You must do the same, for Miss Władzia is timid. *(He takes him under the arm, and leads him away a few steps)* Well?
ŁOŃSKI:	You know what, she's attractive.
KRĘCKI:	Wasn't I right?
ŁOŃSKI:	Extremely attractive.
KRĘCKI:	Just your type.
ŁOŃSKI:	And she's so ... not been ruined yet ... you can tell.
WŁADKA:	I completely messed up my hair.

Władka (Magdalena Kwiatkowska) is shown taking off her boots, which are dirty and worn.

Image copyright: Matt Ager.

Ashanti (1906)

Łoński (Matt van Niftrik) discovers the hole in Władka's stocking (Magdalena Kwiatkowska).

Image copyright: Lib Taylor.

ŁOŃSKI:	Oh, allow me … Here's a mirror, a comb, brushes, everything you need. *(He leads her into the bedroom and returns alone)* Dear Baron, where on earth did you find her?
KRĘCKI:	By accident. Like all the best discoveries.
ŁOŃSKI:	But where?
KRĘCKI:	In the street.
ŁOŃSKI:	In the street?
KRĘCKI:	Like Caesar. I saw, I approached, I recognized.
ŁOŃSKI:	And you escorted.
KRĘCKI:	So I did. One over on Caesar.
ŁOŃSKI:	And now, it's time to go, let me kiss you goodbye. *(They kiss)*
KRĘCKI:	Imagine, when it's dressed, coiffured, learns some etiquette … It's completely wild now. Ashanti girl!

ŁOŃSKI:	*(Laughing)* I like it, let's name her. Ashanti!
KRĘCKI:	Look … I could see you were bored with those, hm, clapped out tarts. For me it's a point of honour that a man, especially my friend, should never get bored.
ŁOŃSKI:	You're priceless.
KRĘCKI:	I thought; let him create a new one. Remember the old adage – a proper toff cannot get by without a tart.
ŁOŃSKI:	Ashanti!
KRĘCKI:	Leave her. She'll be preening in front of the mirror … She's learning … A mirror is woman's trustiest guide.
ŁOŃSKI:	You're probably right … you are, but … *(He runs into the bedroom, returns after a while, leading WŁADKA with him)* We're lovely enough … our hair is combed. Please sit down, do, Ashanti girl.
KRĘCKI:	*(Lights a cigarette, sits by the piano, begins to play with one finger 'The Cat Sat on the Fence')*
WŁADKA:	*(Bursts out laughing)* Oh, it's that nursery rhyme.
ŁOŃSKI:	What sincere laughter …
KRĘCKI:	Yes that's the one … and now I'll play something else. *(He begins to play a 'Cakewalk')*
WŁADKA:	Oh I know, that's …
ŁOŃSKI:	The cakewalk.
WŁADKA:	Cakewalk.
ŁOŃSKI:	Cakewalk … You have to enunciate.
WŁADKA:	Cakewalk … ugh. What a name.
ŁOŃSKI:	Say it again …
WŁADKA:	Cakewalk. Lovely music. *(Starts singing and moves across the stage dancing)*
ŁOŃSKI:	Bravo, bravo, Ashanti girl. Brilliant …
KRĘCKI:	Like a trained ballerina …
WŁADKA:	I taught myself.
ŁOŃSKI:	You did?
WŁADKA:	Oh, I can do any dance … I love it … really I do … I could dance all day and all night.
ŁOŃSKI:	Ashanti girl!
WŁADKA:	What?
ŁOŃSKI:	You're an Ashanti girl.
KRĘCKI:	From the Gold Coast.
WŁADKA:	*(Looks at them suspiciously)* Tut, you gentlemen are laughing at me. I'm not like that one bit.
ŁOŃSKI:	Ha … ha … ha … Perfect! You're not like that!

Ashanti (1906)

Kręcki (George Bull, above) is concerned that Łoński's elderly uncle, who is visiting from the country, will think he procures women for his young protégé, which he indeed does. This is made clear when Łoński goes to his bedroom and returns carrying a pair of shoes for Władka that belonged to his former lover, Nina. Kręcki recognizes the shoes immediately. Łoński's ebullient naïveté is expressed through the dialogue at the start of the play, resulting in a dose of dramatic irony as the playwright creates a strong sense of ambiguity both around Władka's sexual inexperience and Kręcki's relationship with her. Kręcki's rather jaded interest in voyeurism, which connects with his preoccupation with Łoński's sex life, is expressed in the scene where Władka dances to Kręcki's piano rendition of the 'Cakewalk'. In its use of this dance music, this scene engages directly with ideas around the relationship between colonialism and gender politics, within a specifically Polish setting (the 'Cakewalk' originally developed as a plantation dance performed by slaves in the Southern United States). For a director, important decisions that need to be made may relate, firstly, to what, precisely, Nina's shoes look like and, secondly, how Władka dances the 'Cakewalk' since she has clearly never heard of it before. What relationship will the dance style and form have to the music, and how will the actor show the character's motivation while she dances? As a director I chose to have a pair of shoes that were too large for Władka. This affected the way in which she moved and, indeed, her ability to move altogether. The idea of her not quite filling someone else's shoes, as well as additional questions around what Nina may have looked like and why she may no longer be Łoński's 'mistress' were raised by drawing attention to a sizing problem! The colour of Nina's shoes was also very important. I chose a pair that were lilac and dark purple, and that looked clean and new. These qualities linked them schematically to the same colour tones in the two men's outfits. Thus, the suggestion of a relationship unit – a specific type of interconnection – was evoked symbolically, through the use of costume colour-coding.

Image copyright: Matt Ager.

WŁADKA:	Tut. *(She turns her back to him)*
ŁOŃSKI:	Now don't sulk … do stop it … I didn't say anything bad.
WŁADKA:	Then what does it mean?
ŁOŃSKI:	Ashanti? A member of that tribe, a sort of wild creature that lives far … far away, on the shores of a vast sea …
WŁADKA:	*(Laughing)* I live by the Vistula River.
ŁOŃSKI:	That's why … you… are the Ashanti girl … of Warsaw.
WŁADKA:	That's different?
ŁOŃSKI:	Just as dark and even wilder.
WŁADKA:	Tut, don't interrupt, I'm busy listening.
ŁOŃSKI:	Quite right, he's a real pest.
WŁADKA:	Yes, you just play, sir. *(KRĘCKI makes a comic gesture with his arms, turns around and begins to play the waltz)*
WŁADKA:	And then?
ŁOŃSKI:	Then? A white man comes and takes the Ashanti girl into captivity.
WŁADKA:	I wouldn't let him.
ŁOŃSKI:	Suppose you liked him?
WŁADKA:	If I liked him … What do you do in captivity?
ŁOŃSKI:	Listen carefully. Once upon a time, there was an Ashanti girl, just like you, who lived on the banks of the Vistula River. She worked at the factory. Every day she got out of bed and rushed to the other side of town in the rain, the mud or the snow, just to sew, sew and sew. Until her poor head ached.
WŁADKA:	Just like me … But I don't work at the factory any more. *(ŁOŃSKI laughs)* Alright, what happened next …?
ŁOŃSKI:	A white man came and captured her. He shipped her to a country where no rain falls. There is no mud, or snow; it's always warm, the sun shines, like here in June or July. And there the Ashanti girl lived with him in a little marble palace, with a scented garden and she had lots of lovely frocks, pearls and gems, and many servants, and she did nothing for days on end, but play, and laugh and dance …
WŁADKA:	*(Looks at him, after a while)* I would like him, to take me into captivity.
ŁOŃSKI:	Then I shall … why are you blushing?
WŁADKA:	*(Ashamed)* Silly – it just happens. *(Pause)* You talk like a writer.
ŁOŃSKI:	*(Bursts out laughing)* Hear that, Kręcki?
KRĘCKI:	*(Turning towards him at the piano)* What?
ŁOŃSKI:	Władzia says I talk like a writer.
KRĘCKI:	Oh, you practically ooze talent, but is there any drink in the house? You should offer Miss Władzia some refreshment.

Ashanti (1906)

ŁOŃSKI:	Ah, so I should. But is there any point … We're going out for dinner. That was the initial plan. I'm getting hungry.
KRĘCKI:	Will you have enough time …? *(Knocking)*
ŁOŃSKI:	Who is it? *(Runs up to the door)*

The young bachelor (Matt van Niftrik) persuades the ex-factory girl (Magdalena Kwiatkowska) that being 'taken into captivity' is a positive outcome. Note how lighting and colour are being used here to highlight differences between the characters' circumstances and emotions. Blue was used to evoke a sense of the winter scene outside, particularly at the start of the performance, when the window frames also picked up this colour. Władka has come in from the cold outside, but once she is indoors her pallor does not improve. She carries something of the mood from the street with her and as such, the use of this device helps to further disrupt the relationship between indoor and outdoor spaces.

Image copyright: Matt Ager.

Scene Eight

JAN, ŁOŃSKI, KRĘCKI, WŁADKA

JAN:	*(In the doorway)* Pardon me, sir ...
ŁOŃSKI:	Yes?
JAN:	I wanted to fetch the large suitcase and the dress suit from the wardrobe.
ŁOŃSKI:	Oh bloody hell! I clean forgot about the trip with uncle ... we're supposed to be at the theatre.
KRĘCKI:	No time for dinner then.
ŁOŃSKI:	My wash bag is over here ... take it Jan ... I'll give you the clothes later.
WŁADKA:	You're going away?
ŁOŃSKI:	Yes, for a few days. I'm bloody starving ... supposed to be at the theatre ... I'll have no time to eat in peace. *(He comes across one of* WŁADKA's *boots and kicks it with a passion, so that it falls under the sofa)* Whose are these, in the middle of the floor ...?
KRĘCKI:	You're the one who removed them ... Now calm down ... Look how scared she is ...
ŁOŃSKI:	It's true ... Ashanti ... I'm sorry.
KRĘCKI:	My dear man, you rage and storm, but no one's dragging you there ...
ŁOŃSKI:	I can tell you now, I'll be bored witless.
KRĘCKI:	Then why go?
ŁOŃSKI:	I already promised uncle. We're supposed to meet at the theatre.
KRĘCKI:	Then tell the old fellow something's come up, kiss him, stuff him in a train compartment, send him on his way and get back here. Miss Władzia and I will be waiting.
ŁOŃSKI:	Oh, you don't know him ... he'll start ranting ... why get stuck in Warsaw? ... You're wasting your money ... they'll throw you out of Płaczków – the area's gone downhill ... look what happened to Kazio, Tadzio, the devil incarnate, blah, blah, blah. I can bear anything, except his ranting.
KRĘCKI:	Is that what happened earlier?
ŁOŃSKI:	Oh he started gushing ... I agreed, to stem the flow, promised to go along. Thank God he was terribly pushed for time. He's only here for a few hours, on business. *(He turns to* WŁADKA*)* Well, Ashanti?

Ashanti (1906)

WŁADKA:	What a shame, sir.
ŁOŃSKI:	Back in two days or three … we can have more fun.
KRĘCKI:	If you go, they won't let you out.
ŁOŃSKI:	So what shall I do?
KRĘCKI:	In my opinion … just an opinion … write him a letter, to the hotel – you can't go, that's that.
ŁOŃSKI:	We were supposed to meet at the theatre.
KRĘCKI:	Say sorry you couldn't make it.
ŁOŃSKI:	It's not done … We haven't seen each other in a long time.
KRĘCKI:	Well … well … you're not his rightful heir are you!
ŁOŃSKI:	There are in fact other reasons, not that you'd care.
KRĘCKI:	Dear fellow, it's not my fault your uncle fancied coming to Warsaw, and you're so gutless. *(Pause. Everyone is silent.* WŁADKA *goes up to the piano and tries to elicit a melody with one finger)*
ŁOŃSKI:	On the other hand …
KRĘCKI:	What?
ŁOŃSKI:	I could I suppose write a letter … what do you think?
KRĘCKI:	I'd consider it entirely natural.
ŁOŃSKI:	*(After a moment's hesitation)* You know what … I'll write.
KRĘCKI:	Of course … just drop him a line … you're not a child.
ŁOŃSKI:	Huh, what's the point … I don't feel like going, that's that. *(He sits by the bureau, writes.* KRĘCKI *approaches* WŁADKA *and takes her by the hand)*
WŁADKA:	Ah! I got such a fright.
KRĘCKI:	Let me assist you, Miss Władka … *(He moves her hand across the keyboard)*
ŁOŃSKI:	All done! *(He moves away from the bureau)* We'll send Jan right away. *(He rings)*
JAN:	*(Enters)* You rang, sir?
ŁOŃSKI:	Yes. Take this letter to the Hotel Europa, leave it at reception … For Mr Bratkowski.
JAN:	And the suits?
ŁOŃSKI:	No … no … changed my mind … not going … Deliver the letter. *(*JAN *exits)* My heart feels lighter.
KRĘCKI:	Well done.
WŁADKA:	You're not going, then, sir?
ŁOŃSKI:	No, I'm not.
WŁADKA:	How wonderful.
ŁOŃSKI:	Her laugh is so childlike … Right … before we go, let's toast our pleasure with a glass of vermouth … to sharpen our appetites. *(He rings)*

KRĘCKI:	*(Glances at his watch)* I need to leave at quarter past … business in town … you know, that duel … I'll come straight to the restaurant …
JAN:	*(Enters)* You rang, sir.
ŁOŃSKI:	There's one bottle of vermouth. Bring it and fetch some glasses. Then take the letter at once. *(JAN exits – to KRĘCKI)* Quick as you can, then join us.
KRĘCKI:	I won't stand on ceremony. *(Turns in the doorway)* Usual place?
ŁOŃSKI:	The very same.

Scene Nine

JAN, ŁOŃSKI, WŁADKA

JAN enters, brings in a tray with a bottle and glasses, puts them on the small table, and exits.

ŁOŃSKI:	Right, let's drink … *(He fills a glass)* Ashanti, your health … delicious …
WŁADKA:	Ugh … no.
ŁOŃSKI:	You don't like it? … What do you like? …
WŁADKA:	Vodka with a fruit syrup.
ŁOŃSKI:	Wait then, we'll have dinner, and you can have some port …
WŁADKA:	I can't go like this.
ŁOŃSKI:	Why not?
WŁADKA:	You took away my boots, sir …
ŁOŃSKI:	That's true … there's one here … *(He picks the boot up off the ground, hands it to Władzia)* One under the sofa … oh later … Drink, drink up, the first sip is always the worst.
WŁADKA:	How bitter.
ŁOŃSKI:	Wine tastes sweeter … when you kiss … *(He leans towards her, at this moment loud ringing is heard)* Who's that dammit? *(More ringing)* Władzia, darling, go to the bedroom for just one minute, please … *(He exits into the hallway)*

Scene Ten

ŁOŃSKI, BRATKOWSKI

ŁOŃSKI:	*(Offstage)* Oh! It's uncle!
BRATKOWSKI:	*(Entering)* Don't tell me you're alone.
ŁOŃSKI:	I sent Jan to town with a letter.

BRATKOWSKI:	I finished early and I'm free right now … didn't meet Silberstein, to be honest … he's away. Never mind … another time … Had your dinner?
ŁOŃSKI:	Yes … I mean, not yet … To be honest, uncle, I'm ravenous.
BRATKOWSKI:	Delightful coincidence … We'll have dinner, then the show … We need to talk …
ŁOŃSKI:	We do?
BRATKOWSKI:	Yes, yes. I got wind of your little affairs in town and must impart a few home truths.
ŁOŃSKI:	You're determined to believe all that gossip.
BRATKOWSKI:	Gossip or not … the fact is, you're haemorrhaging money.
ŁOŃSKI:	Huh …
BRATKOWSKI:	Remember, when you have land, it's easy to borrow, but to pay it back … Ho … ho! They've got you and you haven't even blinked.
ŁOŃSKI:	Uncle, you always harp on about the same old thing.
BRATKOWSKI:	Because frankly I'm amazed that you spend a whole year, day in, day out, stuck either in Warsaw or somewhere abroad. I can see how anyone else, without a pile, might have trouble settling down, but you …
ŁOŃSKI:	I'm just not made for country living.
BRATKOWSKI:	Then get married …
ŁOŃSKI:	Easy to say.
BRATKOWSKI:	Even easier to do.
ŁOŃSKI:	I'm looking, for a young lady, in Warsaw.
BRATKOWSKI:	In Warsaw … in Warsaw … Dear boy, a man can make love the whole world over but he should tie the knot near home. *(He notices the vermouth)* What's the occasion?
ŁOŃSKI:	It … it … a … friend of mine, had a tipple … Care for a glass, Uncle?
BRATKOWSKI:	Smells like something from a test tube. *(He notices* WŁADKA*'s boot on the chair)* Your friend took his clothes off, I see … *(He lifts up the boot)* He's got devilishly small feet.
ŁOŃSKI:	What? A boot? How strange!
BRATKOWSKI:	I can guess. *(He looks suspiciously around the room)*
ŁOŃSKI:	Let's get dinner, Uncle … I'm dying of hunger …
BRATKOWSKI:	I dread to think of the consequences if this is the state of its footwear?
ŁOŃSKI:	*(Grabs the boot from him, shoves it onto the floor)* Uncle, a very long story … I'll tell you over dinner … come on – let's go, my guts are churning. *(He pulls him towards the exit)*
BRATKOWSKI:	What about your things … we're leaving … No time later.

ŁOŃSKI:	I ... I ... I have it covered, really I do ...
BRATKOWSKI:	Lights staying on ...
ŁOŃSKI:	When Jan gets back, he'll see to it.
BRATKOWSKI:	Shocking waste.
ŁOŃSKI:	I'm putting them out ... alright ... putting them out ... *(Livid, he extinguishes the lamp)* Wait ... it's hellishly dark ... *(He lights a candle and lifts the blinds)* Let's go. *(They exit to the hallway)*

Scene Eleven

ŁOŃSKI, WŁADKA

Light from the streetlamps shines in through the window. A few moments after ŁOŃSKI, *and* BRATKOWSKI *exit,* WŁADKA *appears in the bedroom doorway. Surprised and afraid, she looks around. After a while, in a trembling voice:*

WŁADKA:	Pardon me ... sir! Hello, pardon me! Sir! Oh my God! *(She starts crying loudly. From the hallway enters* ŁOŃSKI *in a hurry, wearing a fur coat and a top hat)*

This is a very interesting moment, since it is possible for a director to show Władka alone in Łoński's apartment. How this opportunity is used, in terms of exposing motivation and in order to comment on her attitude towards being there, is crucial to the development of the character. As a director, I chose to portray her as genuinely frightened at the thought of having been left there alone. However, there are other possibilities, depending very much on what kind of through-line an actor chooses to take in terms of character representation.

ŁOŃSKI:	Bloody hell! Break your bloody neck ... Władzia ... Poor Ashanti ... Now, don't you cry sweetness.
WŁADKA:	I want my boots back.
ŁOŃSKI:	In a tick ... half an hour, an hour at most ... Put on some lights ...
WŁADKA:	No, no, I won't stay!
ŁOŃSKI:	Ashanti ... be good ... my uncle's here, you see ... I have to be at dinner ... You must have heard, how he badgered me ... Stay here, you'll be just fine ... Wait, I'll light the lamp ... Where are the bloody matches?
WŁADKA:	No, no, I'm scared ...

Ashanti (1906)

The structure of the research production depended on a series of transitions, which took place between the acts, and also in the opening and closing moments of the play. These transitions involved movement combined with sound and lighting changes, and were used to convey a sense of journey and a change in location. During these transitions the window frames and dust sheets were once again foregrounded by means of the lighting. Two servants (the actor playing Jan/Franek (Dave Buttle, picture below, and the Maid from Act 3) entered the space, arranging furniture and covering them with dust sheets or uncovering them as appropriate. They did not interact and their movements had a subtle choreographed quality, which was intended to have a de-naturalizing effect. This indicated that these characters were working within the reflexive 'frame' of the performance, whilst also being located within the narrative. I chose to overlay these actions with the recorded sounds of moving steam trains played at varying speeds at different points in the plot. The sounds had multiple functions – realistic, symbolic and dramatic – given their use as an additional 'framing' device.

Image copyright: Lib Taylor.

ŁOŃSKI:	What? A grown up girl like you, scared ...
WŁADKA:	Give me my boots! ...
ŁOŃSKI:	One minute ... no matches anywhere ...
WŁADKA:	I'm so stupid, why did I listen? *(She dissolves into loud weeping)*
ŁOŃSKI:	Władzia ... Poor thing ... Ashanti ... calm down! *(He grasps her round the waist and starts to kiss her passionately)*
WŁADKA:	Give me my boots!
ŁOŃSKI:	One minute ... we'll look for them, don't cry ... whatever you want ... nice dress, a ring, earrings, a brooch ... Ashanti, love ... my uncle can go hang. *(He rapidly pulls off his fur and throws it onto the ground)* Listen. I'm staying ... We'll have dinner ... together ... together, stop crying, please. *(He grasps her round the waist and pulls her towards him)* Ashanti, my own!

Act 2

Florence.

A room in a hotel apartment, occupied by ŁOŃSKI *and* WŁADKA. *To the right, a door to the hallway, to the left, to the bedroom. Backstage, two windows hung with green Italianate shutters. Through the gaps in the shutters sunlight pours into the room.*

A scorching day.

Signs of hurried preparations for departure are evident in the room. Things laid out everywhere, underwear, bits and bobs. In the centre stands an open trunk, on one of the chairs a wash bag etc. WŁADKA *in a negligee is lying with half-shut eyes on a low ottoman.* ŁOŃSKI *with a cigarette between his lips sits by the table. He is silent.*

He is extremely agitated.

Scene One

ŁOŃSKI, WŁADKA

ŁOŃSKI:	*(After a pause)* Władzia ... *(*WŁADKA *does not answer.* ŁOŃSKI *approaches and leans over her)* Are you asleep?
WŁADKA:	*(Touchily)* Leave me alone!
ŁOŃSKI:	*(Returns, sits in his former place)* Nothing's packed. We're supposed to leave in two hours.

Ashanti (1906)

The change in location and the heat of Florence was shown primarily through alterations in lighting, which took on warmer, perhaps rather cloying, tones. This was extended through the costumes and into the actors' performance style, which signified extreme heat. Indeed, an evocation of high temperature in this act is very important. It connects with Łoński's story (Matt van Niftrik, pictured above) in Act 1, when he describes a white man taking Ashanti into captivity. Indeed, one might argue that the couple is now in 'two places'. Literally, they are in Italy – metaphorically, they are in Africa. I explored this confluence of places during the interval, which I located halfway through Act 2. Władka (Magdalena Kwiatkowska, pictured above) was left on stage alone, and as she looked out across the 'fourth wall' into the audience space, the recorded sound of an intense heat wave – which indicated a place other than Florence – was gradually faded in. Within the reflexive parameters of the performance, the implication was that Władka's heightened awareness of her presence in two spaces was sonically accessible to the audience. Additionally, the sound functioned on another level – that is, within the broader frame of the play – and was connected in semantic terms to the sound of trains that featured during the aforementioned transitions. This could be regarded as a systematic use of sound, given that the interval was also given the status of a transition, which helped to manage the performance as a live event.

Image copyright: Lib Taylor.

WŁADKA:	Leave then, my God.
ŁOŃSKI:	*(Rises irritated from the armchair, paces about the room. It's evident he is restraining himself from making an angry outburst. After a while he approaches* WŁADKA*)* Ashanti, why so angry?
WŁADKA:	Get away! It's stifling. I'm half dead and he keeps on pushing …
ŁOŃSKI:	*(Rises, moves to the centre of the room)* How touchy. *(After a pause)* We're not going then? Well? Are we? Basic good manners, just respond.
WŁADKA:	Stuff good manners. I'm common. Alright?
ŁOŃSKI:	You should be really proud.
WŁADKA:	That's how I like it. *(Pause)*
ŁOŃSKI:	Władzia, you're simply horrid, why? I didn't do anything bad … I only want what's best.
WŁADKA:	Why did you take me away from Warsaw?
ŁOŃSKI:	We couldn't have lived together in Warsaw.
WŁADKA:	Really. How coy we are. Not many people 'co-habit' in Warsaw, do they? And grander gents than you.
ŁOŃSKI:	That's not the point. My family … They come to Warsaw all the time. They'd try to split us up, create intrigues, it's better for you that we live abroad. My love, what do you want? This is one of the world's most beautiful cities. You have everything you need. Thousands of people dream all their lives of coming here if only for a short trip.
WŁADKA:	I'll go mad. What's so nice? I'm bored stupid. No one to say two words to and the endless Italian yakking. I can't even go out.
ŁOŃSKI:	Władzia, if you lie on a sofa all day, you will get bored.
WŁADKA:	What am I supposed to do?
ŁOŃSKI:	How about this … you started drawing lessons … with Romkowski. Why did you stop?
WŁADKA:	Study, study, learn, all day long. That's entertainment …
ŁOŃSKI:	Anyway we're leaving. Paris is much more fun.
WŁADKA:	*(In a tearful voice)* It's boiling hot. I can't move a muscle and he wants to coop me up in some train compartment. What made you think of another trip? We live together here or there, it's all the same.
ŁOŃSKI:	I want to take you to the best place, that's all.
WŁADKA:	Here is best for me.
ŁOŃSKI:	We won't be staying on, that's quite clear, is it?
WŁADKA:	So send me back to Warsaw.
ŁOŃSKI:	You'd go?
WŁADKA:	Oh my God. Straight away.

Ashanti (1906)

Magdalena Kwiatkowska as Władka.

Image copyright: Matt Ager.

ŁOŃSKI:	Abandon me without a second thought … (WŁADZIA *does not reply.* ŁOŃSKI *after a pause, rising from his seat*) What's the point of this little performance? Just say it – you're through with me.
WŁADKA:	It's not a little performance.
ŁOŃSKI:	We can't seem to exchange a civilized word. From dawn til dusk – nothing but rows.
WŁADKA:	You're needling me, constantly, that's why.
ŁOŃSKI:	I am?
WŁADKA:	If you wanted to live here, you should've trawled up some Italian woman … I'd have agreed – in Warsaw.
ŁOŃSKI:	Two weeks ago things were different.
WŁADKA:	Not again?
ŁOŃSKI:	Meaning?
WŁADKA	I know exactly what you're going to say. Franek.
ŁOŃSKI:	I asked you not to talk to him. No friendships with hotel waiters.

Magdalena Kwiatkowska as Władka.

Image copyright: Matt Ager.

WŁADKA:	Listen … You're a complete fool. He's a Pole, I can hardly ignore him. I can barely make sense of anyone else.
ŁOŃSKI:	Władzia. It's one thing to be served, another to converse. Common sense. You've got me for companionship and Romkowski … What will they think at the hotel if you take staff into your confidence?
WŁADKA:	Fat lot do I care!
ŁOŃSKI:	But I do. A dirty tramp … the dregs …
WŁADKA:	He is a very poor young man.
ŁOŃSKI:	I've no desire to cultivate this friendship. Understood?
WŁADKA:	You exhaust me with your stupid jealousy … Don't shrug your shoulders – it's true. Top class – quite the done thing – fine gent avoids hotel waiter …

Ashanti (1906)

Władka (Magdalena Kwiatkowska) and Łoński (Matt van Niftrik).

Władka and Łoński are shown here in their hotel apartment in Florence. The trunk in the foreground was significant in relation to the direction of this scene. It had been used in Act 1, when Władka entered Łoński's apartment for the first time. She was helped up onto it – rather like a slave at a market – by Kręcki. Here it is referenced again in different terms that echo its previous usage, during Władka's interactions with an increasingly jealous and suspicious Łoński. Also, it is important to note that the box containing Łoński's gun is positioned on the table, whereas up until this point in the performance, it had been located downstage with the luggage. The colours of the box echo Władka's clothing, providing a noticeable link with her presence. This is of interest since she later takes ownership of it.

Image copyright: Lib Taylor.

ŁOŃSKI:	*(Approaches her, hissing through clenched teeth)* What did you say?
WŁADKA:	*(Leaps startled from the sofa)* Darling ... I was ... I only ... don't be angry ... sweetness ... *(She grasps his hand. ŁOŃSKI tears it away)* Darling, forgive me ... I'm so horrid ... We'll go today ... I'll pack everything myself, straight away ... *(She gathers together the linen and clothing scattered around on the table and chairs in a nervous hurry, begins folding them into the trunk. After a while she sits on the chair and closes her eyes)*
ŁOŃSKI:	What's the matter?
WŁADKA:	Dizzy ... a bit faint.
ŁOŃSKI:	You do seem unwell ... wait ... don't pack those things – lie *down*.
WŁADKA:	You're not angry? *(Kisses his hand)*
ŁOŃSKI:	No ... no ...
WŁADKA:	Horrid Ashanti ... always irritates her sweetheart.
ŁOŃSKI:	Enough ... well – let's forget it. *(He offers his lips to be kissed)*
WŁADKA:	*(Kisses him a few times, then folds her hands as if in prayer)* Muniek.
ŁOŃSKI:	What is it?
WŁADKA:	Let's go tomorrow ... one more day.
ŁOŃSKI:	It makes no sense ... We'll never get anywhere. We decided, today, let's go.
WŁADKA:	I'm so tired; I'll lie down for a while, in bed ... Come on, Muniek. *(She takes his hand and pulls him in the direction of the bedroom)*
ŁOŃSKI:	Darling. We're supposed to be leaving today.
WŁADKA:	Come on ... *(Knocking at the door)*
ŁOŃSKI:	Ah, it's Romkowski.
WŁADKA:	I don't want to talk. Get rid of him quickly and come through. *(She escapes to the bedroom)*

Scene Two

ŁOŃSKI, ROMKOWSKI

ŁOŃSKI:	*(Approaches the door, opens it)* Hello, Stanisław ... Complete mess in here.
ROMKOWSKI:	I can see ... really leaving, then, today?
ŁOŃSKI:	That's right.
ROMKOWSKI:	You won't miss Florence?
ŁOŃSKI:	Ha! Paris will provide a change of scene ... Do sit ... Ashanti's napping, she's tired ... I'll get her in a minute ...
ROMKOWSKI:	I must admit I shall miss you both terribly ... We've had some good times ...

Ashanti (1906)

Romkowski (Chris Montague) arrives wearing his sunglasses, against the heat.

Image copyright: Lib Taylor.

ŁOŃSKI: Perhaps we'll meet in Paris. You will come, won't you?
ROMKOWSKI: Yes, in the autumn, possibly, not sure yet ... have to go back to Kraków first ...
ŁOŃSKI: Sell one of your paintings to a banker, come along.
ROMKOWSKI: Huh, wish I could find one ...
ŁOŃSKI: You'll forgive me, if I pack and talk ...
ROMKOWSKI: Oh, go ahead, can I help?
ŁOŃSKI: No, thanks and when do you leave?
ROMKOWSKI: In a month ... So ... stay in Florence one more month and we'll leave together.
ŁOŃSKI: No, we really must be going.
ROMKOWSKI: *(After a momentary hesitation)* Apropos ... Do send me your Paris address ... I still owe you money.
ŁOŃSKI: Oh, it's nothing, really. Send it when you can, or deliver in person. You must come to Paris ...
ROMKOWSKI: No plans to go back then?
ŁOŃSKI: Not right now ...
ROMKOWSKI: I'd love to meet up in Paris.
ŁOŃSKI: Me too. Believe it! I'll long for your company. We've had such a pleasant time roaming here and there, discussing art. You've changed my perspective on everything.
ROMKOWSKI: You've got talent. With dedication, you could make a very good engraver.
ŁOŃSKI: Too old for that now.
ROMKOWSKI: What do you mean, too old? Men of forty enter the academies. Friend of mine, in Munich. No – you really should, enroll in Paris.
ŁOŃSKI: You're so positive, very inspiring and persuasive. *(He approaches the door, rings)*
ROMKOWSKI: Have a go. You'll see – your passion for work will grow in time. *(Enter FRANEK)*

Scene Three

ŁOŃSKI, FRANEK, ROMKOWSKI, WŁADKA

ŁOŃSKI: *(Spotting FRANEK in the doorway, in a sharp tone)* I rang for room service.
FRANEK: Not available, sir.
ŁOŃSKI: Go to the tailor, and fetch the grey suit, but you won't know ...
FRANEK: I do, I know, sir, I took it over ...
ŁOŃSKI: Straight away. *(FRANEK exits)*

Ashanti (1906)

ROMKOWSKI:	Is he Polish?
ŁOŃSKI:	Can you imagine?
ROMKOWSKI:	I was so surprised when he replied in Polish. That a Pole should be a waiter in a hotel in Florence!
ŁOŃSKI:	Ah well, Polaks are regular globetrotters, aren't they. He's only been here for about two weeks. Footloose and fancy free. Knows Egypt, America, France …
ROMKOWSKI:	You never mentioned. Interesting subject, possibly.
ŁOŃSKI:	Yes, but somehow doesn't fit … Don't like him, or his big vicious mouth.
ROMKOWSKI:	Ashanti must have been delighted.
ŁOŃSKI:	Why?
ROMKOWSKI:	She's always complained about poor communication with staff. Now at least she has a Pole.
ŁOŃSKI:	Well no, she doesn't need to communicate with them because I oblige. Besides we've only just found out he's Polish … I should call Ashanti … *(He calls out to her)* Ashanti, come and join us, its Mr Romkowski …
WŁADKA:	*(From the other room)* One minute … darling … come here, please …
ŁOŃSKI:	Do excuse me. *(Exits)*

Scene Four

ROMKOWSKI, FRANEK

FRANEK:	*(Enters with the suit, puts it on a chair.)*
ROMKOWSKI:	So, you're Polish?
FRANEK:	Yes.
ROMKOWSKI:	From where?
FRANEK:	Galicia, Tarnów.
ROMKOWSKI:	How come you're in Italy?
FRANEK:	Well – been globetrotting. Scarpered to avoid conscription, then – no way back.
ROMKOWSKI:	You don't miss your country?
FRANEK:	Why would I … If you're clever, the world's your oyster.
ROMKOWSKI:	Still, East or West …
FRANEK:	They'll rip you off there, same as here.
ROMKOWSKI:	I've heard you've been to America, and Egypt …
FRANEK:	That's right.

Romkowski (Chris Montague, left), the impoverished artist resident in Florence, expresses fascination when he meets Franek (Dave Buttle, right) in the hotel and finds out that he is a fellow Pole. In this production, Romkowski was presented as an ebullient, rather eccentric character, more open in his expression of emotion than any other man in the play. Within this scene, the playwright shows two highly contrasting male characters – since Franek oozes a performed machismo – engaged in conversation about partitioned Poland. Romkowski's rather romantic view of life in Poland – later expressed in a speech, redolent with Chekhovian nostalgia, about waiting for the train in his village – contrasts starkly with Franek's brutal dissociation from his Polish identity and his potentially defensive (and politically problematic) assertion of his position as a citizen of the world. In this image from the performance, Franek is seen positioned slightly downstage of Romkowski, which allowed the actor playing Romkowski to fully express the latter's bewildered curiosity, and the actor playing Franek to temper this wide-eyed approach with sidelong glances that helped to develop important comedic aspects within the performance style. These comedic aspects featured strongly throughout the performance as a whole, and are important to access in order for the play's satirical tone to be engaged.

Image copyright: Matt Ager.

Ashanti (1906)

ROMKOWSKI:	Egypt must be a wonderful country.
FRANEK:	Huh, really – dust, heat, blink and you're sick. Good for business, though – stay a while, raise money. Eventually, got bored. And besides, I was after this girl.
ROMKOWSKI:	Been in Florence long?
FRANEK:	Only a month, it was Rome before that. But I won't be here long, don't like it …

Scene Five

FRANEK, ŁOŃSKI, WŁADKA, ROMKOWSKI

ŁOŃSKI:	*(Entering)* Aha! You brought the suit – you may leave. *(FRANEK exits)*
WŁADKA:	*(Entering)* Good day to you, sir.
ROMKOWSKI:	Good day, Miss Ashanti. Dreadful pity you're leaving.
WŁADKA:	I'd dig my heels in but Muniek's put his foot down.
ROMKOWSKI:	Why not stay?
ŁOŃSKI:	No … no … no … Stanisław – we have to go. Right then – I should get down to the station and pick up the tickets. Let's all go … We'll stop on the way for a bottle of wine, and drink a toast.
ROMKOWSKI:	Good idea.
ŁOŃSKI:	Really we're quite ready. Whatever's left, we can pack in fifteen minutes. That leaves three whole hours to spare.
WŁADKA:	He's been fretting all day – there's nothing packed. Just before you arrived, he was ranting we'd be late.
ŁOŃSKI:	Just ignore her. Ashanti dearly loves to exaggerate. Well – get dressed – Ashanti.
ROMKOWSKI:	Country folk simply assume they're going to miss the train. I remember my art school days. Each journey back to the city, without fail, my father would set off for the station at the crack of dawn, to see me off. Six hours, sometimes, or even more, until departure, and he'd get itchy feet. 'Come on, my boy, half an hour at the station is better than disappointment'. This little rural habit may have rubbed off on you.
ŁOŃSKI:	No, but Miss Ashanti can be very slow. Like now. Get dressed, Ashanti, better sit in the restaurant.
WŁADKA:	I won't go, I'm tired.
ŁOŃSKI:	Oh, come on.
ROMKOWSKI:	Oh do come, please. It'll be our last outing as a threesome, won't it?

WŁADKA:	No ... no ... no ... I'll be sitting in a train compartment all night long, I want to rest, I'd have to get changed.
ŁOŃSKI:	You look fine.
WŁADKA:	No, Muniek, love, you two go. I'll pack whatever's left, then dress for the journey.
ŁOŃSKI:	Well, perhaps we'll simply remain here. I do need to fetch the tickets though. Stanisław can wait with Ashanti, then.
WŁADKA:	No, no, go together. Stanisław can't stay, I've got to change.
ROMKOWSKI:	What a shame ... we might not see each other for ages.
WŁADKA:	Yes we will ... you shall come to Paris.
ŁOŃSKI:	*(Looks closely at WŁADKA, slowly)* And why do you insist on staying at home?
WŁADKA:	Well, I just want ... Mr Romkowski, do take my side.
ŁOŃSKI:	*(Annoyed)* Come along, Stanisław ... We shan't be long. *(He exits swiftly, ROMKOWSKI follows him)*

Scene Six

WŁADKA, FRANEK

WŁADKA, *after their exit, stretches and slowly approaches the ottoman, lying down on it. After a while the door is pushed ajar quietly, and there appears FRANEK's head.*

FRANEK:	Władka!
WŁADKA:	Wait, Franuś! *(Sits on the ottoman)* Come back later, he'll be here any minute.
FRANEK:	You come to me ....
WŁADKA:	No ... no ... no ... Wait, five minutes.
FRANEK:	He won't come back; they went together.
WŁADKA:	Oho, I know him, he's crafty ... he'll tell the other one he's forgotten something and scamper up the stairs ... Wouldn't be the first time ... even in Warsaw.
FRANEK:	Get rid of him ...
WŁADKA:	Well, he is completely insane ... Aim at a woman and shoot, his type ... Sometimes I watch his great big eyes spark into life, my skin crawls ... I'm not joking. *(She widens her eyes, apparently copying ŁOŃSKI's gaze)* And today we argued, about you.
FRANEK:	*(Laughs with pleasure)* I know he hates me.
WŁADKA:	Don't even imply he's jealous! That's when he'd kill, he won't let me look at anyone else, but he's ashamed.

Ashanti (1906)

Through the character of Franek, Perzyński explores the problems encountered by a working-class man, who has dodged conscription, spent time in travelling, cannot return to Poland and who subsequently uses his rootless existence to create temporary, furtive attachments with sexually dissatisfied women (if we are to believe his stories …).

Władka (Magdalena Kwiatkowska) and Franek (Dave Buttle), the hotel waiter, in Florence.

In this production, Franek's desire for – and class interest in – Władka were shown as compatible with his desire to wreak revenge on Łoński, as a rich man able to return to Poland, by (temporarily) 'possessing' his mistress, as well as (permanently) 'acquiring' a number of his shirts and suits. Like the majority of other characters introduced in the opening acts of the play, Franek seeks to benefit from Łoński's wealth, as well as his sexual predilections (albeit indirectly in this case); Łoński cannot keep anything in his pockets. In the scenes between Władka and Franek, the idea of her experiencing pleasure was very important, and the performance style became increasingly physical during their interactions. Up until this point in the play, there is very little indication of physical pleasure and intimacy but when it is expressed, in the heat of Florence, the electricity of an encounter between equals needs perhaps to be palpable and exciting in performance, in order to contextualize Łoński's jealous rage when he reappears, as much as anything.

Image copyright: Matt Ager.

FRANEK:	The upper classes …
WŁADKA:	Today, I said to him – you make him nervous. Furious, he was. Thought he might hit me.
FRANEK:	*(Approaches the trunk, takes* ŁOŃSKI'S *shirt out)* Just look at his shirts.
WŁADKA:	Take it, Franuś, it's your size, have this one as well … and this …
FRANEK:	He'll notice.
WŁADKA:	He's no idea what's his … Don't worry … wait Franuś, I'll choose something else … now go, go on, he's due back … *(FRANEK exits, carrying the shirt under his jacket. After his exit* WŁADKA *stands by the door listening, if someone is coming along the corridor. After a while she runs on tiptoe towards the trunk and with great enthusiasm begins to tidy up inside it.* ŁOŃSKI *enters quickly)*

Scene Seven

ŁOŃSKI, WŁADKA

ŁOŃSKI:	*(Entering)* I forgot …

Ashanti (1906)

Władka *(Magdalena Kwiatkowska)* and Łoński *(Matt van Niftrik)*.

Image copyright: Matt Ager.

WŁADKA:	Yes?
ŁOŃSKI:	A hankie …. Ridiculous … Ashanti, you were packing.
WŁADKA:	We are supposed to be leaving.
ŁOŃSKI:	My dearest darling child … You're so well-organized.
WŁADKA:	Naughty Muniek … angry with Ashanti … Ashanti must be forgiven … a proper scatterbrain, that's all.
ŁOŃSKI:	No … no … no … I'm not angry. *(He embraces her round the waist and pulls her towards him passionately)* I'm not angry … you'll see, Ashanti, Paris will be so good … should've gone there straight away … not lively enough here. *(Kisses her)* My own Ashanti, sweetheart … leave that packing, and come with us.
WŁADKA:	I might as well finish off … then I'll come.
ŁOŃSKI:	We're going to our wine-bar in the square … You will be there?
WŁADKA:	I will … yes … *(ŁOŃSKI pulls his handkerchief out of his pocket)* Oh, your hankie.
ŁOŃSKI:	That's right, so distracted. *(WŁADKA bursts out laughing)*
ŁOŃSKI:	*(After a while also begins to laugh)* Well … well … you silly creature. *(Kisses her and exits. In the doorway)* We're waiting.

Scene Eight

WŁADKA, FRANEK

WŁADKA, *after ŁOŃSKI's exit, stands for a while, centre stage, with clenched fists, then approaches the door, rings.*

FRANEK:	*(Entering)* Has he been?
WŁADKA:	I did say so …
FRANEK:	And?
WŁADKA:	He's waiting … he kissed my hands … Oh, I'm so stupid!
FRANEK:	You don't love him?
WŁADKA:	Me? If I wasn't scared of prison, I'd have poisoned him ages ago. *(Throwing her arms suddenly round FRANEK's neck)* Franuś! I love you … only you … believe me …
FRANEK:	*(Pushing her away)* Wait … you've pricked me with something sharp … pin or a brooch … *(He examines his hand carefully)*

Ashanti (1906)

WŁADKA:	Where ... let me see ... *(She seizes his hand and kisses it)* Franek, my own Franek ... when I think that in a few hours we'll be parted, my heart nearly bursts ...
FRANEK:	Then stay, you fool.
WŁADKA:	He'd kill me.
FRANEK:	*(Spits with disdain)* Huh, what rubbish ... He's scared of prison too.
władka:	Franuś, I love you so much. You've bewitched me.
FRANEK:	Usual thing, I'm a strapping fellow, girls cannot resist. *(Approaches the trunk)* Władka, I might take this shirt too ...
WŁADKA:	Take it, Franuś, whatever you want ... it's all yours ...
FRANEK:	*(With pleasure)* I give a whistle – ten women appear ... listen, in Paris I worked in a bed and breakfast. This countess fell in love with me ... Long past her prime, but horny as a devil ... aristocrats have secrets ... could've married her, if I'd only wanted ... I'm not joking.
WŁADKA:	I know, Franek, I believe you.
FRANEK:	Gave me a gold pocket watch, many gifts ... went mad for me alright, but was she jealous – oho! ... I couldn't shake her off ...
WŁADKA:	You'd make anyone jealous.
FRANEK:	Nice little earner there ... not for me though ... don't care ... born honest ... I do play around but not like some others, strategic.
WŁADKA:	Because you don't want to Franek, you just don't ... if you did, you could.
FRANEK:	Władka, listen, why put up with Łoński? He keeps you and he's going mad, I give him a year at most ... You've got money saved ... we'll go to Monte Carlo ... We could be happy, really.
WŁADKA:	You'll get a job?
FRANEK:	Anywhere. We'll easily find some gullible ass to chase you around ... Phew ... no problem. *(He puts his hands on her shoulders, then takes a step back and measures her with an expert eye)* Lovely face, good figure ... all curves.
WŁADKA:	I'll stay, Franio, with you ... I just can't leave. I couldn't sleep a wink last night ... kept waking up and when I remembered we're about to part ... grief choked me ... terrible grief, honestly... I could have strangled him and I huddled close to the edge, with this big space between us.
FRANEK:	When I lived at home, in our country, this girl fell in love with me. Know what she did, when I left? Go on, guess ... she poisoned herself. Honestly.

Franek (Dave Buttle) and Władka (Magdalena Kwiatkowska).

Image copyright: Lib Taylor.

Ashanti (1906)

WŁADKA:	I'd do the same, Franek, for you. *(Throwing her arms around his neck)* No ... no, I won't go with him ... I can't live without you.
FRANEK:	I said, drop him and stay ... I'll quit this job and we'll leave together. *(He takes ŁOŃSKI's suit)* This grey suit could be useful.
WŁADKA:	Take it, Franuś, take, whatever you want ...
FRANEK:	Alright, I will ... come to my room ... better there ... some wine ... Dutch courage ... you can tell him – go to hell – on your own!
WŁADKA:	Alright. What will he do?
FRANEK:	Nothing.
WŁADKA:	Let him hit me ... shoot at me ... It's all the same, I've had enough ... am I his dog or what!
FRANEK:	Come on, Władka, you can do it ... that's the spirit ... I love that about you.
WŁADKA:	You love me ... really?
FRANEK:	*(Exiting)* When I tell a woman I love her, then I love her ... what, you think, I'd bother to make things up ... *(For a few moments, the stage is empty)*

Scene Nine

ŁOŃSKI, ROMKOWSKI

ŁOŃSKI:	*(Enters the room hurriedly)* We waited ... We wai- ... *(He crosses into the other room, behind the door he is heard calling)* Ashanti!
ROMKOWSKI:	*(Entering behind him at the same time)* We drank to you and Florence!
ŁOŃSKI:	*(Entering the stage space)* Not here.
ROMKOWSKI:	Miss Ashanti probably went out, ships passing in the night.
ŁOŃSKI:	How's that possible? We surely would have seen her.
ROMKOWSKI:	We did arrange to meet at the wine bar ... We'd better go back and wait. One more bottle, to art. My God, Mr Łoński, if you don't start training when you get to Paris, I'll have you down as a complete philistine ... Frenchmen stay on at the academy for years and apply themselves with rigour. Well – come on – you bought the last round, this one's mine.
ŁOŃSKI:	Let's wait, Stanisław, we'll go with Ashanti.
ROMKOWSKI:	Oh God ... damned shame you're leaving ... charming moments spent together ... I'll write to uncle, asking for money ... I've devised an approach ... might try it ... a month and I'll be in Paris

	... must complete Ashanti's portrait ... fine figure of a woman ... *(He traces a shape in the air with his hand)*
ŁOŃSKI:	It's not packed ... where's she gone?
ROMKOWSKI:	She won't be long. You're under the influence. Not good ... must be overcome ... an artist should never ever ...
ŁOŃSKI:	*(Smiling in spite of himself)* Stanisław, I'm not an artist yet ...
ROMKOWSKI:	You are in spirit ... that's the key ... You have to feel – the rest is just technique. Well, come on, 'nother bottle of wine. Miss Ashanti will join us.
ŁOŃSKI:	One minute, Stanisław ... Let's take a breather ... you're slightly tipsy already...
ROMKOWSKI:	An artist should always ...
ŁOŃSKI:	Just one minute, please ... I'll try the garden ... she may have gone there ... not likely though ... *(Exits; he meets WŁADKA in the doorway)*

Scene Ten

ŁOŃSKI, WŁADKA, ROMKOWSKI

ŁOŃSKI:	There you are. Where've you been?
ROMKOWSKI:	We waited, Miss Ashanti, toasted you and Florence. I've decided Paris, next stop ... I must finish your portrait.
WŁADKA:	*(Paying no attention to ROMKOWSKI, she replies to ŁOŃSKI)* With Franek.
ŁOŃSKI:	What?
WŁADKA:	*(Struggling to calm down)* With Franek ... *(To ROMKOWSKI)* And you shut up ... I'm sick to death of your portrait ... You idiot. *(ŁOŃSKI and ROMKOWSKI look dumbstruck at WŁADKA, who stands facing ŁOŃSKI with her fists clenched, as though at any moment she might throw herself at him)*
ŁOŃSKI:	*(After a pause)* What does this mean?
WŁADKA:	It means, I've had enough ... alright ... enough ... I'm not a dog that you should buy me ... Go to Paris ... wherever you like ... to Warsaw ... I can't look at you any more ...
ŁOŃSKI:	*(Confused)* Władka ... Mr Romkowski ...
WŁADKA:	Oh, fat lot do I care - Mr Romkowski ... what a tramp.
ROMKOWSKI:	Excuse me.
ŁOŃSKI:	You're drunk.

Ashanti (1906)

WŁADKA:	Drunk ... or not, what's it to you ... You can't tell me what to do any more ...
ŁOŃSKI:	Mr Romkowski, leave us alone now please ... terribly sorry ... you see ... I can't quite grasp ...
ROMKOWSKI:	Not to worry at all. *(Exits)*
ŁOŃSKI:	Władka, you've gone mad ...
WŁADKA:	Don't come near me or I'll scratch your eyes out ...
ŁOŃSKI:	For God's sake ... calm down ... stop shouting ...
WŁADKA:	I'll shout ... I will ... will ... will ... I like it.
ŁOŃSKI:	Quietly ... *(He seizes her hands)*
WŁADKA:	Let go ... don't lay a finger on me, you've no right ... I'm yours ... you bought me ... yes? His lordship ... got himself a woman and went abroad, now he can't stand up to a waiter ... ha ... ha ... ha ...
ŁOŃSKI:	Władka ... *(He clasps both hands to his chest as though he is short of breath)*
WŁADKA:	Stop yelling ... you can't just spirit me away under Franek's nose because he's mine ... you stupid fool, you bigot ... I'll hang about, like a dog, at his heels, but I spit on you ... look, all your precious gifts ... *(She grabs a watch from a side table and throws it furiously onto the floor)* There! I love Franek and I've slept with him ... I've always betrayed you ... always .... with the baron, everyone. And all of them laughed at you ...
ŁOŃSKI:	You're lying.
WŁADKA:	That time you had a duel because of me, I told you I was in church that morning, well, I was in actual fact at the hotel ... *(ŁOŃSKI, closing his eyes, pulls a small revolver out of his pocket and blindly shoots in front of him)* Help, somebody ... he'll kill me ... help ... *(She escapes into the corridor)*

In the next image, Łoński (Matt van Niftrik) is seen contemplating the box in which the gun was situated in this production, prior to shooting in Władka's direction, and missing (the reader will notice that the actor playing Władka (Joanna Lucas) in this image is different from the one shown playing her in previous images, with red hair). The box in question reappeared a number of times during the performance. As already described, it was primarily situated downstage, together with a group of trunks and suitcases, which were ever-present, in varying arrangements, either open or closed, in every act. Thus, it was always in full

view of the audience and functioned systematically with other elements of setting to express the play's aforementioned key themes. The box was used symbolically in one key respect. It was clearly shown to be the receptacle for Łoński's gun which, according to the original stage directions, is kept in his pocket. Additionally, later on in the performance, it functioned as a receptacle for a fan, which has been purchased for Władka by a wealthy industrialist seeking to become her 'protector'. During the scene in which Łoński comes to visit Władka in her Warsaw apartment, the actor playing Władka explicitly handled the fan and its emergence from the box using gestures and pacing associated with Łoński's previous treatment of his gun. Directorially, this enabled both an expression of their reversed power relationship and a palimpsestic treatment of the function of the box, which related to the production's evocation of space and location. Władka's self-conscious use of the fan engaged with notions of performativity within gender relations, which connected directly with her earlier dance to Kręcki's 'Cakewalk'. Gender relations are framed and informed within this naturalistic play text by the context of rapid industrialization and financial acquisition within the Russian partition; Warsaw is represented as a 'free-for-all' where people can be easily bought (off).

Ashanti (1906)

Łoński bought Władka and later tried to kill her with a lethal weapon, which, in this production, was kept within and framed by the box. Later, Władka lends Łoński money when he has none left, but he returns it to her. Her weapon against him is her ability to successfully sell herself to a much richer man, who is not a member of the landed gentry, as he himself is, and whose wealth is likely to keep on growing rather than being frittered away. In this production, Władka's threat to Łoński was expressed by her keeping the fan in the same box, which contained and framed it, and this could be read as a symbol of her increased social status and newfound sexual pragmatism. This is reflective of her former lover Franek's approach to his affairs. Essentially, Władka's removal of the fan from the box could be expressed theatrically as a trigger for Łoński's decision to turn his gun on himself, thus implicating her, by association, in his death.

Image copyright: Lib Taylor.

Scene Eleven

ŁOŃSKI, LUTOBORSKI

After WŁADKA *escapes,* ŁOŃSKI *stands motionless for a while, as if frozen. Next he puts the revolver back into his pocket and presses his hands to his brow. He approaches the window and opens it wide. It is sunrise. In the distance, mountains covered with vineyards. Scattered amongst the hills, whitewashed villas. Sweet, late afternoon silence.* ŁOŃSKI *stands gazing in front of him. After a while knocking is heard at the door. It intensifies. Eventually* LUTOBORSKI *enters the space.*

LUTOBORSKI:	Muniek!
ŁOŃSKI:	*(Turning around)* Jesus Christ …
LUTOBORSKI:	No, only me. Been looking for you everywhere. Traipsing around the whole blessed hotel. Knocking on all the doors. No answer. Downstairs, asked some Italian, looked at me like I had no brain … nearly punched him on the nose …
ŁOŃSKI:	How on earth did you get here?
LUTOBORSKI:	Came along with the wife. Just arranged our honeymoon … Well, give us a twirl … how's he looking … *(He takes him round the waist)* Why so pale?
ŁOŃSKI:	Me, pale … no … perhaps a little … slight headache … you've come to Florence, with your wife … Are you really married?

Lutoborski's unrelentingly cheerful demeanour and blustering approach provide the perfect foil for his friend's desperate state. In the production it was possible, given the dialogue, to set off these opposing tendencies against each other and facilitate the full expression of Łoński's despair at the end of this act (Matt van Niftrik, above). Lutoborski (Dan Whateley, above) brings with him ideas about marriage and romantic love, which are very far from his friend's current domestic situation.

Image copyright: Matt Ager.

LUTOBORSKI:	You were supposed to be at my wedding. You didn't come.
ŁOŃSKI:	You're right … Two years ago … I couldn't make it … Something came up … can't remember what …
LUTOBORSKI:	*(Patting him on the back)* There … there … there … Bratkowski's still angry ….
ŁOŃSKI:	Angry?

Ashanti (1906)

After a while, Lutoborski's nostalgia and romantic approach to Italy begins to grate (Dan Whateley, above), in a similar way to Romkowski's cheerful eccentricity. This image gives an idea of how the actor achieved this through his facial expression, which was matched by a light, rather persistent tone. We began to question, during the rehearsal process, whether Lutoborski could actually perceive the extent to which he was wearing his friend down emotionally, in order to achieve some satisfaction that he had in fact 'destroyed his life', and made the 'wrong choice' in leaving Poland.

Image copyright: Matt Ager.

LUTOBORSKI:	He couldn't get over Ashanti … last year, when you sold your estate, he washed his hands of the matter. Got a point if you ask me: stupid thing to do – sell it.
ŁOŃSKI:	They would have thrown me out anyway.
LUTOBORSKI:	I'm completely exhausted. Strenuous times, oho. Just getting round to some sightseeing. What's this? You're leaving?

ŁOŃSKI:	I … don't know yet.
LUTOBORSKI:	You are packing.
ŁOŃSKI:	Oh, yes … Quite right, we were … yes; I will be leaving … maybe even today …
LUTOBORSKI:	What's going on?
ŁOŃSKI:	I … you think I ….
LUTOBORSKI:	Postpone your journey for a few days. Be our tour guide in Florence. The wife's really curious to meet you … Well, she was practically legendary. Especially, when you went abroad. They even said you'd married her … *(ŁOŃSKI shrugs his shoulders)* Never could believe it myself … but people gossiped … Well, go on, introduce me.
ŁOŃSKI:	To whom?
LUTOBORSKI:	What do you mean, whom? Ashanti …
ŁOŃSKI:	Not in … went out …
LUTOBORSKI:	Ah, I've come at a bad time …. I sense a domestic … Go on, you've argued, admit it.
ŁOŃSKI:	No. *(In the distance are heard the quiet strains of a mandolin. The music is gradually audible, becomes increasingly clear)*
LUTOBORSKI:	Why argue in such a marvellous country? Utterly splendid, really is. The wife's enchanted. We've been to Venice, Bologna, from here to Rome, then Napoli. So little time, crying shame … could easily stay for a couple of months …
ŁOŃSKI:	I'm bored with it now …
LUTOBORSKI:	Alright for some. I bet you speak Italian like a native.
ŁOŃSKI:	So so.
LUTOBORSKI:	*(Approaches the window)* Oh, it's that, they sang it on the gondola in Venice. *(Both listen to the serenade in silence for a few minutes)* They slandered you at home, because you went abroad, squandered your fortune … who knows, you may be smarter than the lot. For one moment, just like this … oh, there it is again … *(After a pause)* A woman at your side, the pleasure of all this … In the end, you really knew how to build a life. *(ŁOŃSKI struggles with himself for a moment, finally at LUTOBORSKI's last words he can no longer hide his agitation and he explodes in spasms of fitful weeping. LUTOBORSKI looks at him dumbfounded)* Łoński, what's happened to you?

Ashanti (1906)

Łoński's (Matt van Niftrik) time in Italy has ended with a bang …

Image copyright: Lib Taylor.

Act 3

The setting is a room in WŁADKA LUBARTOWSKA'S *apartment. Backstage, a door leading to the bedroom. Through it, a large French bed is visible. Above the door, colourful portieres. To the left, two windows, to the right, a door to the adjoining room. Between the windows an ottoman, in front of it a small table and two small armchairs. On the table albums and an epergne for visiting cards. In the centre a large, round table, covered with a tablecloth. On the table a lamp, various odds and ends. On the right, between the entrance door and the bedroom door, a large palm tree. In the foreground to the right a fireplace, shielded by a screen. To the left, in the corner, between the window and the bedroom door, elegant bookshelves, on which there are lots of photographs and various odds and ends. On the walls, a few pictures. On the round table, in the centre of the room, lies a big doll wearing a pink dress.*

Scene One

MRS LUBARTOWSKA, MAID

As the curtain rises, MRS LUBARTOWSKA *and the* MAID *are on stage.* MRS LUBARTOWSKA *sits on the very edge of the sofa. The* MAID *stands in the centre of the room, holding a dress.*

MRS LUBARTOWSKA:	So, you did pawn that gemstone brooch.
MAID:	Would I make it up? Yes I pawned it.
MRS LUBARTOWSKA:	Get much for it, did you?
MAID:	Three hundred and fifty roubles.
MRS LUBARTOWSKA:	Well … Well … dear God … Three hundred and fifty … What's she done with that?
MAID:	Blew it all, at the races.
MRS LUBARTOWSKA:	All of it?
MAID:	Whole blessed lot. As of this morning, no money in the house. *(She returns the dress to the bedroom and comes back)* Miss Władzia's no idea how to keep it close … Oh no … Anyone else in her position would've made her fortune long ago … And what about us?
MRS LUBARTOWSKA:	I've told her. She won't be pert forever … and who'll give her anything when she sags, the madam … stack it up while you're fresh – they won't cough up later.
MAID:	Everyone wants money … No free lunches for an old hag, eh?
MRS LUBARTOWSKA:	Completely mad … up in the air … she's got nothing and won't spare a thought for her blessed mother.
MAID:	Oh well, as her blessed mother I suppose you'd expect a good cut.
MRS LUBARTOWSKA:	What's it to you … a Mother, that's something! Get what I can … and can't take it with me, alright?
MAID:	And then there's Łoński, still hovering about.
MRS LUBARTOWSKA:	He's been here?
MAID:	All the time …
MRS LUBARTOWSKA:	He's got nothing now.
MAID:	Not a loaf …
MRS LUBARTOWSKA:	And the count?
MAID:	Gone abroad … there's still the mahgrabi ….
MRS LUBARTOWSKA:	Is that better than a count?
MAID:	Oh much better … Anyone can be a count … Even those without a single crumb ….
MRS LUBARTOWSKA:	And what's the richest one called?
MAID:	An ordynat.
MRS LUBARTOWSKA:	Does Władka see one of *them*?

Ashanti (1906)

MAID:	Oh they can have German women, French women ….
MRS LUBARTOWSKA:	How are people meant to be happy in their own country? They let their native women die of hunger and stuff money into some foreigner … better value, is it?
MAID:	Course not … that's how it goes. God decides who gets what. One woman is ugly as sin and makes her career – they find she's special – another, ten times prettier, must work her fingers to the bone …
MRS LUBARTOWSKA:	Oh, yes, yes, life's completely senseless, ah me … *(Door bell is heard)*
MAID:	Go to the kitchen – the mistress doesn't like it when you sit in here … *(They exit)*

Scene Two

ŁOŃSKI, MAID

ŁOŃSKI:	*(Elegantly dressed, but the clothing is worn)* Is she in?
MAID:	No.
ŁOŃSKI:	Where's she gone?
MAID:	To town, and then it's Miss Hela's for dinner. She'll be a while, daresay.
ŁOŃSKI:	Damn. I've come on serious business … I'll write it down, find me a pen and paper … *(MAID exits; after a while she brings a pen and paper, ŁOŃSKI begins to write, and speaks as he writes)* Well – did she lose a lot?
MAID:	Everything, down to the last grosz.
ŁOŃSKI:	We'd no luck either … stripped clean … We'll make it up tomorrow …
MAID:	I'm not sure she'll even be at the races.
ŁOŃSKI:	Oh, she will.
MAID:	*(Curious)* Why's that? *(Doorbell)*
ŁOŃSKI:	Maybe it's her?
MAID:	We'll soon see … *(Exits)*

Scene Three

ŁOŃSKI, VIOLA

VIOLA:	*(Enters quickly)* How are you, Łoński? Ashanti not back?
ŁOŃSKI:	Apparently she's gone to Hela's for dinner.

The scene between Viola (Anne Keogh) and Łoński (Matt van Niftrik) was one of the most challenging for me as a director to realize, yet one of the most rewarding to work on. As a translator, this was also the scene that I re-drafted most frequently, since the more the actors worked through issues relating to Stanislavskian concepts of 'given circumstances' and 'objectives', the more the translation needed to shift in terms of inflection, tone and rhythm, in order to express and allow for future re-embodiment of the discoveries we were making in rehearsal. At this point in the play, Łoński's character is well-developed, though the ellipses in time between acts do present significant complexity for all actors (especially those playing Łoński, Władka and Kręcki) in terms of character development. In other words, it is important for them to have a sense of an inter-act narrative for their character and there are, of course, various possibilities. In my experience it is this scene, however, that contains astonishing levels of depth and complexity in terms of allowing the director and actors to 'mine' subtext and explore motivation, as well as engage with the play's thematic structure. Łoński and Viola clearly know each other fairly well and so there is a question of 'back story' here as well. However, given its location in the plot, this scene presents numerous opportunities for evoking subtle shifts in power dynamics that allow the actor playing Łoński

Ashanti (1906)

in particular to express changes in his character as well as explore the character's various neuroses. Also of interest is the idea that he is now attempting to reproduce his former relationship with Kręcki in a number of different contexts; there are aspects of his interaction with Viola that allow for an expression of addictive tendencies and co-dependency, which are brought to the fore because he has no money left. In short, the idea of psychology as a mechanism for producing characterization reaches its full development in this scene.

Image copyright: Matt Ager.

VIOLA:	I saw her at three, in town, driving along the boulevard in an open-topped carriage. What are you writing?
ŁOŃSKI:	A note to Ashanti. Proposition.
VIOLA:	Shifty business?
ŁOŃSKI:	Listen, Viola, if you're so darned clever, you'll age really quickly and no one will give you a second glance … *(He seals the note and gets up)*
VIOLA:	That old rubbish …
ŁOŃSKI:	If you behave yourself, I might introduce you to a lovely boy. He's in Warsaw for the races.
VIOLA:	How rich?
ŁOŃSKI:	Immeasurably …
VIOLA:	How old?
ŁOŃSKI:	Moderately.
VIOLA:	How intelligent?
ŁOŃSKI:	Minimally … *(They both burst out laughing)*
VIOLA:	It's a bit like you, when you started with Ashanti … Now come on – don't be angry, I forgot you don't like it, when people remind you …
ŁOŃSKI:	You're beastly but I like you … As such you're entitled to special privileges … *(He wants to embrace her and kiss her)*
VIOLA:	Now, now, back off …
ŁOŃSKI:	Not as if you'll lose anything …
VIOLA:	That's not the point, whether I lose anything, it's the principle. Well – sit over there. Tell me, about this proposition, for Ashanti …
ŁOŃSKI:	I'll kiss and tell.
VIOLA:	Oh, Łoński, Łoński, how strange you men are, it upsets me to think. If I, like you, had lost everything, all because of women, I don't think I could look at one again … But you're still the same

Anne Keogh as Viola.

Image copyright: Matt Ager.

	… If someone said you'd catch a glimpse of ankle at Wilanów … you'd rush there, on foot … when will you get some sense?
ŁOŃSKI:	Never, dear Violeta, never … from cradle to grave, like this.
VIOLA:	Well, don't come any closer, or I'll tell Ashanti … You say that women are stupid but I've never seen a single man who had, well, even *this* much sense … And I've had a few you know … the sort who pass as intelligent, even a university professor.
ŁOŃSKI:	University professor.
VIOLA:	Don't interrupt. You – you can pester Ashanti endlessly, but for me, or any other woman who gives someone a wink in the street, there's hell to pay. When I lived with Kociek … I was so depressed … a lifetime of problems, all in one man! … With him I repented

Ashanti (1906)

Matt van Niftrik as Łońksi and Anne Keogh as Viola.

Image copyright: Matt Ager.

	for all my sins ... And why? Because I betrayed him from time to time. Well – think about that and tell me, where's the harm? ... He knew I loved him because I really did love him ... I'd never loved anyone like that, in my whole life, so what harm could it do that apart from what he gave me, I also collected some extra pin money.
ŁOŃSKI:	Viola, you're magnificent ...
VIOLA:	Get away ... He was so-o jealous ... Ugh ... *(She makes a face and a gesture with her hands, which is supposed to represent the jealousy of the said 'Kociek')* And if only he'd listened, he wouldn't have caught typhus either, and everything would have worked out perfectly alright ...
ŁOŃSKI:	No, Viola, I must embrace you ...

Matt van Niftrik as Łońksi and Anne Keogh as Viola.

Image copyright: Matt Ager.

VIOLA:	Get away, you'll crease my suit … Here, kiss, kiss, but be careful … Again … you can … kiss … if you want to … again … again …
ŁOŃSKI:	Wait … I'm breathless …
VIOLA:	No - do it all in one round … Kiss me once then leave me alone …
ŁOŃSKI:	How strategic … when you speak, you appear quite temperamental …
VIOLA:	I am, but I have to save that up, to conserve my resources. Well, kiss.
ŁOŃSKI:	Not like this.
VIOLA:	Kiss me at once.
ŁOŃSKI:	No …
VIOLA:	Well, thank God, peace at last … *(She stretches)* You know Łoński, you're a good kisser … Shame you're so bald …

Scene Four

MAID, ŁOŃSKI, VIOLA

ŁOŃSKI *wants to reply, but the* MAID *interrupts him, as she enters the room carrying a large bunch of flowers.*

VIOLA:	What's that?
MAID:	A letter and some flowers … I'll arrange them here on the table. Lovely.
ŁOŃSKI:	Who brought them?
MAID:	The hotel courier.
VIOLA:	Completely useless … If someone sent me flowers, he'd be out in a trice …
ŁOŃSKI:	Don't you like flowers?
VIOLA:	Oh I do, but I can buy them at the market … waste of money … two whole złotys … tell your mistress I called, I'll be back in an hour, or maybe less …
ŁOŃSKI:	Don't go … *(maid exits)*
VIOLA:	I'm anxious, you're far too aroused … Good day! *(She exits, stopping in the doorway)* Ah but, listen, when will you acquaint me with your friend? Were you in earnest?
ŁOŃSKI:	Completely.
VIOLA:	Bring him over to my place … Tomorrow at four … Alright? *(Doorbell)* Oh, could be Ashanti … *(She is heard talking outside the door)* Baron, how are you … Do go through, Łoński's here … *(Enter* KRĘCKI*)*

Scene Five

ŁOŃSKI, KRĘCKI

KRĘCKI:	*(Entering)* Bonjour ….
ŁOŃSKI:	*(With his back to him)* Good day …
KRĘCKI:	What are you doing here?
ŁOŃSKI:	Sitting down.
KRĘCKI:	Business with Ashanti …
ŁOŃSKI:	Yes, business. *(For a few moments, they don't speak to each other.* ŁOŃSKI *looks through a book.* KRĘCKI *whistles softly)* No point waiting for Ashanti … She'll be gone a while.

KRĘCKI:	Never mind. I'll keep you company, so you don't get bored.
ŁOŃSKI:	*(After a longer pause, during which time one of them flicks through a book, and the other whistles, he turns rapidly)* Listen. Kręcki, what are you doing here?
KRĘCKI:	Cards on the table – I came to invite Ashanti to dinner.
ŁOŃSKI:	Same as me.
KRĘCKI:	Age before beauty.
ŁOŃSKI:	You may have a point …
KRĘCKI:	Well …
ŁOŃSKI:	What?
KRĘCKI:	Why are you scowling? There was a time when I arranged dinners for you, there was a time when other people arranged them for me, well, and now we're both arranging them for everyone else … That's how history unfolds …
ŁOŃSKI:	Kręcki …
KRĘCKI:	It's quite alright … We're alone, don't hold back … I like your tone of voice …
ŁOŃSKI:	Don't push me, Kręcki …
KRĘCKI:	Calm down … please … she chewed you up and spat you out, just get used to it …
ŁOŃSKI:	*(Roused, going towards him)* Listen … if you don't get out this minute …
KRĘCKI:	*(Frightened, hides behind the chair)* Łoński … you've gone mad …
ŁOŃSKI:	*(Sits heavily by the table, leans his head on his hands)* Oh my God … oh God … oh God …
KRĘCKI:	Sorry if I touched a nerve …
ŁOŃSKI:	You're right … completely … it's all true … if I'd any scrap of dignity I'd have blown my brains out long ago … And yours especially, like a dog's … don't you see … I could have been *decent* …
KRĘCKI:	No … you're too agitated … *(Exits; next, he leans back round the door)* You'll regret it … *(ŁOŃSKI, terribly agitated, stands by the window and looks out into the yard)*

Scene Six

ŁOŃSKI, MAID

KRĘCKI exits hurriedly.

MAID:	The baron was white as a sheet.
ŁOŃSKI:	I said some hurtful things.

Ashanti (1906)

As a cast we took a great deal of enjoyment from creating this image of Kręcki behind the settee. The image was intended to evoke Kręcki's sense of himself, redolent with an underlying paranoia. The image also connects with the caricature of the distant Gold Coast, which he and Łoński evoke in Act 1, when Ashanti first arrives in Łoński's apartment: Kręcki (George Bull, above) thinks he is in an 'exotic' place, threatened by the untamed beast, Łoński. He is in fact in Warsaw, where, in his own mind, a pseudo-Darwinian struggle for survival is being played out through a process of transaction and exchange. Though it may have appeared to Łoński that he and Kręcki were putting Władka in the position of 'slave' in Act 1, as it turns out, it is Łoński who was captured, then abandoned by Kręcki. At this point, the effect I sought to evoke was humorous, insofar as this image comments reflexively on the play's thematic structure as well as functioning plausibly with the naturalistic frame of the action.

Image copyright: Matt Ager.

MAID:	*(Laughing)* Oh, good for you, sir …
ŁOŃSKI:	Don't you like him?
MAID:	Hideous creature … you'd think he'd offer me a tip when I open the door …
ŁOŃSKI:	He …
MAID:	You'll be waiting for the mistress, sir?
ŁOŃSKI:	A while. Yes, yes, my dear … life is hard …
MAID:	Huh – as if for you it's hard.
ŁOŃSKI:	*(Bats his hand, lights a cigarette, after a while repeats mechanically)* Life is hard … *(After a while, as if he was finishing out loud some unarticulated thought)* Huh, what the hell, there must be some cognac or vodka in that credenza, any on offer …
MAID:	The mistress'll say I drank it …
ŁOŃSKI:	No … she won't … *(Doorbell rings abruptly)*
MAID:	Oh, that must be her this time …
ŁOŃSKI:	Could be … it's her ring … *(MAID exits)*

Scene Seven

MAID, ŁOŃSKI, WŁADKA

Offstage lively humming of an Italian melody. WŁADKA *runs in wearing a spring outfit, weighed down by parcels.*

WŁADKA:	How are you, Muniek? I'm in such a good mood … *(To* MAID*)* Any callers?
MAID:	Miss Viola and the Baron …
WŁADKA:	What did he want?
MAID:	No idea … then this bouquet, with a letter.
WŁADKA:	From where?
MAID:	Hotel.
WŁADKA:	*(Tears open the envelope, starts reading the letter, throws it onto the ground)* Stupid ass …
ŁOŃSKI:	A man in love?
WŁADKA:	Hm … *(She contorts her face in a mocking way)* We know all about those, don't we, Łoński? *(To* MAID*)* Will Miss Viola come back?
ŁOŃSKI:	Within the hour, she said …

Ashanti (1906)

The Maid (Magdalena Kwiatkowska) and Władka (Joanna Lucas).

Image copyright: Lib Taylor.

One of the pleasures of realizing the final act theatrically is that some degree of balance is restored in relation to the gender politics played out in the first act, without a diminishing of their complexity. Władka's lodgings are a partial reflection of Łoński's – she has established a bachelorette apartment where a matriarchal structure prevails. Władka's maid is an equivalent to Łoński's Jan and of course the introduction of Mrs Lubartowska (played by Emma Meade-Chapman), her mother, in the initial scene of Act 3 is perhaps somewhat unexpected; her presence echoes the intrusions into Łoński's life of Uncle Bratkowski in Act 1. Whether one presents Mrs Lubartowska as a former washerwoman (as Władka suggests in Act 1), or an experienced former prostitute, or a factory worker now dependent on her daughter – or a combination of all three – is of course a specific directorial choice, and costume plays a very important signifier in this regard. Crucially, the fact that Władka allows her to share her space is significant. For an audience, one of the most interesting things about Act 3 is attempting to work out what has happened to Władka since Łoński shot in her direction and missed (whether deliberately or accidentally) in Act 2. There is no mention of Franek or the demise of her relationship with him – not many textual clues are offered for the actor. Our ensemble speculated a great deal about whether Władka's feelings of sickness in Act 2 were entirely the result of heat, or whether she was in fact pregnant as well. Once this idea surfaced, it was difficult not to connect it to her reference to the doll in her apartment, in the Director's presence. Although these ideas may not be explicit in the dialogue, the possibility exists for actors to work with them and import them into performance through performance style and emotional timbre.

WŁADKA:	*(Sits on a chair, unwraps a parcel)* I bought two pairs of silk stockings … *(She takes another parcel)* And frankfurters. I saw them in the window, got such an appetite …
MAID:	Were you out to dinner?
WŁADKA:	At Miss Hela's. *(To ŁOŃSKI)* Darling, pass me my shoes, they're under the bed … *(Starts singing again)*
MAID:	You're in a good mood today.
WŁADKA:	So, so … Pass me a frankfurter please … *(She tears a piece and starts to eat)* Go on, Muniek, it's delicious …
ŁOŃSKI:	Thank you, I'm not hungry.
WŁADKA:	Lay them on a small dish … ready for supper … *(MAID exits, WŁADKA takes off her boot and changes her stockings)* Guess what … strolling along the boulevard, Nowy Świat, two schoolboys, I think, next to me … one of them says: 'look, that's Ashanti' … They'll call me that 'til the day I die …
ŁOŃSKI:	You see … I summed you up …

Ashanti (1906)

Władka (Joanna Lucas) holding the fan, which she brings from her room in this scene.

Image copyright: Matt Ager.

WŁADKA:	Remember, when you said it … A wild creature that lives in the woods by the sea … and a white man comes and takes her into captivity …
ŁOŃSKI:	It wasn't quite like that …
WŁADKA:	Do you know, it's two years to the day, since you tried to shoot me … Remember?
ŁOŃSKI:	Let's just forget …
WŁADKA:	You're ashamed … I'm so good … most women would bear a grudge.
ŁOŃSKI:	I also wanted to blow my brains out.
WŁADKA:	Really … you can do that any time … *(Looks out of the window)* Oh, it's raining … Just managed to avoid it, hair's breadth …

ŁOŃSKI:	What rain ... *(He approaches the window, opens it and breathes in deeply)* Hm.
WŁADKA:	Why open the window?
ŁOŃSKI:	Smell that?
WŁADKA:	You're mad ... you'll wet my floor ...
ŁOŃSKI:	It's alright ... *(Shuts the window, after a while with lazy dreaminess in his voice)* Rain ... rain ...
WŁADKA:	*(Bitingly)* You liked it ...
ŁOŃSKI:	*(Doesn't reply, stands by the window, gazing at the rain. After a while he turns, paces the room once and then again, then suddenly)* You know what, Władka, if I don't hang myself today ...
WŁADKA:	Then what? Tell me ...
ŁOŃSKI:	Oh, it's silly ... not worth saying ... really ... what's done is done ... Right? Best to move on, stay positive.
WŁADKA:	Why bother reminiscing?
ŁOŃSKI:	Huh ... Listen, Władka, tell me ... listen quietly, I'm not blaming you ... I'm just talking, I wonder ...
WŁADKA:	What?
ŁOŃSKI:	Do you ... well, you saw how I was, how I am ... put simply, have you any idea how much you've hurt me?
WŁADKA:	Oh, leave me alone ... If that's why you've come, to bore me, forget it.
ŁOŃSKI:	No, I came to invite you to dinner ...
WŁADKA:	I won't come ...
ŁOŃSKI:	Why not?
WŁADKA:	No time ... No time today ...
ŁOŃSKI:	What are you doing?
WŁADKA:	Oh, what's on my list ... You're so funny. You think that without your help I'll struggle to make contacts.
ŁOŃSKI:	As you wish ... An old friend was eager to meet you ... He'll be in Warsaw for two whole days.
WŁADKA:	I'll give that a miss.
ŁOŃSKI:	I see ... *(After a while, with irony)* Władzia, you've not fallen in love again?
WŁADKA:	Łoński ... you're becoming increasingly tedious.
ŁOŃSKI:	Well ... let's not argue ... confide in me, your old friend.
WŁADKA:	It's a long story. Before you came back to Warsaw ... Last winter I was invited to a masquerade ball, I had no fan and went to buy one ... I'm in a hired carriage and following me in a trap, this old man ... he was following, I knew, because I'd seen him

	earlier, in the street. I arrive at the square beside the theatre, pause in front of a shop and he stops too. I go in, so does he. There, on the counter, an ostrich feather fan – this one here, you see. *(She runs to the bedroom, returning after a while with a large white fan)*
ŁOŃSKI:	*(Examining the fan)* It's lovely.
WŁADKA:	I feel there's something in the air, but no. I pretend to be very prim … 'How much is the fan?' I ask. 'Seventy five roubles' … 'Oh', I say, 'that's much too dear, something more modest' … Then the old fellow says: 'please wrap this one, for me'. I paid for mine, got in the carriage, he approaches: 'Would you accept this token of my esteem'. 'But I don't know you, sir'. 'This evening, we'll become acquainted, at the ball'. 'That's altogether different, in that case I accept'. I winked so hard, these veins here nearly burst … *(She points to her eye)* … grabbed the fan and off we go. And you know what – it's very silly – I didn't actually go to the ball. I regretted that later, a lot, I couldn't find out who he was and just you imagine, yesterday we met at Dolina.
ŁOŃSKI:	He didn't reproach you?
ŁADKA:	Hah, he was absolutely delighted … mark my word … *(She narrows her eyes meaningfully)* Cream of the crop.
ŁOŃSKI:	Who is he?
WŁADKA:	Curiosity killed the cat … and now, my love, you really must go. He'll be here any minute and shouldn't meet a soul … Go on … don't be angry … I'm not getting rid of you … you do understand …
ŁOŃSKI:	*(Rising slowly)* I understand … There was something else.
WŁADKA:	Well?
ŁOŃSKI:	I …
WŁADKA:	Come on … out with it.
ŁOŃSKI:	Władka, I'm desperate … Lend me twenty five roubles.
WŁADKA:	I've got no money.
ŁOŃSKI:	You have. I know you got some today.
WŁADKA:	I need that myself. *(Long pause)* If you like, I can lend you ten … No more … I don't have it.
ŁOŃSKI:	*(Quietly)* I'll have it.
WŁADKA:	*(Giving him the money)* Now leave … my love …
ŁOŃSKI:	Alright yes … Goodbye … *(He exits. The bell is heard simultaneously)*
WŁADKA:	*(Runs towards the door following ŁOŃSKI)* Hide in the kitchen, don't leave now.

Evident in this image are the gradual shifts in colour tone in the lighting, particularly an intensification of red, which occurred throughout Act 3. Although the indication, through dialogue, is that outside the apartment it is raining and not terribly warm, an atmosphere of emotional 'heat' and foreboding 'indoors' can be built up through expressionistic means. In this research performance, given the establishment of reflexive framing devices such as the inter-act transitions, it was possible to systematically provide extra-textual commentary through a variety of theatrical channels of communication, including lighting. Also visible in the photograph is the box from which Łoński earlier removed his gun. This was the box in which, in this production, Władka (Joanna Lucas, pictured above) also kept her fan. As she brought it into the room, Łoński appeared to recognize it.

Image copyright: Matt Ager.

Scene Eight

THE MANAGING DIRECTOR, WŁADKA, VIOLA, MAID

DIRECTOR:	*(Enters, pauses in the doorway with his hat in his hand)* May I?
WŁADKA:	I've been waiting for you … Come closer … I was worried you'd change your mind.
DIRECTOR:	Oh … what a pretty hand. *(Greeting her, he caresses* WŁADKA'S *hand)* A small, pretty hand … Each finger deserves a tiny kiss … And now …
WŁADKA:	Yes?
DIRECTOR:	Since, as they say in France, small gifts consolidate a friendship, will you accept, lovely Miss Władzia, this small token of my esteem? *(He gives her a box)*
WŁADKA:	Oh, how lovely … thank you (She gives him her hand)
DIRECTOR:	Now, let's kiss those little fingers in reverse order … Like so … and so … and so … *(Doorbell)* Is there someone at the door?
WŁADKA:	It's round the back, through the kitchen.
DIRECTOR:	I'm not likely to meet anyone.
WŁADKA:	Of course not.
DIRECTOR:	Because people's tongues do wag and I must mind my reputation.
WŁADKA:	Not to worry. It's practically a convent … you'll see … *(She rings. Enter* MAID*)* Who rang?
MAID:	The messenger.
WŁADKA:	With a letter?
MAID:	No … He brought ten roubles.
WŁADKA:	Ten roubles?
MAID:	Yes, he said a man had told him to return the money … Here, outside the house.
DIRECTOR:	A debt …
WŁADKA:	*(Confused)* No … Keep the money … He'll soon be back I'm sure. It must be some mistake. I'm certain.
DIRECTOR:	You're expecting a payment?
WŁADKA:	Ha … ha … ha … Me? It would be lovely if I could lend people money. *(Wishing to change the subject she seizes the doll)* Let me introduce my daughter … My daughter Jadzia. *(She covers the doll with kisses)* My darling, my sweet – the only thing I love.
DIRECTOR:	Not real people?
WŁADKA:	Sometimes, when they deserve it. Will you take tea?

My idea to use unusual boxes – which do not appear to fit the visual style of the naturalistic environment being evoked – as receptacles for significant items, came from the stage direction above, describing the fact that the Director (Dan Whateley) gives Władka a box. The box is not described by the playwright, nor do the stage directions indicate that she opens it. Given the significance within this research production of the larger box in earlier scenes, its association with the gun and the fan, as well as Łoński and Władka's complex relationship, it became important to echo the potential for similar complications in Władka's relationship with the Director. The box signifies the unknown – the uncanny, perhaps – which is at first 'hidden' but remains ever-present. It was also significant that the smaller box presented by the Director was gold in colour, evoking the African metaphors used earlier on in the play by Łoński and Kręcki, but also that it was shaped like a miniature trunk. My intention was to echo the larger trunk, which was always present downstage amongst the luggage, and which Władka had been asked to stand on by Łoński and Kręcki when she first arrived in Łoński's apartment. Through the use of this prop, Władka's integration into the Warsaw 'slave trade' is expressed as having been in some sense 'consolidated'. She has moved from a battered leather trunk to a miniature representation of trunk that looks as though it might be solid gold and is passed to her rather like a prize.

Image copyright: Matt Ager.

Ashanti (1906)

DIRECTOR:	Thank you. I must be going … I've some errands in town and won't be free till later.
WŁADKA:	Oh, I shan't let you go just yet.
DIRECTOR:	No, Miss Władzia. Really, I must … But I hope we can spend the evening together. We'll have dinner. *(Doorbell)* More ringing.
WŁADKA:	It's my friend, I can tell by the tone.
DIRECTOR:	How distracting, but if it's a friend, please introduce us.
WŁADKA:	*(Opening the door)* Viola, is that you?
VIOLA:	How do you do?
WŁADKA:	My friend, Miss Viola.
VIOLA:	Enchanted.
DIRECTOR:	Upon my word, the loveliest friends in Warsaw! Miss Władzia and I have a dinner date this evening. Perhaps you'd care to join us?
VIOLA:	Only if you escort me to my door. I get frightened on my own at night.
DIRECTOR:	We'll find a solution. I'm counting on you …
VIOLA:	Alright. To be honest, mother never lets me out, but I'll sneak away.
DIRECTOR:	In that case around nine or ten, I'll pick you up, Miss Władzia, yes?
VIOLA:	We'll meet at the theatre.
DIRECTOR:	No … no … no … at the theatre one meets friends, I'd prefer incognito … Humour me … If you would …
VIOLA:	Oh, your wish is our command … *(She puts her arms around* WŁADKA's *waist)*
DIRECTOR:	Delightful pair … a living picture … Happy the man who steals both those hearts.
WŁADKA:	Oh, that's a challenge.
DIRECTOR:	Some well-born youth.
WŁADKA:	Youth? Never!
DIRECTOR:	You don't like young men.
VIOLA:	Brr … young men? Alright for adolescent girls … We're far less flighty.
WŁADKA:	Very well-grounded.
DIRECTOR:	This evening, then? And now I'll kiss your pretty little paws … This and that … And see you later … about ten o'clock … You'll be ready …
WŁADKA:	Yes, we will.
DIRECTOR:	See you later. *(Blows kisses from the doorway)*

VIOLA:	*(A few moments after the* DIRECTOR'*s exit)* Amusing old codger.
WŁADKA:	Stop it – he's got money.
VIOLA:	Paranoid ones like that are the best.
WŁADKA:	You have to wheedle your way into everything.
VIOLA:	Wheedle my way in … I've introduced you to my friends on more than one occasion. Well?
WŁADKA:	The same goes for me.
VIOLA:	But I didn't bear grudges.
WŁADKA:	I don't either … Anyway, he's hooked … he won't wriggle free … but there is Łoński. Next time, I'll have him thrown out.
VIOLA:	Well?
WŁADKA:	He was here.
VIOLA:	I know, because I was too.
WŁADKA:	He whined about having no money, please lend him twenty five roubles. I gave him ten. He took it, got offended, and then sent it back by messenger … Right in front of the director …
VIOLA:	He's a director?
WŁADKA:	Yes – of some factory … I was so embarrassed; I didn't know what to do. Well? I barely know the man, God knows what he thought. And that maid, stupid woman, sees a strange man sitting here and won't shut up. No, I won't let that Łoński in again.
VIOLA:	Ashanti, you are aware that it's a bad idea to get involved with anyone who's put up money.
WŁADKA:	I felt sorry for him. Look what he's done. You try your best … *(Approaches the window)* It's pouring outside.
VIOLA:	Ashanti, you should get that old codger to buy you a piano. You could use one in here.
WŁADKA:	Already thought of that.
VIOLA:	And a summer trip, I think … How tired I am of Warsaw … aah … *(She stretches and yawns)*
WŁADKA:	You're sleepy?
VIOLA:	A little … went to bed late … that old man's a chore, you know … hard work.
WŁADKA:	Just you wait – we've led the horse to water, now he'll drink on his own.
VIOLA:	Tell him, I've got a second-hand coat, too small for me now. He should buy it, sell it on, and we'll split the proceeds … alright?
WŁADKA:	Alright then. I need the money … I must win some back at the races.

Ashanti (1906)

Anne Keogh as Viola and George Bull as Kręcki.

What is particularly intriguing about this scene is the fact that the circumstances of the shooting are reported by the Baron, who also acknowledges that he recently thought about challenging Łoński to a duel. The audience's knowledge that Kręcki has previously survived a duel – this is made clear in Act 1 – problematizes the news that Łoński is likely to die of self-inflicted wounds on his way to hospital. Was Kręcki involved and, if so, how? Establishing Kręcki as the bearer of the news serves to obfuscate Łoński's motivation and creates a further sense of ambivalence and confusion around the relationship of these two men. Directorially, establishing a tone for this scene proved to be challenging, particularly since there are a number of ways that Kręcki can be represented within it and also because it is essentially anti-climactic. Indeed, the somewhat botched shooting – presumably a suicide – feeds into what has been a gradually evolving discourse around Łoński's political, financial and sexual impotence. This in turn is rooted thematically within ideas concerning traditional Polish masculinity and class. As Łoński squanders his inherited Polish fortune, wealthier men who are, in association with the imperial occupiers, building factories are also swiftly changing the rules of sexual engagement. And, of course Władka – now known to all as Ashanti – once worked in a factory situated on the Vistula River.

Image copyright: Matt Ager.

Scene Nine

As before, KRĘCKI

KRĘCKI:	*(Runs onto the stage hurriedly in a hat and a coat)* Ashanti, do you know?
WŁADKA:	What?
KRĘCKI:	Łoński. Shot himself.
WŁADKA:	Oh my God! *(She covers her face with her hands, at her cry MRS LUBARTOWSKA and the MAID rush in)*
KRĘCKI:	The ambulance came, took him to hospital … Pitiful sight … *(A serious moment of silence, WŁADKA sits by the table, suddenly starts crying)*
VIOLA:	Don't worry … It's not your fault … wake up Mrs Lubartowska – glass of water.
MAID:	No fear of God. Suicide.
KRĘCKI:	*(Goes to the front of the stage with VIOLA, lowering his voice)* I was with him an hour before his death. Terribly agitated … he provoked me, I even considered challenging him to a duel … Dear me …
MRS LUBARTOWSKA:	*(Handing WŁADKA a glass of water)* Władzia, drink this …
VIOLA:	*(To KRĘCKI)* Always had a feeling. You could see it in his eyes.
KRĘCKI:	Well, he was mad … Terrible shame … knew him all those years.
VIOLA:	He may recover …
KRĘCKI:	Doubt it … They said he wouldn't make it to the hospital.
VIOLA:	Poor Ashanti … we had plans for dinner … *(Long pause. MRS LUBARTOWSKA whispers something quietly to the MAID. WŁADKA sits at the table with her face in her hands)*
KRĘCKI:	*(Approaches the window)* A little brighter … *(No one answers. He sits down on a chair, lights a cigarette)*
VIOLA:	*(After a while, to WŁADKA)* Władka, enough … you'll strain your eyes …
WŁADKA:	*(Leaps up from the chair, to KRĘCKI, livid)* You might have told me tomorrow! You stupid fool! You never change.

Ashanti (1906)

Joanna Lucas as Władka.

Locating a tone for the ending of the performance was a challenge. Władka's outburst, directed at Kręcki, is deliberately awkward, and draws the play to a close with a sense of irresolution. Should Władka (Joanna Lucas, pictured above) blame herself? Given the play's complex evocation of issues relating to motivation, heredity and environment, this is a potent question. The notions of free will and responsibility come to the fore. Can Kręcki be held responsible for Łoński's death? Should he blame himself? Is Władka still beholden to him in some way? What is the precise nature of his power? The fact that Perzyński sets these questions against the backdrop of partitioned Poland renders the play's political import particularly complex and difficult to evoke in intercultural, trans-historical terms as a translator but – especially – as a director. This is particularly the case given the fact that, in my own cultural context, Polish history of this period is not particularly well-known in non-Polish contexts and therefore the play's naturalism can be seen as anachronistic in a variety of ways. What I discovered in directing the ending, however, is that I could not evoke a scenario in which the actor playing Władka was 'livid', as required by the stage directions. The production choices I had made appeared to lead me, quite logically, to present a woman who spoke her final line with poise and control, against a backdrop of the sound of falling rain outside, which intensified as the reddish lights dimmed.

Image copyright: Matt Ager.

Invisible Country

Cast and Technical Support List for the Research Performance of Ashanti, 2009/10

Actors

EDMUND ŁOŃSKI *Matt van Niftrik*
BRATKOWSKI *Chris Montague*
BARON KRĘCKI *George Mawji-Bull*
ROMKOWSKI *Chris Montague*
LUTOBORSKI *Dan Whateley*
DIRECTOR *Dan Whateley*
JAN *Dave Buttle*
MESSENGER *Dan Whateley*
FRANEK *Dave Buttle*
MRS LUBARTOWSKA *Emma Meade-Chapman*
WŁADKA *Magdalena Kwiatkowska/Joanna Lucas*
MAID *Joanna Lucas/Magdalena Kwiatkowska*

Technicians and Designers

Doug Pye
Pam Wiggin
Chris O'Shea
Ashley Thorpe
Phoebe Garrett
Phoebe Higgins
Emma Devenish

In a Small House (1904)

Tadeusz Rittner

W Małym Domku (1903)

Tadeusz Rittner

Dramatis Personae

DOCTOR (LOLEK, LOLUŚ)
MARIA (MARYŚ, MARYNIA), his wife
WANDA (WANDECZKA, WANDZIA), his cousin
SIELSKI, a teacher
JURKIEWICZ (STASIO, STASZEK), engineer
JUDGE
JUDGE'S WIFE
NOTARY
NOTARY'S WIFE
KOSICKI, pharmacist's assistant
KASIA, servant
SZYMON, railwayman
Little ANTEK (ANTOŚ), Maria's son

The action takes place in a small Galician town.

Act 1

At the doctor's. The house is located not far from the railway. The windows (opposite the auditorium) are open – a little greenery and malvas, tall and straight, are visible through them. On the walls, simple oil prints. A smoking room – one can almost smell the cigar fumes – besides which there is also a consulting room, to which a door leads on the left. In the corner is a bureau cluttered with everything except for papers: a little apron, a toy clown etc. Above the bureau are stag horns, swords, rifles, also a shelf with books. In the centre a table made from pale wood. On the right-hand side a door leading to the hallway, a credenza, on the wall a portrait of the doctor, under the left-hand wall, a black oilcloth sofa.

Scene One

MARIA, KASIA, ANTEK

MARIA and KASIA, who is holding a child, are standing by the window; six-year-old ANTEK is sitting on the floor with a book.

MARIA:	The courier left … just gone four thirty, the Doctor set off at three, on foot.
KASIA:	They've sent for him twice already.
MARIA:	You never listen, Kasia, do you … the washing needs to come down. It's going to rain. My head aches yet you're still contrary.
KASIA:	Pharmacist's wife said it won't rain.
MARIA:	And I'm telling you, the washing needs to come down. It'll be just like last week, when the two twelve freight train went past.
KASIA:	He won't make it to the town hall. They could wait, I suppose? Would they choose a mayor without him? The pharmacist gave his serving girl a month's notice – for mixing with that Franek, from the carpenter's.
MARIA:	Now it's thundering … in the distance … like a cart crossing a bridge.
ANTEK:	*(From the floor)* Mama, where does thunder come from?
KASIA:	A letter and parcel arrived today for the master – from that officer's wife he's been treating, I expect.
MARIA:	Prepare the samovar, please, so tea is ready when he gets back?
ANTEK:	*(Clamouring)* Mama, where does thunder come from?
KASIA:	Cigars in that parcel, I expect. Something different every day … wine … yesterday, flowers … bless me …
MARIA:	Who from? Why aren't they in here? I used to get flowers at mother's in Kraków … roses, they sent, and confectionaries … Yes, our student lodger gave me a bouquet once and some bonbons *(She sighs)* There – now it's raining …
ANTEK:	*(As above, repeating as if playing a game)* Mama, where Mama, where … Mama, where does it come from …
MARIA:	*(To the boy)* Be quiet! *(To Kasia)* There, it's raining; didn't I say, Kasia? Well?
KASIA:	*(Wanting to leave)* At the double!
MARIA:	Now? It's too late, the courier's gone … the tea needs brewing …
KASIA:	Alright *(To the child)* Chop-chop! Well? Prefer to loiter by the window?
MARIA:	*(Almost tearfully)* Kasia, would you listen, just this once?

In a Small House (1904)

KASIA:	*(Taking the child)* I'm going, aren't I …
MARIA:	At mother's in Kraków, I was fancy free … now … Am I a servant, like you, or someone else? … I can't tell … why do you needle me, Kasia? Why that story about the pharmacist, the servant, the carpenter? What's it to me? You do address me like another servant.
KASIA:	Well, you were listening, and now …
MARIA:	What do I care for your stories, Kasia? I am the mistress here and you … Kasia … *(She looks down at the same time at her dress)* What's this?
KASIA:	All ripped …
MARIA:	Really! To sink so low … *(In a changed tone, almost pleasantly)* Before I married, I was stylish … wore something red, without fail, Kasia, you know?
KASIA:	I do.
MARIA:	The doctor lived with us then … Red suits your complexion, he'd say. A student in one room, the doctor next door. Didn't used to have a beard … looks older now.
KASIA:	Not a single day over twenty-five, says the pharmacist's wife.
MARIA:	*(As above)* Back then he sported this small, black moustache. So handsome! He could've had all the girls – every one.
KASIA:	Oh, they're still after him … and not just girls … I must prepare that samovar.
MARIA:	*(Detaining her in spite of herself)* The young proprietress of a tenement-building fell in love with him.
KASIA:	*(With astonished admiration)* Oooh?!
MARIA:	Yes and another young lady, general's daughter … that's right.
KASIA:	*(As above)* Oooh … a general's daughter?
MARIA:	He didn't want a single one … oh no … just me.
KASIA:	*(Quickly)* Yes … yes … I know … well he didn't have much choice.
MARIA:	What? He loved *me*, Kasia, alright? I was the only one!
KASIA:	Yes, yes.
MARIA:	He sacrificed everything … what did you say, Kasia? What's that? *(Angrily)* Still here, Kasia?
KASIA:	On my way … I'm going now! *(She leaves the room holding the child. The boy rises, throws down his toy soldier and follows her)*
MARIA:	*(To the boy)* What do you want? The garden? Well? To get drenched? In the pouring rain? *(She goes to exit through the door to the right, leading to the hallway, but in the doorway meets* JURKIEWICZ*)*

Scene Two

MARIA, JURKIEWICZ, ANTEK

JURKIEWICZ:	*(He speaks in a rather sweet, teasing voice. Carefully dressed, wearing a pince-nez, he takes her for a servant)* Won't you let me in, my sweet?
MARIA:	*(Taking a few steps back)* Pardon?
JURKIEWICZ:	Don't panic. What's your name?
MARIA:	*(With a troubled laugh)* Me?
JURKIEWICZ:	Of course … we must become acquainted. I'm moving in.
MARIA:	Here?
JURKIEWICZ:	Yes, to the doctor's. *(He approaches as though to take her under the chin.* MARIA *backs away)*
ANTEK:	Mama, I want to go to the garden … to-the-gar-den …
JURKIEWICZ:	*(Confused)* What? Oh lord … terribly sorry! That's rich … I thought you were …
MARIA:	*(Reddening, laughing)* Kasia, sir. *(Antek, seeing that they are paying him no attention, runs out into the garden)*
JURKIEWICZ:	*(As above)* Perish the thought … that is … I don't even know Kasia but … *(He bows low)* I'm Jurkiewicz. *(He kisses her hand with gallantry)* Don't be angry … your husband said nothing … Jurkiewicz, the engineer … I'm building a bridge … perhaps you've heard, basic suspension type … kettenkonstruktion … The doctor, that is, your husband …
MARIA:	My husband …
JURKIEWICZ:	Is letting a room to me for several weeks … that is, 'til September the fiftteenth. Completion date for the bridge.
MARIA:	He said nothing.
JURKIEWICZ:	If you object …
MARIA:	No … of course not … You're welcome to stay if Lolek wishes it. Did you arrive on the eight fifty?
JURKIEWICZ:	I've already been here a week or so in terribly cramped lodgings, a single room with my friend Kosicki …
MARIA:	With that … assistant, from the pharmacy?
JURKIEWICZ:	Yes, him … Your husband must be at a council meeting? They're choosing a mayor.
MARIA:	No, he's performing an operation.
JURKIEWICZ:	Delightful place. I love it. Small white house … sweet little windows … framed by red malvas.
MARIA:	I don't like malvas … they're common; I wanted roses.

In a Small House (1904)

JURKIEWICZ:	Me and this house, love at first sight … 'This is the place!' I told myself. My friend Kosicki advised against it, what with the railway so close by … but I said to myself, 'I shall live here!'
MARIA:	Once a night, that's all you hear. The eleven o-five express.
JURKIEWICZ:	You know all the trains? You often stand by the window then, looking at the railway. I did wonder – aren't you sad, so far from the world?
MARIA:	Far from the world? I don't mind.
JURKIEWICZ:	Have you lived here long, in this small town?
MARIA:	Since I got married – eight years.
JURKIEWICZ:	So glad I can stay. Always live with a family … in a town … yes, yes … without fail … I love the closeness.
MARIA:	Yes.
JURKIEWICZ:	Yes, dear lady. I've never cared for lodgings with a discrete entrance or ugly furniture.
MARIA:	Our furniture is old. We've always had the same. In my husband's consulting room, that's new, it's floral.
JURKIEWICZ:	A house presided over by a woman is beautiful. You can feel loveliness in the air … whatever the upholstery. This house exudes it! Delightful! *(He looks into her eyes)*
MARIA:	*(Senses his gaze, reddens and looks at her torn dress; from this moment on she attempts to arrange it so that the tears at the bottom are not visible)* Why my husband isn't back.
JURKIEWICZ:	Remarkable man, your husband. Respected universally and praised.
MARIA:	They won't give him any peace; he's away the whole day long.
JURKIEWICZ:	Duty, dear lady … the medical profession … and to the town itself. I envy him … for me its work, work, work … for him its work, work … home … These windows, framed by malvas, greet him from afar, and lo! A pair of azure eyes …
MARIA:	All morning he's at the hospital. Azure eyes in the window? Then they arrive … is the doctor in? Is the doctor in?

Scene Three

MARIA, JURKIEWICZ, ANTEK, KOSICKI.

KOSICKI:	*(Appears, breathless, in the garden doorway)* Is the doctor in?
MARIA:	*(Laughing)* There, you see. No – he's performing an operation.
JURKIEWICZ:	*(Gesturing towards KOSICKI)* My friend.

MARIA:	Ah yes …
KOSICKI:	Sent here by the pharmacist. *(To Jurkiewicz)* Hm, how are you? Everyone's at the council chambers … not long 'til the vote.
MARIA:	Tell them please, my husband is not available.
KOSICKI:	Oh! Such an important meeting …
MARIA:	Well, he is performing an operation.
KOSICKI:	*(To JURKIEWICZ)* Moved in already, Stasio?
JURKIEWICZ:	On the verge, as you see.
MARIA:	*(Rising)* I don't even know if your room's alright … that's Lolek's fault, he should've said … He never says … one minute.
JURKIEWICZ:	Don't take any trouble …
MARIA:	I'll go and see. *(She exits)*

Scene Four

KOSICKI, JURKIEWICZ

KOSICKI:	Well, how is it?
JURKIEWICZ:	Good … just recently, very good.
KOSICKI:	Meaning?
JURKIEWICZ:	Oh nothing, really. I like her.
KOSICKI:	Who? The doctor's wife?
JURKIEWICZ:	At last, a woman! That's all I wanted. First proper woman I've seen round here.
KOSICKI:	For heaven's sake!
JURKIEWICZ:	Surprised?
KOSICKI:	You can live here for years and the doctor's wife won't even cross your mind! That's how it is. Ask the notary, commissary, anyone you like.
JURKIEWICZ:	Hm! … Why not?
KOSICKI:	Because … don't know really … she's not quite there.
JURKIEWICZ:	What do you mean, not quite there? My soul quivered and blanched, like a maiden … and you tell me, she's not quite there.
KOSICKI:	There's only her husband, our great doctor.
JURKIEWICZ:	If he really is so great, I'm off – I can't stand greatness … especially in a small town.
KOSICKI:	She's barely ever mentioned; it's vaguely inappropriate.
JURKIEWICZ:	How so?

KOSICKI:	Certain … oh, never mind. Besides, she's stupid as well.
JURKIEWICZ:	Stupid? How quaint!
KOSICKI:	No, in my opinion … well, Miss Wanda, doctor's cousin … have you met her?
JURKIEWICZ:	No, misses don't interest me. Why is the doctor's wife barely ever mentioned?
KOSICKI:	Hm … as a couple …
JURKIEWICZ:	*(Interested)* They're not in love?
KOSICKI:	That's not the issue.
JURKIEWICZ:	*(As above)* It's not?
KOSICKI:	Imagine … a chap with such fine career prospects … had to marry, just like that!
JURKIEWICZ:	*(As above)* Had to?
KOSICKI:	Well, yes. There once was a widow from Kraków and she lived with her daughter near the university, providing student lets. A doctor lodged with them as well. It seems mama failed to keep a close eye on her young daughter and, well …
JURKIEWICZ:	Ah, really?
KOSICKI:	You saw the sweet little boy playing outside? They married approximately one month prior to his birth.
JURKIEWICZ:	*(Almost with delight)* Curious household … interesting.
KOSICKI:	What a man, to have married her – don't you think? Sacrificed everything! Anyone else in his position would have cast her off, no question, but he's a character …
JURKIEWICZ:	*(As above)* It's true, that's right!
KOSICKI:	I gave up on any kind of future. He actually dug himself into this hole. He'll never get out now … children and so on … same as me … if only I hadn't flunked my exams. He'll stay here forever – understand?
JURKIEWICZ:	*(Rubbing his hands together, paces the room)* As I see it, he's not so badly off. Everywhere you go the second word is 'doctor' – he gets out and about and she stays at home with the servant, the children … she, who's barely ever mentioned, sits alone by the window watching the trains go by … express, freight, passenger train … eight thirty … two twenty …
KOSICKI:	He's a vital creature – fine temperament – genuine talent for organization … lord of the manor! He's going to be mayor, of that I'm certain. Why so pleased?
JURKIEWICZ:	Me? Because the doctor will be mayor, of course … what an honour, to reside in such a household.

KOSICKI:	Well, it's not over yet – there is competition.
JURKIEWICZ:	No, listen, there's more … I relish this type of household. She feels so worthless; I mistook her for a servant. A house like this, absolutely priceless.
KOSICKI:	Why so?
JURKIEWICZ:	Because ladies of the manor are frightfully dull … they're not women. Slaves like this I simply adore. Their petals burst open with a dizzying scent, like roses, when you utter those magic words: you rule my heart.
KOSICKI:	You're a strange fellow. Ask around, she's practically invisible.
JURKIEWICZ:	To kneel at her feet and tell her …
KOSICKI:	You are a strange fellow.
JURKIEWICZ:	Tell her morning, noon and night: how lovely you are!
KOSICKI:	No one will even think of her.
JURKIEWICZ:	I can certainly believe that.
KOSICKI:	Let's go down to the square.
JURKIEWICZ:	What for?
KOSICKI:	To watch the crowd by the town hall …
JURKIEWICZ:	That's interesting? (*Taking his hat*) Well, alright. Let's go. What's her name?
KOSICKI:	Maria.
JURKIEWICZ:	Two reliable strategies. The first – applicable to proud women – they're the ones you brutalise: ideal for chaps with nerves of steel. For me, your sensitive new man … the doctor's wife – her type – a perfect match. In her presence, one kneels and says …
KOSICKI:	Ha ha! I know: you rule my heart. Honestly, you! I'd be terrified of the doctor.
JURKIEWICZ:	Let's go down to the square.

Scene Five

KOSICKI, JURKIEWICZ, MARIA

MARIA:	(*Entering through the door on the right*) The room is perfectly alright but it will be a squeeze … don't be at all surprised if it's a squeeze …
KOSICKI:	We're going down to the square.
JURKIEWICZ:	To rally support for your husband.
KOSICKI:	No point really – the doctor shall be mayor, no question.

In a Small House (1904)

MARIA:	Him? I really couldn't say ... my husband tells me the notary will get it.
JURKIEWICZ:	Wouldn't you like to be crowned Mayoress?
MARIA:	Me? I don't mind.
JURKIEWICZ:	Don't mind? Not again? Again? You're young, you really should mind ... *(He bows low before her)* Mayoress.
MARIA:	*(Laughing)* Oh! What are you doing? *(KOSICKI and JURKIEWICZ exit)*

Scene Six

MARIA, WANDA, DOCTOR

MARIA:	*(Goes to the bureau and tidies, stands for a moment in front of the mirror and regards her torn dress, takes a needle and thread and begins to mend the torn frill, all the while shaking her head, as though she has suddenly perceived that the whole dress is old and ugly.* WANDA *runs in from the right, passes quickly across the stage without looking at* MARIA, *who is seated on the sofa)* Wanda!
WANDA:	*(Without turning runs into the garden. In the central doorway she replies)* Just a minute! *(She disappears)*
MARIA:	*(Puts down the needle and thread, goes to the window, suddenly calls through the window)* Oh! Lolek! Did you get soaked? *(In the garden doorway* WANDA *appears and behind her the* DOCTOR*)*
WANDA:	I saw you from the upstairs window.
DOCTOR:	*(Entering)* Touched by the welcome.
MARIA:	Did you get soaked?
WANDA:	He arrived in the notary's trap.
DOCTOR:	*(To* MARIA*)* Why so drowsy?
MARIA:	I'm drowsy?
DOCTOR:	Ha ha! You've probably been standing by that window all day.
MARIA:	Well really! You were called on twice, by the town hall. A parcel arrived. Our new lodger came – that engineer.
DOCTOR:	Is that so? Right then! Town hall ... parcel ... engineer ... *(He puts his case on the bureau and hums in a half-tone)* I won't bother attending the meeting ... it's too late ... What a palaver! There I was, hacking into that woman, a full half hour. I've scored, though, Wanda – one hundred złotys, for the hospital.
WANDA:	From old Blumenfeld.
DOCTOR:	Yes ... I pressed him 'til he croaked: I saved your daughter's life, old miser, now pay up! Ha ha! He'd no choice ...

MARIA:	One hundred złotys, for the hospital? What'll you do with that?
DOCTOR:	*(Mockingly)* A ball! We'll arrange a ball and invite you.
MARIA:	Two letters came. The judge's wife asked if you'd be in today. The assistant from the pharmacy said they'd be sure to choose you.
DOCTOR:	*(Distracted)* He did? Really?
MARIA:	Why didn't you tell me about letting a room?
DOCTOR:	*(As above)* Hm … my darling … what was it I… *(He looks through the letters on the bureau)* Fetch me some tea … *(MARIA exits; the DOCTOR watches her, laughing)* Lovely frock! Is that Turkish cloth or Indian?
MARIA:	*(Standing in the doorway)* What?
DOCTOR:	*(Laughing)* Nothing … nothing at all … *(He steps towards her suddenly and bends her head back)*
MARIA:	*(In a half-drowsy, half-surprised voice)* What?
DOCTOR:	*(Kisses her neck briefly but passionately)* Off you trot! Bring the tea! *(MARIA exits. He, humming all the time, approaches WANDA)* I've remembered that quadrille they played at the governor's … la la la …

Scene Seven

DOCTOR, WANDA

WANDA:	*(Tactfully)* You've no interest in the selection process?
DOCTOR:	Don't have to be there to get selected.
WANDA:	Don't pretend you don't care. I'm sure there's little else on your mind.
DOCTOR:	Ah, how wrong you are. We can now modernize the operating theatre, that's what I'm thinking.
WANDA:	Hm …
DOCTOR:	That's right. *(Pacing the room)* Why would I want to be there when the votes are cast? *(Looks nervously at his watch)* Anyway, it's too late now.
WANDA:	*(With a touch of irony)* Yes – especially since you don't care.
DOCTOR:	Hm! *(Suddenly)* How about the engineer? Your opinion of that charming, cosmopolitan young man?
WANDA:	Oh, the one letting the room? I didn't see him – he spoke to Marynia.
DOCTOR:	*(With irony)* A frightfully elegant youth! Naturally, a gentleman like that from the big city is very special. Permit me to signal my

In a Small House (1904)

	delight at the prospect of his performance. He's bound to be very entertaining.
WANDA:	Aha! European ...
DOCTOR:	Exactly ... That gentleman's every utterance, reaches us from the nexus of civilization. He wants to take me in, of course, by gushing.

Scene Eight

MARIA, WANDA, DOCTOR

MARIA carries in the tea and pours it.

DOCTOR:	He adores everything: lovely station, lovely post office, lovely hospital ... Just like Marynia, in Italy ... *(MARYNIA looks askance at the DOCTOR)* 'What do you like best, Maryś, my darling. The Vatican, San Marco, the Palazzo Pitti?' And she: 'It's all lovely!' *(He laughs)*
MARIA:	*(Confused, suspiciously)* Because it was lovely.
WANDA:	*(Scowling)* I adore it when you're so witty.
MARIA:	*(As above)* Because what .... Well? Why would I say it wasn't, when I liked it?
DOCTOR:	Elementary, ha, ha! Why would you ...
MARIA:	Want some sugar?
DOCTOR:	Enough! *(MARIA exits)*

Scene Nine

WANDA, DOCTOR

WANDA:	At least Marynia's sincere.
DOCTOR:	*(Lighting a cigarette)* Oh, absolutely.
WANDA:	And you ... get me a light ... you're insincere.
DOCTOR:	Huh?
WANDA:	For example, you pretend to be cheerful ... you laugh all the time, you joke around ...
DOCTOR:	But I'm not cheerful.
WANDA:	No.
DOCTOR:	So what am I?
WANDA:	Exactly. Right now I only know you're pretending ... very taxing. I'd love to know what's really going on with you.

DOCTOR:	Ha, ha!
WANDA:	*(Covering her ears)* Not again! It gets on my nerves.
DOCTOR:	Oh! You have nerves, madam? Pardon me, how long has this been going on?
WANDA:	What?
DOCTOR:	Well – your analysis.
WANDA:	Since you brought me here from school.
DOCTOR:	I'm speechless with pride.
WANDA:	Yes, and I also think you're careless and enjoy getting attention.
DOCTOR:	Everyone does.
WANDA:	You love it when local ladies gossip about how interesting you are and that's why you converse with them so often.
DOCTOR:	Yes – I talk to people a lot … well? I'm gregarious – no crime there, surely? But what Miss Wanda fails to comprehend …
WANDA:	Gregarious people make Miss Wanda very suspicious.
DOCTOR:	Gracious! She probably thinks anyone seeking contact is a pickpocket, or worse.
WANDA:	More or less.
DOCTOR:	I prefer people – even the stupidest – to boredom.
WANDA:	You even favour complete fools because they flatter you more.
DOCTOR:	I favour complete fools because they shout more. I like loud noise, cacophony.
WANDA:	Aha! They'll shout, for example, long live the mayor! Long live the mayor!
DOCTOR:	Ha, ha! Doesn't matter what, so long as they do! I detest silence, that's all.
WANDA:	*(Innocently, lightly, leaning her head on her hands and looking into his eyes)* Aha, must have been tough here, to begin with, after the big city.
DOCTOR:	To begin with? Maybe … but not for long … because I can't bear silence. Gradually I roused people – you know – I can do that. Things started happening … activity … life … I won't let them rest and of course they like me.
WANDA:	You're popular. Yes. It must feel like a glass-house. I stood at the window upstairs today, it was fun watching people doff their caps … *(Suddenly half-serious)* But then it struck me, Marynia was at the downstairs window, spoiling the whole effect … She could look nicer, like the wife of a mayor-to-be.
DOCTOR:	You tell her: Marynia, my dear, I'm ashamed of your clothes.
WANDA:	*(Suddenly, almost nonchalantly)* Do you love her?
DOCTOR:	*(Getting up)* What? *(He bursts out laughing)*

In a Small House (1904)

WANDA:	*(Impatiently, rapidly)* Stop laughing … don't laugh.
DOCTOR:	I'm listening.
WANDA:	Do you love Marynia?
DOCTOR:	Yes – it's a given.
WANDA:	*(As above)* Alright – only don't start. You were being honest – you were – yes.
DOCTOR:	Your point?
WANDA:	Nothing. If someone loved me, I'd dress and comport myself like a princess.
DOCTOR:	*(With teasing seriousness)* Nobody loves you?
WANDA:	No-one has told me so.
DOCTOR:	Maybe someone does.
WANDA:	No, you have to say it.
DOCTOR:	That's imperative?
WANDA:	Yes – and more than once. If I were a wife, my husband would have to tell me every day.
DOCTOR:	Really! Every day! Make an effort every day. Ha, ha! Isn't my wife mine?
WANDA:	*(With irony)* It's a given … your property … as surely as this house, for example, which is insured.
DOCTOR:	Ha, ha! Of course! The premium's too high already! *(The door to the garden opens and* SIELSKI *enters suddenly, unnoticed)*

Scene Ten

DOCTOR, WANDA, SIELSKI

SIELSKI:	*(A fair beard, blue eyes; he speaks quite quietly, looking ahead sometimes, as if deep in thought)* Good evening!
DOCTOR:	*(Stops laughing)* Sweet Jesus!
SIELSKI:	*(Bowing to* WANDA*)* Good evening, Miss!
WANDA:	*(Giving him her hand)* You move like a cat.
SIELSKI:	Forgive me …
DOCTOR:	For God's sake, what's happened?
SIELSKI:	Happened? Nothing; I came to tell you our society now exists. *(Without looking at them, he moves quite quickly but very quietly about the room)*
DOCTOR:	Society? What? Don't you prefer to sit?
SIELSKI:	We've four regular members … day before yesterday … Our name … a pity … didn't go with my idea … In the days of King

	Pericles there lived a man who dedicated his life to the cause of compassion.
DOCTOR:	Didn't Pericles have him thrown in a madhouse?
SIELSKI:	No, sir. His name was Agathon. I wanted to name our society after him, my idea was rejected.
DOCTOR:	Professor, I wouldn't want you drying tears in this town.
SIELSKI:	*(Losing himself in thought)* Why ever not? I was planning to suggest that you enrol; as secretary. You're a medical man, you've dedicated your life to suffering humanity.
DOCTOR:	If you're planning to encourage sloth in this town, I'll have you locked up. You're a dangerous lunatic – enemy of order, because you give money to lazy people.
SIELSKI:	*(Not listening, lost in thought, to WANDA)* Did you read that book I brought yesterday, Miss?
WANDA:	*(Animatedly)* I did … it's lovely … only, I like the truth. I'm practically desperate to learn something truthful. Don't give me those books any more … because I'm … tuned to a different key … alright?
SIELSKI:	You want the truth, things as they are? No taste for idealism? I do apologize …
DOCTOR:	You don't know life, that's why, you've no respect for things as they are …
SIELSKI:	By God! I detest things as they are!
DOCTOR:	*(With irony)* How interesting!
SIELSKI:	I was passing the town hall when I discovered we're to have a new mayor.
WANDA:	*(Laughing)* Only just? I'm sure your pupils knew ages ago!
SIELSKI:	It's possible. What children don't know.
DOCTOR:	And the news had an impact?
SIELSKI:	I thought, if we really must have a new one …
DOCTOR:	Ha, ha!
SIELSKI:	Then the best choice would be Wółkowicz, the trader, on account of his boundless compassion.
DOCTOR:	Who?
SIELSKI:	The trader Wółkowicz … that is … he's not a trader any more because he lost everything … he was severely tried by God.
WANDA:	Is that the Wółkowicz ….
DOCTOR:	*(With an artificial laugh)* Indeed … But the professor thinks we can still choose him. No, it's superb! Brilliant!
SIELSKI:	*(Quietly, raising his eyes in surprise)* We can't? Why not?
DOCTOR:	*(Trying to remain calm)* Well, only because he's been in prison. Didn't you know?

SIELSKI:	*(Slowly, sadly)* I did … yes. I heard of his terrible misfortune. It happened to the best man in the world. So merciful, father of beggars. He kept thousands alive.
DOCTOR:	*(As above)* You're wrong … his acolytes paid the price … he had so many, the balance finally tipped. What a thought! Are you joking? Why him anyway?
SIELSKI:	Because he's so good – endlessly good, because he thinks more of others than of himself … and only such a man can head a council – not a shred of self-interest, just brotherly love – so much love ….
DOCTOR:	*(With absolute, poorly concealed irritation)* Are you still a child? Don't you feel that a man who's been in prison … *(gestures dismissively)* Tut! …
SIELSKI:	*(As above)* People are swift to judge; they fail to see the heart. And if they judged him once, isn't it time to stop? Oh, I know you feel the same, deep down. Listen to your inner voice – you can rise above what other people say.
DOCTOR:	Sir – forget your inner voice, and listen exclusively to what people say, because it's usually sensible and healthy … because those people make the laws we all live by. You're completely clueless – morally insane. Basically you're an anarchist. *(MARIA's voice is heard in the garden)*
WANDA:	Ha, ha! Poor thing!
DOCTOR:	Yes, an anarchist! With a tender Christ-like smile, what's more … and they're the worst … *(Takes a few steps towards the door to the garden, all the time listening, then says to MARIA through the window)* What? For me? Alright … to the town hall? On my way. Say I'll be there in a minute … *(He takes his hat and cane)* I have to go! Excuse me! My regards. Don't expend too much energy on Wółkowicz's behalf. Ha, ha! *(Exiting)* Good day to you, Professor, old chap!

Scene Eleven

WANDA, SIELSKI

SIELSKI:	Good day! *(Pause)* I'm sorry … so sorry …
WANDA:	*(Laughing)* Because he got angry? … Really … how naïve … to confess everything … how could you say all that, to him?
SIELSKI:	What, miss?

WANDA:	Well – that Wółkowicz would make the best mayor! You could have said that to anyone but him!
SIELSKI:	Why?
WANDA:	*(As above)* Because … oh, you'll see … soon enough. Don't you know anything? Ha, ha! *(With sudden mildness)* Don't worry, sir, it'll pass …
SIELSKI:	I only care whose side you're on.
WANDA:	*(Interested)* Me? How is that relevant?
SIELSKI:	All I could think of during that conversation was whether you share my feelings or his.
WANDA:	More often, yours … because you are, hmm … *(Laughs)* … more feminine … you are gentle … mild-tempered …
SIELSKI:	And he?
WANDA:	Oh, he's one of those men. Basically, born to govern. Don't you think he's a just man?
SIELSKI:	What is justice?
WANDA:	You feel it.
SIELSKI:	You see, you feel it … *(He indicates his breast)* … feel it here. Why does he value man-made laws so highly? Why does he depend on them? Why does a man like him not stand alone in a crowd? He's afraid of himself.
WANDA:	What do you mean – afraid of himself?
SIELSKI:	Sometimes I feel it. When someone hasn't the courage to face himself, he talks to other people … he fears the dark room, of his soul. Just like a child, he flees towards the light, to forget its existence.
WANDA:	*(After a pause, with some hesitation)* I don't understand.
SIELSKI:	*(Quietly, calmly)* Yes you do, though you're unaware. You understand me because … it's all I long for … I love you.
WANDA:	What? *(As though eavesdropping, quietly)* Did you say?
SIELSKI:	I love you.
WANDA:	*(Laughs abruptly in sudden confusion)* No … how strange … since when?
SIELSKI:	I've no idea … a long time, perhaps.
WANDA:	And now … suddenly … why didn't I know?
SIELSKI:	To me this moment seems just like a dream. Everything depends on you … my awakening, depends on you …
WANDA:	*(With sudden child-like fear)* On me? But I don't know. I'd like to say something, to you, but I don't know … I feel nothing … Is it my fault? Well? Let's not talk about this … ever!
SIELSKI:	*(As if in a dream)* It's not your fault … you feel nothing. I apologize.

In a Small House (1904)

WANDA:	*(Troubled, helplessly)* I'm so sorry … if you thought …
SIELSKI:	No, I didn't … I'm sorry … I don't know … what just happened.
WANDA:	*(As above)* Truly? What just happened? *(Laughing suddenly)* No, one never knows with you … Sometimes you say such unexpected things …
SIELSKI:	*(Melancholically)* I apologize for everything, I really do *(Rises suddenly, takes his hat, bows)* Goodbye!
WANDA:	*(As above)* Good … Why so soon? *(She offers her hand hesitantly)*

Scene Twelve

SIELSKI, WANDA, MARIA

MARIA:	*(Speaks on entering)* … didn't I tell her to take down the washing … *(Suddenly seeing SIELSKI)* Oh, it's you! I can't do anything with Antek. What goes on in your school?
SIELSKI:	*(Sad, distracted)* At school … Antek … sweet child … very good …
MARIA:	Dear God! A tell-tale! I told him, work out that sum …
WANDA:	*(Quietly, to SIELSKI)* You're not angry?
SIELSKI:	*(As above)* No … no … I apologize … I must be …
MARIA:	Keep a close eye on him, sir. Ask him, please, why he hasn't done his homework.
SIELSKI:	*(Leaving, as above)* Yes … yes … sweet child … very good … *(He trips in the doorway)* Good bye! *(He leaves)*

Scene Thirteen

MARIA, WANDA

MARIA:	*(Looks after him, shaking her head)* Merciful heavens! What a fool! Lolek was right.
WANDA:	Marynia!
MARIA:	What?
WANDA:	Do you still remember when Lolek told you he loved you?
MARIA:	*(With slight bitterness, rapidly)* No, not any more. And now he's no time to talk. Why do you ask? What's going on?
WANDA:	Because … it doesn't make the slightest impression.
MARIA:	What doesn't?

WANDA:	I thought the heavens would open when someone said 'I love you' … but it's nothing … it doesn't make the slightest impression.
MARIA:	*(Interested)* What do you mean? Who told you that?
WANDA:	*(Pointing at the door through which Sielski has exited)* He did …
MARIA:	The teacher?
WANDA:	Yes.
MARIA	And what did you say?
WANDA:	Me? Nothing …
MARIA:	*(Shaking her head, sits)* No! … Really? *(Pause)* Lolek would never allow it. Is there any point? He has no money. Besides …
WANDA:	I wouldn't dream of it …
MARIA:	*(Rapidly)* Lolek would never allow it … you're a good catch, like a china doll. Everyone likes you. Look, I go about in a tatty frock … but I don't care. No, really, he'd prefer to mind his pupils. Guess what Antek did? Tore up his school book in a rage! When I scold him, he just laughs. *(WANDA not replying walks about the room)* Does Lolek bat an eyelid? No, he just talks to those ladies who pretend to be ill. He laughs at my frock … is it my fault? He'll be furious, when you tell him; you'll see … Have you told him already?
WANDA:	*(In confusion)* No.
MARIA:	You really must … only when I'm there – I'd like to hear what he says. You never talk seriously when I'm in the room. I'm not that stupid of course. Mark my word, the judge's wife thinks, I see nothing … she is in love with him … she pretends to be sick … and there's nothing wrong.
WANDA:	Who knows? You can never tell.
MARIA:	Ha, ha! Nothing! Every day she comes to Lolek … I can hear it, when they laugh. Ask Kasia, she'll tell you, how my head ached yesterday.
WANDA:	*(As above)* Really?
MARIA:	Kasia's getting headstrong … Those servants see me as an equal now. Because I'm in the kitchen all day long or with the children.

Scene Fourteen

MARIA, WANDA, KOSICKI, JURKIEWICZ

KOSICKI:	*(Appears suddenly in the doorway to the garden)* Long live the mayor!

In a Small House (1904)

WANDA:	*(Animated)* What? It's over already?
KOSICKI:	You've no idea what's happening in the square … people are shouting, it's madness!
WANDA:	Who? Tell us, who's the one?
KOSICKI:	Take a guess.
JURKIEWICZ:	*(Entering)* My congratulations, madam.
MARIA:	Ah! Lolek?!
WANDA:	Objection!
MARIA :	*(Introducing him)* Mr Jurkiewicz, engineer.
JURKIEWICZ:	Congratulations, ladies! Entirely predictable, to be honest … un secret de polichinelle … very public secret … but it's always … I'm enormously pleased.
WANDA:	Thank you! Is my cousin on his way?
JURKIEWICZ:	Mobbed by a crowd of beautiful ladies and dignitaries.
WANDA:	*(Scowling)* Oh dear!
KOSICKI:	Don't worry … I'll go with you … please … (WANDA *hesitates a while, eventually goes – they exit*)

Scene Fifteen

MARIA, JURKIEWICZ

JURKIEWICZ:	*(Taking* MARIA *by the hand)* Allow me to pay tribute? *(Kisses her hand)*
MARIA:	*(Confused)* To me? Oh … what's this I …
JURKIEWICZ:	*(With a smile)* Because now you are most honourable.
MARIA:	*(As above)* Me? My husband … I don't really count, do I? What are you staring at?
JURKIEWICZ:	When first I saw you I felt fear and admiration, all at once, as in the presence of something so … far above me.
MARIA:	*(As above)* Oh, hardly! You thought I was Kasia, not something way up there or whatever …
JURKIEWICZ:	*(Sadly)* I am always tactless … through lack of confidence … only when you left … did I say to my friend Kosicki: now have I seen a unique woman!
MARIA:	No shortage of women here. You haven't seen the judge's wife, I suppose, or the commander's.
JURKIEWICZ:	Ha, ha! The judge's wife, the commander's!
MARIA:	What's so funny? Haven't you seen them? When they speak to me I get so muddled, I don't know what to say, they frighten me.

JURKIEWICZ:	Well perhaps they're scared of you … because you're the most beautiful, the nicest … They envy you and isn't your husband just as important as a judge or a commander?
MARIA:	I don't know … I don't … you shouldn't say that! They just frighten me … that's all. Why won't they speak to me, normally? Why does the judge's wife only talk to my husband? Everyone's the same! You treat me differently, sir, because you've just arrived. But after a while …
JURKIEWICZ:	Long may I stay! Ah, you've no idea, how I love it, right here, right now! *(In a lowered tone)* Since meeting you, madam.
MARIA:	*(Confused)* Me? What are you staring at? My clothes? I know they're …
JURKIEWICZ:	I'm so sorry … you're enchantingly naïve … so fresh, so young … so sorry, may I? *(He takes her hand again)*
MARIA:	*(Retreating, blushing)* No, you've already kissed my hand, sir. *(She turns, suddenly)* Oh! Here they are! They're coming! My husband!

Scene Sixteen

MARIA, JURKIEWICZ, DOCTOR, JUDGE'S WIFE, JUDGE, NOTARY, NOTARY'S WIFE, WANDA, *then* SIELSKI

DOCTOR:	*(With evident excitement)* Ha, ha! What are you doing! I feel rather silly! Ha, ha!
JUDGE'S WIFE:	*(Artificially)* Aha! We must congratulate the dear lady! *(She gives her hand somewhat forcefully to MARIA)* Our Mayoress … *(Half-turning to the NOTARY'S WIFE, self-consciously, with delicate irony)* Ha, ha! Our Mayoress!
NOTARY'S WIFE:	*(The same)* Ah yes … naturally … congratulations are due … *(Gives MARIA her fingers, carefully)* Our Mayoress … *(She turns to the JUDGE'S WIFE)* Yes, ha, ha! Our Mayoress! *(She stands in the corner with the JUDGE'S WIFE and whispers)*
JUDGE:	Congratulations, congratulations … are due!
NOTARY:	*(Bowing stiffly, militarily, briefly)* Best regards.
DOCTOR:	Oh, our engineer! *(Introduces JURKIEWICZ)* Mr Jurkiewicz, the engineer, my lodger.
JUDGE:	Ah … not from these parts? Hmm … it happens … delighted! You're building our great bridge?
JURKIEWICZ:	Basic little suspension type, kettenkonstruktion.

SIELSKI:	*(Enters unobserved, quietly)* Good evening! I've just been told ... *(Expressing the highest degree of awe)* Is it true? I couldn't believe it.
DOCTOR:	*(Laughing sincerely)* Ha, ha! Those eyes!
SIELSKI:	*(Surprised, looking around)* Good evening! Good evening!
WANDA:	*(Rescuing the situation)* Well, why not congratulate Lolek nicely?
SIELSKI:	*(Approaching the doctor)* Yes, well? *(Giving him his hand slowly, quietly)* Congratulations!
DOCTOR:	*(Patting his shoulder)* Ha, ha! And Wółkowicz? Because, if you prefer him, I'll resign. *(WANDA pours the vodka; DOCTOR taking a glass)* And here's to you, dear judge!
JURKIEWICZ:	*(Quietly, to MARIA)* Chin up – look around. Survey and rule ... yes, for you are a queen.
MARIA:	Ah, not so loud! *(Laughing, red-faced)* A queen! No one's ever said that to me.
JUDGE:	*(Raising his glass)* Beautiful ladies! Dear gentlemen!
VOICES:	Listen, listen!
JUDGE:	Hmm ... hmm ... I'm no orator ... it happens. But you can believe that what I say flows from the bottom of my ... hmm ... heart. I am the oldest person here ... but a strangely joyous ... hmm ... a joyous, spring-like feeling overwhelms my soul, when I think that this town, where once my cradle stood, this town, where ... hmm ... *(During the JUDGE's speech, the curtain falls)*

Act 2

The same room at the DOCTOR's. Evening, twilight. The door to the veranda is open; a table and chairs are visible on the veranda. In the distance, the red and green lights of the railway. The room is tidier than in the previous act, adorned here and there with flowers.

Scene One

WANDA, SZYMON

WANDA stands by the credenza. For a while the very quiet, vibrating sound of the electronic signal from the station is heard. Suddenly SZYMON appears in the doorway to the veranda, in a railwayman's uniform, in a coat thrown over his shoulders and a cap in his hand.

WANDA:	*(Turning around)* Who is it?
RAILWAYMAN:	It's Szymon, Miss, the railwayman.

WANDA:	What's the matter? How's your wife?
RAILWAYMAN:	She's fretting … very worried, no doctor, for two weeks.
WANDA:	He couldn't come; he's been away.
RAILWAYMAN:	She thinks there's no one to help, even the doctor has abandoned us.
WANDA:	She should calm down. He couldn't visit; he just got back, today.
RAILWAYMAN:	I'll tell her, miss, I'll tell her. *(SIELSKI enters)*
WANDA:	*(Pleased)* Once is enough! *(To the RAILWAYMAN, who is kissing her hand)* Take care now! *(She gives SIELSKI her hand)* Have you forgotten us completely? *(The RAILWAYMAN exits)*

Scene Two

WANDA, SIELSKI

SIELSKI:	*(Avoiding her gaze)* Didn't want to cause aggravation. I'm here to see the doctor's wife about Antek. Is she in?
WANDA:	Yes; wait here … don't be afraid …
SIELSKI:	*(As above)* I only wanted to see Maria.
WANDA:	*(Laughing)* Alright, and not me, I know.
SIELSKI:	That's not what I meant. Maria asked me to tell her how Antek's doing at school.
WANDA:	How's everything?
SIELSKI:	*(Sighing)* Oh, alright. *(After a while)* And here? Really well, I think, recently.
WANDA:	Why's that?
SIELSKI:	I've been hearing happy voices in the garden. Maria's been laughing and singing for several days.
WANDA:	Several days?
SIELSKI:	Whereas before …
WANDA:	I'd no idea this was one of your research areas.
SIELSKI:	No, I like it, when people are happy.
WANDA:	And you think … Why now?
SIELSKI:	I couldn't say … In general I sense more than I actually know.
WANDA:	Do say …
SIELSKI:	A bit nervous … So delicate, these matters … I only feel, she must be happy now.
WANDA:	You had doubts?
SIELSKI:	No … no … only … she needs a lot of sunshine … that kind of creature … affection, and so far …

WANDA:	What?
SIELSKI:	… The doctor's been spreading himself thin … Never at home … I saw it … I think he's undergone a huge transformation.
WANDA:	That may be true … what kind?
SIELSKI:	*(Triumphantly)* I haven't been here for some time. But it's enough to look at the house … even from a distance … in the evening. It's like a human face … either happy or sad. Up 'til now this house was dark in the evenings, and for the last few days … ten, maybe … the windows have been gleaming.
WANDA:	Ten days …
SIELSKI:	I see it clearly. And there's more. Yesterday evening, passing by the window … should I? … The white drapes were down, but the outline … you can see silhouettes … I saw her and the doctor together …
WANDA:	*(Disbelieving)* Yesterday? …
SIELSKI:	I saw clearly … *(He rises)* … here, like this … a man stood here … and she, here … Such a beautiful, happy couple, so much …
WANDA:	*(Interrupting him energetically)* But yesterday …
SIELSKI:	*(Rather surprised)* What? I'm certain. *(WANDA looks at him for a while; suddenly it's obvious that something has occurred to her, some suspicion, some premonition. Silently she turns away, in order to hide her confusion)* But maybe … *(He falls silent)* Please forgive me, private matters, not my business … *(WANDA stands immobile, her face turned towards the window)* I apologize … I only came about Antek …
WANDA:	*(Turning)* What about him?
SIELSKI:	*(Tentatively, confused by WANDA's behaviour)* It strikes me that for some time he has learnt nothing. Yesterday, he missed religious studies. I don't want to complain … but I've been worried he might be ill …
WANDA:	No … that is … perhaps … a little under the weather. I'll see to him … myself. Don't tell Lolek, sir, he's so strict … terribly strict … and Marynia is so busy. *(With a smile)* Do you trust me?
SIELSKI:	Yes, of course …

Scene Three

SIELSKI, WANDA, DOCTOR

DOCTOR:	*(Entering from the left, from his room)* Who trusts you? … So dark in here, can't see a thing. *(Looking suspiciously at SIELSKI and*

	WANDA) Professor? Well, a consultation? What's going on? … Fell asleep for three hours … Dammit!
WANDA:	*(Rapidly)* I'll just light a lamp.
DOCTOR:	What for? Not much point now … Someone calling me, I think … half heard it in a dream …
WANDA:	*(As above)* No … not a soul … only the railwayman, you know, with the sick wife.
DOCTOR:	Szymon again? … What does he want? Is the old girl worse?
WANDA:	No, only … *(Looking askance at SIELSKI)* … he was surprised you hadn't called in a while.
DOCTOR:	*(With irony)* Surprised? That's rich … *(To SIELSKI, with a short laugh)* They love me here, don't they? Can't budge for two weeks. Get back today – and behold! Seven stalkers.
SIELSKI:	*(Surprised, quietly)* You weren't here? … You just got back, today?
DOCTOR:	Didn't you know? No interest in local news?
SIELSKI:	*(As above)* Today … *(WANDA stands opposite him in such a way that the DOCTOR cannot see her, and looks into his eyes; the 'silhouettes in the window' are clearly on SIELSKI's mind but, understanding WANDA instinctively, in confusion, he falls silent)*
DOCTOR:	You want to dry people's tears … you don't really care. For once, be honest! How come I know what's happening in every home in this town and you don't? For example, what's new at your own school?
SIELSKI:	Oh well, at school …
DOCTOR:	Well, well … How many children does your friend Rzemień have?
SIELSKI:	Three.
DOCTOR:	But that's not true, you see … because today, a fourth came into the world. I haven't been here for two weeks and I know … *(Looks at his watch)* I know some interesting things about you as well.
SIELSKI:	About me?
DOCTOR:	Yes, yes … we'll discuss it further … very soon … hm! … I'm going to see the railwayman.
WANDA:	Now? You could take the day off.
DOCTOR:	To hell with that … It's not far, just a short walk.
SIELSKI:	I should get going too … *(Approaching WANDA)*
DOCTOR:	We shall make our way together …
WANDA:	*(Giving SIELSKI her hand)* Good bye! *(MARIA's laughter is heard)*

In a Small House (1904)

Scene Four

SIELSKI, WANDA, DOCTOR, MARIA

MARIA:	*(Dressed far more carefully than in the previous act, enters blushing, bursting with laughter)* Ha, ha, ha!
DOCTOR:	Well? … Well? …
MARIA:	Nothing … ha, ha, Jur … kie …
DOCTOR:	Well, what?
MARIA:	Jurkiewicz has climbed the tree … ha, ha!
DOCTOR:	*(Holding her under the chin)* That's terribly amusing! Terribly …
MARIA:	*(Wiping away tears of laughter)* Because Antek's balloon got stuck up there … and first we tried with a cane, then with … Ha, ha, ha! …
DOCTOR:	You can finish telling me when I get back, no time. You'd be better off making sure that scamp does his homework. Dreadfully spoilt in my absence, I imagine. I'll deal with him … Won't you say hello to the professor?
MARIA:	*(Through her tears, giving* SIELSKI *her hand)* I didn't see … Good evening! *(*SIELSKI *bows)*
DOCTOR:	Curious manners, that woman. *(To* SIELSKI*)* Avanti! Avanti! *(They exit)*

Scene Five

MARIA, JURKIEWICZ

JURKIEWICZ:	*(Enters after a while, brushing his clothes)* Be quiet! For God's sake! What are you doing? Stop laughing and shouting, and …
MARIA:	*(Stepping up to him, longingly)* Aah, you …
JURKIEWICZ:	*(Fearfully, quietly, looking around)* The doctor was here?
MARIA:	He was … yes … but he's gone.
JURKIEWICZ:	I thought so … Anyone else?
MARIA:	No … only Sielski.
JURKIEWICZ:	You're not being cautious … not remotely …
MARIA:	*(Humbly, with a smile)* I apologize …
JURKIEWICZ:	*(Anxiously)* Well? The doctor said nothing? He didn't see?
MARIA:	No, no …
JURKIEWICZ:	You'll be the … You're not cautious. Have you any idea what I said just now?

MARIA:	I know … I know … *(Suddenly, forgetting herself, joyfully)* Ha! I'm so happy!
JURKIEWICZ:	Be quiet! Wanda's in the next room, yes?
MARIA:	No, she's not … Just before dawn, I awoke; it was still dark … and all at once I was so overcome with happiness I burst out laughing … why do I feel so good, I asked myself? Why do I suddenly feel so good? And I remembered everything … that I have you and always will … you see? My handkerchief smells of you and that's why …
JURKIEWICZ:	Just remember, he's back; don't forget, our freedom has ended.
MARIA:	Alright, yes. All I know is I love you! Come what may! Perhaps in the garden it's autumn already? I know nothing. Let winter come … let it come. I love you!
JURKIEWICZ:	As I do you … of course. And remember, Maryś, self-control is essential – alright? Otherwise, it could all go badly wrong.
MARIA:	Yes, alright … Might it be best to not call me Maryś?
JURKIEWICZ:	As you wish. Don't be surprised, if I'm cautious. You may be wondering if I'm afraid? I need intelligence enough for two, that's all – you may as well be sleepwalking.
MARIA:	Alright, yes. He calls me Maryś and you can call me what you did before. You're so youthful! When you were up in that tree … ha, ha! So vigorous … and mine! You've such small, delicate hands … show me.
JURKIEWICZ:	Your eyes are shining … too much – that's bad … Gives an odd impression … Take care how you look. Your face is flushed … your voice is different, you move …
MARIA:	*(With naïve flirtatiousness)* Am I pretty?
JURKIEWICZ:	Very … very … But you don't know what you're doing … or saying … He's bound to spot it … I haven't the stomach for scandal … he's brutal. I just cannot put up with that kind of thing, really.
MARIA:	Please, don't be gloomy … smile. Since you became mine, I don't know, what's going on around me … nothing bothers me … I don't know if it's Thursday, or Friday, I don't know if it's autumn or summer …
JURKIEWICZ:	*(Lost in thought)* Autumn … not yet, but soon. We must prepare for the end. The project might be finished any time and then …
MARIA:	Then what? What then?
JURKIEWICZ:	Well, you do know I've never loved anyone like this; I swear it, not a soul! I am terribly … how can I put it … sensitive … I'll never forget you, my entire life! *(Muttering suddenly)* Tut, I've ripped my trousers up that wretched tree.

MARIA:	But you'll stay … you will stay … We have to be together – the two of us.
JURKIEWICZ:	Yes, hm … of course, for now … naturally I'll stay 'til I finish the bridge … who'll do it for me? A month … maybe longer … Oh yes, a little while, easily arranged.
MARIA:	Well? I'm not afraid. If you leave, I'll go with you, alright?
JURKIEWICZ:	Hmm … it's getting dark … we should perhaps ….
MARIA:	If you leave, I'll go with you. What will you do without me? Go on, tell me … It's the truth; you feel the same. I don't want to live as I used to … I can't do that now … I won't give in! Because you have told me that I'm your queen … *(Laughing quietly and edging towards him)* You see! Kiss me, come on, kiss me. Now I always want to be her majesty.
JURKIEWICZ:	*(Kissing her distractedly and looking about him uneasily)* If the doctor returns, suddenly … it's dark in here … perhaps …
MARIA:	Stay, or just for the winter. That's when I feel I'm dying. It's dark, and the windows are like stone walls, no one talks to me, Karol comes and goes. 'What is it, Maryś? How are you Maryś?' That's all. I am alone and I sleep. When you leave, no one will love me. Stay for the winter. You told me I'm pretty, no-one used to. I love you.
JURKIEWICZ:	*(As above)* For the winter? Why not? But listen. Happiness must be concealed, alright? Now don't laugh, just listen …
MARIA:	Ah, I could shout for joy! I fear no one. Only stay …
JURKIEWICZ:	*(Listening)* Quiet! Someone's coming … quickly … where's the lamp? I'm off.
MARIA:	Wait! It's Wanda.
JURKIEWICZ:	*(Nervously)* Back in a minute … in the garden *(He exits rapidly)*

Scene Six

MARIA, WANDA

WANDA:	*(Entering)* What's this? Why so dark?
MARIA:	Oh, nothing.
WANDA:	*(Lights the lamp and looks askance at* MARIA*)* You've taken to wearing a new frock.
MARIA:	Nice, isn't it?
WANDA:	*(Non-committal)* Not bad. *(Sits, lightly)* Is Lolek here?
MARIA:	No.

WANDA:	Thank God these two weeks are over.
MARIA:	Why?
WANDA:	Oh, just in general.
MARIA:	Tell me.
WANDA:	No man in the house, don't like it – lack of order.
MARIA:	*(Stands in front of the mirror)* Not bad, you say? Maybe a white belt would look better – do you think? The Judge's wife has a nice one. *(Suddenly)* He likes it.
WANDA:	Who does?
MARIA:	Well – Jurkiewicz.
WANDA:	*(With irony)* He probably knows as much about these things as a woman – he wears a bracelet.
MARIA:	He has lovely hands, doesn't he?
WANDA:	No, not really. Someone like him is simply off my scale.
MARIA:	Why's that?
WANDA:	He's a clown! Now he's tiptoeing around, ha, ha! Because there's a man in the house, and before Lolek came back, the place was full to the brim with Jurkiewicz; he walked about with his hands in his pockets and whistled. I'm not remotely fond of gentlemen like him. *(She rises)*
MARIA:	*(Pleadingly, softly)* Don't say that, don't …
WANDA:	Why not?
MARIA:	*(Puts her arms around WANDA's neck suddenly and kisses her gently)* Just don't – please! Because now I like everyone, because now, for some reason, for me, the world is a better place! Ha, ha! Wandzia, don't look so cold, so horrible … I like everyone now, everyone …
WANDA:	Let go! *(Moves away from her, after a while, drily, quietly, looking at her askance)* Go to your room … bathe your eyes.
MARIA:	What for?
WANDA:	Because you've been crying … I don't know … your eyes, and wash your face …
MARIA:	*(Laughing)* I haven't been crying.
WANDA:	No? Forgive me … perhaps … there's just something about your eyes and face … *(After a while)* Where's Antek?
MARIA:	I don't know.
WANDA:	What do you mean you don't know? Sielski was here complaining that he's done no schoolwork; where's Antek?
MARIA:	*(Lightly)* Probably in the garden.
WANDA:	*(Impatiently)* Probably. You don't have a clue! *(She turns away)*

In a Small House (1904)

Scene Seven

MARIA, WANDA, DOCTOR

DOCTOR:	*(Entering, looks from WANDA to MARIA)* Well?
WANDA:	*(Suddenly very animated, artificially, lightly)* How are you? Did you visit Szymon's wife? How's everything? You won't be going anywhere else, will you?
DOCTOR:	No, I won't. Listen Wanda, what's between you and Sielski?
WANDA:	How do you mean? I don't understand.
DOCTOR:	Don't give me that, young miss, I don't like it. What's the story? I tackled him over it, man to man, and he …
WANDA:	*(Reddening)* What did you say? By what right?
DOCTOR:	Aha! The right … the right, young woman that you are here, in my house! And that I am your guardian! I like clarity!
WANDA:	Marynia must have told you he made a declaration.
DOCTOR:	There it is! And your answer was?
WANDA:	*(Through clenched teeth)* She probably told you that as well?
DOCTOR:	*(Abrasively)* I'm talking about you.
WANDA:	*(Aggravated)* Calm down, alright. I won't have him, no. He means nothing … absolutely nothing.
DOCTOR:	*(Angrily)* Listen, girl, if you address me in that tone of voice, I won't be held accountable …
WANDA:	*(As above, her head in her hands)* Oh my God! Oh God!
DOCTOR:	And crying as well? That bookworm of yours cried too!
WANDA:	What?
DOCTOR:	For that alone I wouldn't let you have him. I was upfront, direct. It's beyond me!
MARIA:	Not me though. If you love someone intensely …
DOCTOR:	*(With irony)* Oh an expert? How do you know?
WANDA:	Anyway, he's not likely to come here again.
DOCTOR:	And? No regrets on my part! The Judge will be here later, by the way, with his wife. I invited them, for some wine from Siekerski's, superior to that poison they serve up.
WANDA:	The Judge's wife made enquiries yesterday, are you back.
DOCTOR:	She's been feeling faint again?
WANDA:	Same as usual, more or less.
MARIA:	*(Laughing)* She couldn't wait.
DOCTOR:	Really? Marynia's being witty, look everyone!
WANDA:	Anyone else coming?

DOCTOR:	I issued no invitations; if they want to, let them come.
WANDA:	So how many places should I set?
DOCTOR:	Kosicki might come; he's always with them. Well, and Jurkiewicz, of course. What's he up to?
WANDA:	*(Shrugging her shoulders)* Wandering about indoors.
DOCTOR:	*(Ironically)* Nothing then?
MARIA:	Oh, but he's never here.
WANDA:	*(Laying the table)* Four ... two ... seven ... *(Pause)*
DOCTOR:	Well, Maryś?
MARIA:	Nothing. Jurkiewicz is never here.
DOCTOR:	I know that. What's new at home?
MARIA:	*(Mechanically)* Oh, nothing ... (WANDA *exits*)

Scene Eight

MARIA, DOCTOR

DOCTOR:	Why so distant?
MARIA:	*(As above, approaching slowly)* No reason.
DOCTOR:	Children alright?
MARIA:	Yes.
DOCTOR:	Antek does his schoolwork?
MARIA:	Yes.
DOCTOR:	*(Taking her hand)* Let me look at you ... *(Looks at her)* I haven't given you my once over.
MARIA:	*(Looking at her dress)* Just the usual.
DOCTOR:	*(Embracing her)* Usual what?
MARIA:	*(As above)* Frock.
DOCTOR:	You've such dark eyes. Why's that?
MARIA:	Don't know.
DOCTOR:	You remind me. That time in Kraków, you were sixteen.
MARIA:	*(In confusion)* Jurkiewicz says, in a month, he'll finish that bridge.
DOCTOR:	Ah, yes? What have you been doing?
MARIA:	*(As above)* Oh, nothing. He took me once, to the bridge.
DOCTOR:	Where are you going? Look at me.
MARIA:	I am.
DOCTOR:	*(Pulling her towards him)* I like you.
MARIA:	*(Resisting)* Please ... please ...
DOCTOR:	What's the matter?

MARIA:	My frock's rumpled.
DOCTOR:	To hell with that! What's on your mind? Look at me!
MARIA:	I am looking.
DOCTOR:	*(Half jokingly, half passionately)* No, no! … *(Wants to kiss her)*
MARIA:	*(Pulling away, gradually, quietly, with an expression of disgust on her face)* Please … please …
DOCTOR:	Oh, yes … pulling faces … what's this?
MARIA:	Nothing.
DOCTOR:	I'll teach you … I go gently, I'm good, and you … *(He squeezes her hand)*
MARIA:	Let go, it hurts …
DOCTOR:	Really? It should … When I make love to you and you turn away, it should hurt … *(He pulls her towards him again)* Well?
MARIA:	*(Hissing with pain)* Ah, you …
DOCTOR:	There! Taste your own medicine. When I arrived in the courtyard today, the dogs leapt on me and licked my hands. If they'd barked at me instead, I'd have beaten them – understand?
MARIA:	*(Turning her head away)* You …
DOCTOR:	Never mind: there's a good reason why men have wives. I'll show you! Don't like me? How infantile! Ha, ha! You think I won't get it! That's rich! *(He takes her head in his hands and moves her towards him)* Damn you! … What lurks in those eyes … dark, mysterious … If I could just know, where you are … Well, will I get it? Doesn't matter now, if you like me or not … you have to, because I want it … *(He moves her lips to his with force)* … because I want it.
MARIA:	*(Pulling away)* Please … please …

Scene Nine

MARIA, DOCTOR, JUDGE, JUDGE'S WIFE, *then* WANDA *and* KASIA

JUDGE'S WIFE:	*(Entering)* Ha, ha, ha!
JUDGE:	Ah, ah!
DOCTOR:	Good evening! Please, come in! …
JUDGE'S WIFE:	*(Stopping where she is)* Husband, let's go home!
DOCTOR:	No need for that!
JUDGE:	*(Looking enticingly at the DOCTOR and MARIA)* They haven't seen each other in two weeks … it happens.
JUDGE'S WIFE:	Yes, it does … but not after years of marriage. *(She gives MARIA her hand)* Why didn't you want to be kissed? *(MARIA, troubled,*

	laughs; the JUDGE'S WIFE, *looking at her through her lorgnette)* Ah, charming smile ... so placid ... *(To* WANDA, *who enters with bottles)* And how are you, my child?
WANDA:	Good evening. *(Behind her enters* KASIA, *who places dishes on the table, after which she leaves)*
DOCTOR:	Ladies, gentlemen, let's sit down.

Scene Ten

MARIA, DOCTOR, JUDGE, JUDGE'S WIFE, WANDA, KASIA, KOSICKI, *then* JURKIEWICZ

KOSICKI:	*(Entering)* I'm sorry ... no idea, there'd be so many people.
DOCTOR:	Not at all, sir, please! Couldn't wait to see you. You've such a down-to-earth pharmaceutical smell ... how I long for you ...
JUDGE:	Good grief ... how bizarre ... *(They sit)*
JUDGE'S WIFE:	Come along, you well-stocked medicine chest, I'm desperate for some wine.
KOSICKI:	Jurkiewicz is hot on my heels.
DOCTOR:	Really? *(He goes to the door)* Where is he? Dawdling? *(He goes out onto the veranda)*
JUDGE:	No rest for the mayor ... he can't sit still.
WANDA:	You're right there.
KOSICKI:	Jurkiewicz is slow because he walks with distinction.
WANDA:	Ha, ha!
JUDGE'S WIFE:	*(To* MARIA*)* Is your husband also in love with Jurkiewicz?
WANDA:	Who else is in love with him?
JUDGE'S WIFE:	Well, he's very good looking. Isn't he? *(She looks fleetingly at* MARIA*)* Ha, ha, ha!
DOCTOR:	*(Greeting* JURKIEWICZ *with somewhat artificial sincerity)* Where did you wander off to in the dark? We're waiting ...
MARIA:	*(Rises and says rather too loudly and joyfully)* We're waiting ...
JURKIEWICZ:	*(Pretending he cannot hear* MARIA, *very politely to the* DOCTOR*)* The mayor's recuperation is complete! Excellent! You look better I think Doctor ... better than when you left.
DOCTOR:	*(Looking at* MARIA, *drily)* Really, I always look good.
KOSICKI:	Come on, Staszek ...
JUDGE'S WIFE:	*(In half-tones, jokingly)* Come on, Staszek ...
MARIA:	*(The same)* Come on, Sta ... *(All at once becomes confused and falls silent)*
JUDGE'S WIFE:	*(Looking at her quickly, with a smile)* Well?

MARIA:	Ha, ha! *(Suddenly calling to JURKIEWICZ too loudly, as before)* There's an empty seat next to me ... *(JURKIEWICZ, clearly confused, hesitates for a while, and then sits next to her)* Yes, that's right ... *(She moves closer to him and begins to whisper something to him; he listens with nervous distraction)*
DOCTOR:	*(Almost sharply)* Maryś!
MARIA:	*(Having trembled)* What?
DOCTOR:	*(As above)* Be more attentive to your guests ... serve the Judge's wife ...
JUDGE'S WIFE:	*(Calming him ironically)* Now, now! *(To MARIA)* I do like you terribly ... I have discovered you for the first time! Is it true that you passed by our house, day before yesterday?
MARIA:	*(Confused)* Yes ... possibly ...
JUDGE'S WIFE:	*(Looking at her again through her lorgnette)* Or now, the sudden blush ... well? Charmante! Spontaneously, like a maiden! Tres gentille! You were passing by, laughing and twittering like a little bird ... Who were you with?
MARIA:	*(Quietly, indistinctly)* Mr Jurkiewicz ...
JUDGE'S WIFE:	*(Loudly)* With whom? *(Leaning towards her)*
JURKIEWICZ:	*(To the DOCTOR, quickly, to talk her down)* Did you travel by road or rail?
DOCTOR:	*(Looking distractedly at the JUDGE'S WIFE and MARIA)* Yes ... yes ... by train ... that is ... what was the question? *(He rises abruptly, abrasively to MARIA)* Are you blind! *(When MARIA frightened wants to pour wine in her neighbour's glass, he snatches the bottle from her hand; quietly)* What are you looking at? What's on your mind? *(He pours)* Well, how's the wine?
JURKIEWICZ:	*(Very quickly)* Excellent! Marvellous!
DOCTOR:	So effusive. And the Judge?
JUDGE:	*(With a complacent smile)* So, so ...
JUDGE'S WIFE:	*(In a tired voice)* I require a certain dose of alcohol. I know it's bad for me, doctor, right? But without it I'd immediately expire.
MARIA:	*(To JURKIEWICZ)* Where were you? Why did you leave the house so suddenly and go out walking .... God knows where?
JUDGE'S WIFE:	Oh, so harsh!
JURKIEWICZ:	*(Nervously to MARIA)* What did you say? Where have I been? Urgent business. *(He turns to the DOCTOR)* Did the doctor have a pleasant fortnight?
DOCTOR:	*(Looking at him askance)* Ah, yes ... it was ... quite pleasant ... Why these inane questions, fit for some young girl, in a drawing room?

JURKIEWICZ:	*(Confused)* Hu, hu! Very funny! No, I'm only curious about the Symposium, was it of interest?
DOCTOR:	*(Laughing ironically)* Absolutely. Endless hours of wisdom ... I prefer five serious operations.
JUDGE'S WIFE:	Brr! The doctor's eyes practically glow when he says 'five serious operations' – like a tiger's.
JUDGE:	Who were the delegates?
DOCTOR:	Great men, that's who! You can imagine, me, a poor provincial soul. My former colleagues from Kraków were there, including that short fellow Pałecki. Luck is everything! The poor mite barely made it through his final viva ... and now he's a university professor. Ha, ha! He even wants to take me in hand.
WANDA:	What do you mean?
DOCTOR:	Well, he and some others have urged me to move to Lwów – I have your attention now – to write something clever, try for a professorship ...
WANDA:	*(Animatedly)* Well, and?
JURKIEWICZ:	I am convinced, should the mayor wish it ...
DOCTOR:	*(With irony)* Think so, do you? Should I wish it? ...
JUDGE:	I protest! As an inhabitant of this town. We won't let you go.
DOCTOR:	Tut, it's all talk ... how could I, now? A bit late! A man does of course get stupider with age. As if I need their good advice! *(More quietly)* As if I hadn't ... hm ... myself ... *(Falls silent, after a while, to JURKIEWICZ)* Think this place isn't enough for me? Your pity – that's all I'm worth?
JURKIEWICZ:	On the contrary, I was only ...
JUDGE:	And we're very happy with you ... perfect match! My respects, dear Mayor! They're jealous – it happens! You are the ... erm ... king ... here. What does some measly professor matter? Well, not a jot!
WANDA:	I suppose if it's something you wanted.
DOCTOR:	I really don't. What for? Not my cup of tea. Pałecki's type thrives on it.
JURKIEWICZ:	Generally speaking, large towns are perfectly suitable for the rabble; a decent person does not push and shove ... *(With emphasis)* ... he dwells in solitude, far from the crowd.
WANDA:	*(With light irony)* Do you dwell in solitude, Lolek?
DOCTOR:	*(Insincerely)* I'm not demanding. I have enough. A group of true friends ...
JUDGE'S WIFE:	A loving wife.
WANDA:	I'd pay a fortune to learn if he's telling the truth.

DOCTOR:	*(Artificially, lightly)* My darling wife, when you've finished talking to Mr Jurkiewicz, do pass round the cigars.
JURKIEWICZ:	*(Jumping up)* Please … here … a cigar … here … a cigar …
DOCTOR:	Oh, sir, you exert yourself.
JUDGE'S WIFE:	Not quite sure what gives this away but I don't think long journeys agree with our doctor.
DOCTOR:	Why so?
JUDGE'S WIFE:	Your mode of communication is today persistently unpleasant.
DOCTOR:	It is? How interesting.
MARIA:	*(To JURKIEWICZ, animatedly, loudly)* Why don't you have this piece … I'll serve it myself.
JURKIEWICZ:	No, thank you … Thank you …
MARIA:	*(As above, so that she draws attention to herself)* Or I won't eat a thing myself … *(Laughing she lays her knife and fork on the plate)* Like so.
JURKIEWICZ:	*(As above)* Oh, what are you doing? *(He takes it quickly, looking around with a certain trepidation)*
JUDGE'S WIFE:	*(To the DOCTOR, who has been closely scrutinizing JURKIEWICZ)* So lovely and cheerful, your wife, I almost envy her.
MARIA:	*(As above, raising her glass, to JURKIEWICZ)* With me … if you please, with me …
JURKIEWICZ:	*(Turns, pretending that he cannot hear)* Since I arrived … all summer, I've not read a single newspaper … surprising relief …
JUDGE'S WIFE:	*(Wanting to draw his attention to MARIA)* Are you deaf, sir?
KOSICKI:	Jurkiewicz could settle here easily; small towns flatter his complexion.
DOCTOR:	*(With light irony)* Nonsense! Man of the world, 'European' …
JURKIEWICZ:	Really … You never know.
MARIA:	*(Louder)* Sir! … Sir!
KOSICKI:	He enjoys being near a 'close-knit' family; that's his habit.
MARIA:	*(Tugging at JURKIEWICZ's sleeve)* With me!
JURKIEWICZ:	*(Rapidly, pretending to have only just noticed this)* Ah! *(They clink glasses)*
MARIA:	*(Laughing)* No, that's not what you do.
JURKIEWICZ:	*(Very confused, laughing artificially)* Is this alright, then? *(He clinks clumsily, glaring at MARIA, livid)*
MARIA:	*(Suddenly plonks her glass down on the table, sulky)* No, that is not alright *(Pause)*
DOCTOR:	*(Nervously)* Why is no one drinking? Judge! *(Scrutinizing MARIA in spite of himself)*
JUDGE:	Yes, yes … of course … I still have a drop …

KOSICKI:	How absent-minded … I must be at the pharmacy tomorrow for eight and I need nine hours of sleep.
JUDGE'S WIFE:	You still have time, 'til eleven.
MARIA:	We always know the time because of the trains; at eleven you hear the express whistle.
JURKIEWICZ:	It heads north.
MARIA:	Yes … far away … I always wake when it whistles at night.
KOSICKI:	How unpleasant.
MARIA:	I like it very well. I always think I'll go on a long journey … a very long one …
KOSICKI:	To the end of the track, right?
MARIA:	I have longed for it, since I came here.
JUDGE:	It happens. Women always long for something.
DOCTOR:	*(Who has all the time been looking at MARIA)* Maryś!
JUDGE:	What's she done this time?
DOCTOR:	Maryś, some time we'll travel together on the eleven o'clock express.
JUDGE'S WIFE:	Ah! Listen to that!
MARIA:	*(Paying the DOCTOR no attention, she tilts her head and looks alluringly into JURKIEWICZ's eyes with a smile)* So far away … To the north … where it's warm … and fragrant … where the sky is blue … far away …
DOCTOR:	*(Rapidly, quietly)* Maryś!
MARIA:	*(As if waking from a dream)* What?
JUDGE'S WIFE:	Nothing … nothing … the doctor's angry, you don't want to go with him.
DOCTOR:	*(Following an internal struggle, with a strange smile)* Ha! … If she doesn't want to … *(Pause)* Please, drink up.
MARIA:	*(To JURKIEWICZ)* You're angry with me. I don't like it!
DOCTOR:	*(Sarcastically, aggravated)* Tell us, do, why you're angry.
JURKIEWICZ:	*(Confused)* But, sir …
DOCTOR:	*(As above)* So you're not? God be praised!
WANDA:	*(Quietly)* Lolek!
JURKIEWICZ:	*(As above)* You imagined it, that's all … really …
DOCTOR:	*(As above)* Aha, that's good, I'd be devastated, if you were. *(Pause)* Please, drink up … please …
JUDGE:	*(Clearing his throat)* Hmm … hmm … thank you …
KOSICKI:	*(The same)* Hmm … thank you … getting late …
JUDGE:	Yes … hmm … should be going …
DOCTOR:	What's all this? And why? You see, they won't drink because you're angry. It's all your fault.

In a Small House (1904)

WANDA:	*(As above)* Lolek, please, I ask you!
JURKIEWICZ:	*(After a while, with a final burst of energy)* Oh, I apologize for being rather maudlin ... but there was talk of beautiful journeys ... my heart positively sank ... at some point I would so love to ...
DOCTOR:	*(Drinking, his eyes shining)* Really? Well I never! Why not take a trip? If I were in your position I wouldn't stay in this God-forsaken hole – no way! It's good enough for me, for Kosicki ...
KOSICKI:	Er hemm!
DOCTOR:	... e tutti quanti, most certainly not for a 'European' ... ha, ha, ha!
JURKIEWICZ:	*(As above, paling)* Hm ... you're joking ...
DOCTOR:	You think so? I'm a jovial ass from a small town, right? *(He laughs quietly)* Naturally, a complete ass.
JURKIEWICZ:	*(As above)* Sir, honestly. I fail to comprehend ...
WANDA:	*(Rises suddenly)* I propose that we retire to the veranda.
DOCTOR:	*(Paying no attention, to JURKIEWICZ, loudly)* Do you think I could become a 'European' ... hmm? Perhaps not everyone can, hmm?
JURKIEWICZ:	*(Very uneasy)* But of course we are all ...
WANDA:	*(Nervously)* Let's move onto the veranda, it's stuffy in here. *(All rise)*
DOCTOR:	*(To JURKIEWICZ)* A small glass, one more, with me?
JURKIEWICZ:	*(As above)* No, no, really. *(All pass onto the veranda; last are JURKIEWICZ and MARIA and for a while they are alone in the room. At the entrance to the veranda, the DOCTOR turns once quickly to look at them)*

Scene Eleven

MARIA, JURKIEWICZ

MARIA:	*(Brushing against JURKIEWICZ's shoulder)* I love you ... I love you ... I want you ...
JURKIEWICZ:	*(Aggravated)* What are you doing? He was looking over ... he sees everything ... he's jealous.
MARIA:	*(Longingly)* Don't be angry ... At the table I was holding back from shouting all the time, I love you ...
JURKIEWICZ:	*(With his head in his hands)* Oh God! Oh my God!
MARIA:	What's the matter?

JURKIEWICZ:	*(Tearing himself away, in a despairing voice)* Just go! Please, remove yourself! Go! I need some space … They're all outside … Go! *(MARIA goes with some hesitation; JURKIEWICZ alone on the stage, sits in a chair, hangs his head and covers his face with his hand)*

Scene Twelve

JURKIEWICZ, KOSICKI

KOSICKI:	*(Pacing quietly with his hat in his hand)* I am currently playing the role of an Englishman … off I go, home to my castle … Cheerio! *(In the doorway he stops suddenly, looking at JURKIEWICZ)* Cheerio! *(Approaches him)* What's all this? Migraine?
JURKIEWICZ:	Listen … I'm out of here.
KOSICKI:	What?
JURKIEWICZ:	I'm out of here … I'm leaving!
KOSICKI:	So suddenly?
JURKIEWICZ:	*(With a strange smile)* You must sense what's going on?
KOSICKI:	*(Scrutinizes him for a while)* Hm … just a hunch.
JURKIEWICZ:	But now you're certain, right? *(Laughs angrily, abruptly)* She's making it too obvious! *(Rises)* Ha! Nothing for it! *(Looks at his watch)* The bridge isn't finished … but I can't … devil himself can finish it, I'm jumping off!
KOSICKI:	Hm … wait … think carefully …
JURKIEWICZ:	*(Quietly, in a voice trembling with emotion)* I don't want a scandal. I don't! I've always lived a quiet life and she'll destroy me … she's a child. Oh, I know women … what a catastrophe … no thanks!
KOSICKI:	I did warn you … Don't be angry, but it was a stupid thing to do.
JURKIEWICZ:	Maybe … Maybe so … I should have stuck firmly to my principles – only women from good company. Principle number one – follow convention.
KOSICKI:	Too late now …
JURKIEWICZ:	Too late!
KOSICKI:	*(Looking around)* Pst! Cheerio! *(He leaves, as he arrived, pacing quietly through the right-hand door. JURKIEWICZ stands immobile for a while, deep in thought, eventually sees the DOCTOR and JUDGE'S WIFE entering, vanishes through the same door as KOSICKI did a while ago)*

In a Small House (1904)

Scene Thirteen

JUDGE'S WIFE, DOCTOR

JUDGE'S WIFE:	*(Putting down her hat and gloves)* There's no need, really … Your polite attentions are merely a symptom of alcohol-induced arousal.
DOCTOR:	Oh dear.
JUDGE'S WIFE:	In any case we're going home.
DOCTOR:	Already? Why?
JUDGE'S WIFE:	Surely you are aware that I'm a sick woman. Allow me to jog your memory, if I may.
DOCTOR:	I'm listening.
JUDGE'S WIFE:	*(Quietly)* When was it now? 5 March, in the afternoon, your consulting room.
DOCTOR:	What does that mean?
JUDGE'S WIFE:	To you it almost certainly means nothing, but I remember … because it's the day I endured my life's greatest humiliation.
DOCTOR:	Ah!
JUDGE'S WIFE:	It registers I see … what a relief! Oh, my husband is saying goodbye to the ladies … There's just one thing.
DOCTOR:	I'm listening.
JUDGE'S WIFE:	Today, would I re–… *(She calls out)* Just coming! *(To the DOCTOR quietly, with a smile, in a trembling voice)* Today, would I receive a similar rebuttal? I've a feeling, you'd be different now …
DOCTOR:	Why so?
JUDGE'S WIFE:	*(As above)* Revenge.
DOCTOR:	*(Paling)* On whom?
JUDGE'S WIFE:	You don't know? *(Pause)*
DOCTOR:	*(Controlling himself with difficulty, with laughter)* Ha, ha! I understand. Now you're the one taking revenge.
JUDGE'S WIFE:	I am? Surely you must know I'm a sick woman.
DOCTOR:	I don't believe you.
JUDGE'S WIFE:	*(Pulling on her gloves)* You don't? Then why did you understand at once?
DOCTOR:	You can see that I remain composed.
JUDGE'S WIFE:	Good for you. *(Louder)* We're going home now.
DOCTOR:	You can see that I am laughing.
JUDGE'S WIFE:	I can. *(Louder)* Goodnight! We're on our way!
DOCTOR:	*(Going with her, his voice suddenly catching in his throat)* What do you know?

JUDGE'S WIFE:	No – I'm sorry. Dear husband, where is my umbrella?
DOCTOR:	*(Laughing quietly)* How small everything is ... How funny ...
JUDGE'S WIFE:	*(Yawning)* Yes, it is always funny.
DOCTOR:	You've failed ... I don't believe you.
JUDGE'S WIFE:	Goodnight.
MARIA:	*(In the doorway to the veranda)* No, don't leave just yet ... the express hasn't gone by ...
JUDGE'S WIFE:	Lovely lady, my express went by a long time ago ... You're still young and healthy – long journey ahead of you.
JUDGE:	Goodnight! Goodnight! *(They say goodbye on the veranda)*
DOCTOR:	*(On the veranda)* This way, through the garden ... I'll light your way.

Scene Fourteen

MARIA, WANDA, DOCTOR

MARIA enters after a while, stands lost in thought for some time, as if listening intently to the increasingly distant voices of the guests, then she goes to the forestage and lies down on the sofa.

WANDA:	*(Approaching the table)* Shall I clear?
MARIA:	*(Stretching)* Ah. No ... leave it.
WANDA:	As you wish.
MARIA:	In the morning ... in the morning.
WANDA:	In that case ... *(She wants to leave)*
MARIA:	Wanda!
WANDA:	What?
MARIA:	You're going?
WANDA:	Yes.
MARIA:	It's sometimes really sad when an evening ends ...
WANDA:	Was this one so pleasant?
MARIA:	No – no – but it's ending and that's really sad ...
WANDA:	Goodnight!
MARIA:	*(In a slightly sleepy voice)* You've seemed angry with me today.
WANDA:	Me? I have no reason.
MARIA:	You've seemed ... *(WANDA leaves; after a while the DOCTOR's voice is heard)*
DOCTOR:	*(Offstage)* Where's Jurkiewicz? Kasia, where's Mr Jurkiewicz, do you know?

In a Small House (1904)

Scene Fifteen

DOCTOR, MARIA

DOCTOR:	*(Enters, whistling, puts the lamp on the table, then looks around)* No Jurkiewicz ... *(Seeing MARIA)* Ah ... You're lying down ... *(Stands in front of her)* You're tired, drowsy ... aren't you?
MARIA:	*(Without opening her eyes)* Extremely.
DOCTOR:	That's odd ... just then you were talking, laughing away, and now you're reclining, with your eyes closed. Sorry, I'm in the mood for a chat ... I wanted a word with Jurkiewicz – can you imagine – he's not in.
MARIA:	Not in?
DOCTOR:	Oh! You've opened your eyes ... Jurkiewicz's room is empty ... no one knows where he is ... never mind ... You did say yourself, that he's never in ... I remember, you said it ... twice, even ... right?
MARIA:	I may have done.
DOCTOR:	*(Suddenly)* But are you drowsy? No – eyes open? Today, you have dark eyes. You don't seem like my wife at all ... why not? You're like a strange woman. But you are handsome ... handsome. *(Loudly)* Get up, I'll tell you something ...
MARIA:	*(Rising drowsily)* My God ... what? What?
DOCTOR:	You seem strange.
MARIA:	*(In a sleepy, tearful voice, like a child)* How can I help it.
DOCTOR:	People are speaking ill of you.
MARIA:	*(As above)* How can I help it?
DOCTOR:	I don't know if you can. People know everything ... the Judge's wife said ...
MARIA:	*(As above)* What ... the Judge's wife? What do you want from me?
DOCTOR:	Nothing. Just tell me you love me ... lie, that you love me and I'll leave you in peace.
MARIA:	*(As above)* I'm so tired ... so, so tired ...
DOCTOR:	But you can talk. You're a child ... Are you afraid? I know, you're innocent. What are you scared of?
MARIA:	*(As above)* Let me go ...
DOCTOR:	I know ... do you hear? I can feel it's not true! Say something, anything ... what's happened while I've been away. Tell me!
MARIA:	*(As above)* Let me go, Lolek! You'd be better off without me. You don't love me ... no one here loves me ... not you, or Wanda ... or those people ... Let me go!

DOCTOR:	You want to leave me? Altogether? Like this, now? But surely I must learn the truth. This house – is you! Understand? If you've betrayed me then so has all this, betrayed me … say it!
MARIA:	*(As above)* Let me go, Lolek!
DOCTOR:	Come on, then … Jurkiewicz? Is it true? You don't know me … you think I'm forgiving? No, never, not anyone! Listen. If it's true … if it is … ah! … You! *(He goes to the bureau and takes out a revolver)* Look!
MARIA:	*(Crying covers her face with her hands)* No … no … no … no …
DOCTOR:	Look!
MARIA:	*(As above)* Drop it, Lolek! Drop it, Lolek!
DOCTOR:	Tell the truth, then I'll drop it … *(Lowers his hand)* Maryś … *(He kisses her eyes, lips and neck passionately)* My sweet … sweetness … People lie … is it true that you're mine? Tell me!
MARIA:	Let it go! Let it go! *(She lies down and cries)*
DOCTOR:	People lie … you are a child … you can't have tricked me.
MARIA:	People don't like me … no one likes me.
DOCTOR:	I love you!
MARIA:	*(In a sleepy voice)* No, Lolek, no!
DOCTOR:	I believe in your shining eyes more than I do in other people.
MARIA:	*(As above)* Yes … people don't … he says that people …
DOCTOR:	What? What?
MARIA:	*(As above)* He says that happiness should be hidden.
DOCTOR:	Who does?
MARIA:	*(As above)* Him … he does …
DOCTOR:	*(His voice catching)* Jurkiewicz?
MARIA:	*(As above)* Yes.
DOCTOR:	*(As above)* Ha ha! Of course! My beauty! My innocent! You're thinking of him …
MARIA:	*(As above)* Of him …
DOCTOR:	At this very moment?
MARIA:	Always.
DOCTOR:	*(Like a wounded animal)* You!
MARIA:	How can I help it?
DOCTOR:	*(Quietly)* When I was away, he stole you! The first best man came along and he stole you …
MARIA:	Lolek, I was never yours.
DOCTOR:	You were … yes, you were … I paid …
MARIA:	Why did you take me, Lolek? Why? I thought it had to be that way. I didn't know that some time … some time … I knew nothing then, at mother's in Kraków.

DOCTOR:	Don't look at me like that! You think I'm still the same person who paid with his entire life for one solitary night with you? I gave up everything for you and you … The first best … *(He takes the revolver, which he had previously dropped)* Wake up, you … wake up, do you hear? Look at me.
MARIA:	*(Shouting)* Lo … lek!
DOCTOR:	Look me in the eye, you … my shame … my curse … my withered life …
MARIA:	*(As above)* Lolek, I want to live – to live – let me go … I'll flee like a dog!
DOCTOR:	You … *(Shoots)* You … *(Shoots a second time)*
MARIA:	*(Falling down)* Lolek *(The DOCTOR lets his hand drop; the revolver falls to the ground; he approaches. She whispers, dying)* Why did you … take … me … why … did … you … take … me …
DOCTOR:	*(Bending over her, quietly)* Maryś … *(Lifts up her hand, which drops, lifeless)* Maryś … *(He rises and looks about him, as if suddenly waking from a dream. At this moment the prolonged, distant whistle of the eleven o-five express is heard, on which* MARYNIA *wanted to leave on a long journey. Curtain falls)*

Act 3

The same room. Early spring. The same arrangement, but the room appears emptier, uninhabited; everywhere sterile order, each item in its place as though no one has touched it, no one has used it.

Scene One

JUDGE'S WIFE, KASIA

A while after the curtain is raised, the JUDGE'S WIFE *enters, behind her* KASIA.

JUDGE'S WIFE:	Well now, is the young lady here? Ah, dear, so chilly!
KASIA:	She's not in.
JUDGE'S WIFE:	Again? There's a draught. That's the second time I've missed her. How are things? News from the master?
KASIA:	*(Hesitates)* From the master? News?
JUDGE'S WIFE:	Yes … of course? Apparently he's due back any day.
KASIA:	*(Confused)* I don't know … I'm sorry … no one told me …

JUDGE'S WIFE:	Really? That's odd, my dear. Hmm ... terribly cold ... (*She looks around and wants to leave, when suddenly from the right-hand side* SIELSKI *enters, leading* ANTOŚ *by the hand*)

Scene Two

JUDGE'S WIFE, SIELSKI, ANTEK

SIELSKI:	(*Without looking at the* JUDGE'S WIFE) I didn't know you'd get tired so quickly ... if you'd prefer to go to the garden now, instead of writing, then you may. I don't want to force you ...
JUDGE'S WIFE:	(*Looking at* SIELSKI *through her lorgnette*) Good evening!
SIELSKI:	(*Distracted*) Good evening ... (*To* ANTEK) Run about in the garden for as long as you like and when you want to write again, just tell me – I'll wait. (ANTEK *runs into the garden*)
JUDGE'S WIFE:	(*Approaching* SIELSKI *slowly*) You're very lenient with Antek ... Perfectly right, that poor child, no mother ... Well, he never really had one.
SIELSKI:	What do you mean, never?
JUDGE'S WIFE:	Let's not talk about that. I came because I missed Wandeczka. But she's not here, is she?
SIELSKI:	Seems not.
JUDGE'S WIFE:	You come here often, is that right? I haven't been for three whole months ... since the trial. I couldn't attend the actual hearing, I had neuralgia in my head. I am still sick. But when I learned how the hearing had gone, I was so delighted, I cannot describe it. Shall we sit?
SIELSKI:	(*Indicating a chair distractedly*) Please ... here or there ... I must go and check on Antek, in the garden ... soon.
JUDGE'S WIFE:	Last night I thought I was dying; and anyway I came here because I dearly love Wandeczka. Everyone loves this house, don't they?
SIELSKI:	Possibly ... I don't know what people think and feel because I live alone ...
JUDGE'S WIFE:	Oh yes, everyone does ... that's obvious ... when the verdict was read the whole town rejoiced ... like when the doctor became mayor ... everyone was behind him ... a panel of twelve jurors, salt of the earth as my husband would say – pronounced not guilty. He left the courthouse victorious.
SIELSKI:	(*Looking about him uneasily*) That's a bit much ... victorious! It's all so upsetting ...

In a Small House (1904)

JUDGE'S WIFE:	No, sir, it's beautiful! Beautiful! Once again I can believe in fairness! Terrible draught! An undeserving woman presided over this house ... unworthy of such a man!
SIELSKI:	*(Suddenly, quietly)* That's not true!
JUDGE'S WIFE:	*(Mortified)* What? What do you mean?
SIELSKI:	I do apologize but it's not true! And no one may say so.
JUDGE'S WIFE:	Ha ha! Energetic defense. Forcefully expressed.
SIELSKI:	*(Humbly)* I really am sorry but I can't say otherwise. It hurts when someone speaks like that ... it's cruel, unjust ... especially in this house ... yes, in this house, which remains hers ... One should speak quietly here ... very quietly ...
JUDGE'S WIFE:	*(Artificially, lightly, but in spite of herself more quietly)* You are strange ... you always defend everyone ... and hold a unique opinion.
SIELSKI:	Yes, always a unique opinion. Terribly sorry.
JUDGE'S WIFE:	But you're a friend of the doctor's ... at least, I thought so.
SIELSKI:	A friend? I don't know ... but that's irrelevant. I wish him well.
JUDGE'S WIFE:	Sir, perhaps you'll tell me ... the Doctor is still away? He left straight after the court-hearing ... yes ... they released him in the autumn ... four months ago ... he's still on his travels? Hm? *(After a while of narrowing her eyes, slowly, quietly)* Because people say he's coming back. A rumour went round today ... *(Leaning towards Sielski, uneasily, quickly)* Is it true?
SIELSKI:	*(Confused)* I don't know ... I don't know ...
JUDGE'S WIFE:	*(With apparent joviality)* Ha, ha! I suspect you know something ... but you've been briefed ... Forgive me ... you are so good ...
SIELSKI:	*(As above)* No ... nothing ... best avoided ... please!
JUDGE'S WIFE:	Oh! You can't hide. I see from your face it's true. And that would be strange. No one thought he'd come back ... everyone respects him, of course, as they did before, and will greet him with joy, I'm sure. But I had the impression he wouldn't really want to; he wasn't blessed with those talents, to be walled up here, well? When she lived, he had no choice ... she was his misfortune ... his ball and chain!
SIELSKI:	That's not true! My God! It's not true! You don't know who she was ... no one does ...
JUDGE'S WIFE:	*(Crossly)* Oh I think we do. May I be so bold as to claim ... forgive me ... We knew long ago, before that woman repaid her husband so charmingly for his virtue.

SIELSKI:	What virtue?
JUDGE'S WIFE:	Well, to begin with, he did marry her. It was his duty, that's true … but are there many men sensible of that?
SIELSKI:	I don't know, I suppose, not many, that would be terrible! Yes, I understand now … You expressed it well … Duty prompted the doctor to marry … that's what people expect … the done thing. Completely true. His entire life was an expression of what your circle considers right and proper.
JUDGE'S WIFE:	*(Sharply, with a smile)* And what's your view of propriety?
SIELSKI:	Doesn't bother me … don't hear what people say … I'm self-sufficient … I have peace and quiet. But he always needed you, and your life – was his life … he loved you more than himself – and when you instructed him to kill her …
JUDGE'S WIFE:	*(In an outburst)* That is outrageous! Madness! Who instructed him?
SIELSKI:	*(Looking around uneasily, quietly)* Not so loud … please … you ask me, who? Your system … yes, I'll tell you in confidence – your justice system! Didn't twelve jurors confirm he'd done the right thing …
JUDGE'S WIFE:	*(As above)* Enough! My husband will learn what you have said … the whole town will know …
SIELSKI:	*(Distracted)* Alright, alright … keep your voice down; he might be next door …
JUDGE'S WIFE:	Who? *(With sudden fear)* The doctor? He's here?
SIELSKI:	*(Tempering himself)* My God! What have I said! Yes, the doctor … is here!
JUDGE'S WIFE:	*(Backing away)* Ah, yes … ah, yes …
SIELSKI:	It pains me to say so … I was asked directly … he didn't want to see anyone …
JUDGE'S WIFE:	*(Nervously, quickly donning her hat)* Really? So he's here? Doesn't want to see anyone?
SIELSKI:	*(With growing concern)* It pains me … I'm so absent-minded … will you wait for Wanda? … *(Wanting to somehow make up for his tactlessness)* Madam … madam …
JUDGE'S WIFE:	*(As above)* No, thank you … another time … must dash …
SIELSKI:	*(Approaching the window)* She may be somewhere in the garden … *(Calling)* Wanda!
JUDGE'S WIFE:	*(As above, in the doorway, gesticulating fearfully)* No! No! Don't call her! Off I go! *(Leaving)* Another time … *(She disappears)*
SIELSKI:	*(Alone, calling even more loudly through the window)* Wanda!

In a Small House (1904)

Scene Three

DOCTOR, SIELSKI

DOCTOR:	*(Appears suddenly in the left-hand doorway. On the face of it he has not changed at all since the previous act, even the same swift movements, the same voice, and sometimes laugh, but as though everything is parodied, as if he is only playing the previous* DOCTOR *and in doing so, exaggerating a little; besides he has grown a little paler and is less neatly dressed)* What's going on? You …
SIELSKI:	*(Turns with a light cry)* Ah … nothing … I'm sorry …
DOCTOR:	What the hell do you mean, nothing? You, here, alone? I could've sworn you were talking to someone! What's going on? Huh? Closer … come closer … sit down … You should visit more often … a cigar?
SIELSKI:	No, thank you – the Judge's wife was here.
DOCTOR:	What, the Judge's wife?
SIELSKI:	Yes … I told her you'd arrived.
DOCTOR:	*(After a while)* Oh honestly, you … you told her?
SIELSKI:	Yes … just slipped out … I'm sorry … I realize you don't want people to know … but I can't … just slipped out …
DOCTOR:	*(Laughing, as though angrily)* Ha, ha! Very nice, I must say.
SIELSKI:	I am miserable.
DOCTOR:	*(As above, hiding with difficulty a growing excitement, almost joy)* Look at that! You're miserable! Never mind! Born diplomat. Just slipped out? Thank you, sir … *(Pacing quickly about the room)* Ha, ha! You entrust him with a secret … Know what'll happen? Any minute they'll arrive in droves … you'll see … droves …
SIELSKI:	You think so …
DOCTOR:	Absolutely. The Judge's wife will blab. The whole town will know. *(Looks at his watch)* You old gossip! *(Rubbing his hands)* Misery … trouble … Can't conceal a thing! *(Unable to hide his sudden joy)* To hell with it! Misery!
SIELSKI:	Truly I apologize … I am so sorry … Perhaps no one will come.
DOCTOR:	*(Standing before* SIELSKI*)* What? No one? *(Almost sharply)* May I ask why not?
SIELSKI:	I am assuming … I clearly told the Judge's wife …
DOCTOR:	*(Uneasily)* What? What did you say?
SIELSKI:	That you don't want to see anyone … yes, I said it clearly.

DOCTOR:	*(Coldly, with unpleasant calmness)* That wasn't strictly necessary … honestly … over the top every single time. I didn't need someone to act as a deterrent.
SIELSKI:	*(After a while, quietly)* Wanda told me, you weren't receiving guests.
DOCTOR:	*(Batting his hand)* Eh … of course, at first … but now … I'm not going to lock myself away forever … *(Suddenly depressed)* You think no-one will come?
SIELSKI:	*(Quietly, uncertainly)* I don't know …
DOCTOR:	*(Impatiently)* What?
SIELSKI:	*(As above)* I'm sorry … I don't know … *(Pause)*
DOCTOR:	*(Looking at his watch)* Fifteen minutes … yes, long enough for the Judge's wife to arrive home and tell her husband. Perhaps on the way she met an acquaintance – 'Did you know? The Doctor's arrived'. And that acquaintance tells another … and she another … it spreads quickly … as if by telegraph … And soon, the entire town knows. Do you think?
SIELSKI:	Maybe … I don't know …
DOCTOR:	You don't know anything. You're ignorant about the world, relationships … how annoying. I care nothing for your philosophy, oh no. My Antek knows more about the world and people than you do. Why assume that no one will come?
SIELSKI:	I didn't say that.
DOCTOR:	But you thought it. You can't fool me. You're a laughing stock. *(After a while with angry laughter)* Do you think I'd let a daughter of mine marry you, well?
SIELSKI:	We're not talking about that. *(He rises)*
DOCTOR:	You're right! We're not – besides, I don't have a daughter. But you think I'd let you have, Wanda? Ha, ha!
SIELSKI:	What … we're not discussing that either.
DOCTOR:	*(Laughing insincerely)* Dash it all! Really? Then what? Perhaps we're dumb? I've forgotten how to speak. Here a week seems like a year. What's happened to everyone? Huh … *(Quietly, sadly)* Wanda's very talkative as well. Not even the children make a huge racket, like other people's. I raised them too well, it seems, welcome – my sad old age. To hell with it! The whole house … the *whole* house … *(Suddenly, in an altered tone)* I'd like to be active again, dammit! Something's keeping me from life … and it's all this … I want to work again!
SIELSKI:	That I understand.
DOCTOR:	Lucky old you. If I can't have people, then patients will do, you see? But what's the use when you chase everyone away! *(He rises)* This

	is what stands between me and life! *(Suddenly)* Did the Judge's wife say she was sick?
SIELSKI:	She said nothing.
DOCTOR:	*(Looking at his watch)* Twenty-five minutes *(Stands by the window)* Here comes Szymon ... from the railway ... Wanda tells me his wife's still frail. When he learns I'm here, he'll come at once. Aha! He's one of the rabble ... the masses ... can't get rid of them ... *(After a while)* He can't see me ... he's bowing ... he's recognized me ... *(Uneasily)* But he's moving on ... keeping his distance ... I must ... embolden him a little ... Hey! Szymon! You see? He needs encouragement ... *(Wants to go out – on the doorstep he meets WANDA)* How are you ... wait ... let me out!
WANDA:	*(Entering)* Where to?
DOCTOR:	*(Exiting quickly)* Nowhere ... nothing ... back in a minute ... *(He leaves)*

Scene Four

WANDA, SIELSKI

WANDA:	*(Looks after the DOCTOR, then to SIELSKI)* Where's he gone?
SIELSKI:	To get someone ... don't know ... doesn't matter ... He saw Szymon, went after him. He wants to talk.
WANDA:	Ah yes ...
SIELSKI:	Yes, he can't live without them ... doesn't really matter who ... Szymon or the Judge's Wife.
WANDA:	Ah, yes.
SIELSKI:	I knew it. Just one question ...
WANDA:	Don't ... It'll be dreadful, I know. He can't live without them ... but they ...
SIELSKI:	Exactly ... they live without him and will carry on.
WANDA:	Don't.
SIELSKI:	You feel it yourself ... you know.
WANDA:	*(Sits with a sigh and drops her hands on her knees)* Our greatest fears, they come to pass.
SIELSKI:	What's this?
WANDA:	Oh nothing. I saw it in my nightmares, as a child.
SIELSKI:	Not that long ago.
WANDA:	I don't know. Everything seems long ago ... far behind me, even what happened, less than a year ... Even the time, when this house

	lived ... when Marynia walked and talked, laughed and shouted at the children ... and was like a child herself. *(She falls silent for a while, from a distance the quiet, prolonged chuff of the train, which is lost without meaning)* His greatest fear was always loneliness. And now ...
SIELSKI:	Your sad, quiet tone appalls me ... this cannot be ... you're so young ... in you there's something stronger than all the fears combined ... there's life beyond this lifeless house. You'll leave, go into the world ... the sunshine ... you'll blossom ...
WANDA:	This is the problem. I wanted to stay here with the children, until he got back ... and now ...
SIELSKI:	Well?
WANDA:	You must sense that he cannot be alone.
SIESLKI:	Him?
WANDA:	Yes ... not the children, him. *(She suddenly smiles sadly)* Seems strange ... impossible, that he should be alone ... illogical ... him, a recluse! Seems inevitable that people will be drawn to him ... I feel that ... and will repeat it still.
SIELSKI:	Yes ... like singing alone in a valley.
WANDA:	They will ... because he draws them ... he'll compel them, won't he? He willed them once with all the life that's in him, and he'll overcome them a second time. You'll see.
SIELSKI:	*(Quietly, meaningfully, slowly)* Because he is a real man.
WANDA:	*(Suddenly, with a smile)* Ah! A good memory, very good!
SIELSKI:	Not always; only for certain things. I even know when you said that. Do you? When I discovered ... that you ... *(Thoughtfully, pointedly, as if reading quietly)* ... feel nothing for me ... feel nothing ... hmm ... *(He falls silent and covers his face with his hands)*
WANDA:	*(Turning her head)* Let's not talk about that, alright?
SIELSKI:	*(Uncovers his face and looks her straight in the eye)* Why not? It's all I think of. Do you suppose it frightens me? That would be ... like fearing to mention the sunlight ... or that my heart is beating ... it's all I think of!
WANDA:	*(Suddenly troubled, she lowers her eyes)* Ah ... let's not talk about this ... *(She turns away)*
SIELSKI:	*(Surely, though with a voice slightly trembling with emotion)* Why won't you look at me ... just look at me ... am I not calm?
WANDA:	*(Raises her gaze slowly, smiling obscurely, more and more brightly)* Yes, you really are ... *(Almost with admiration)* You have a gentle disposition, too much composure, you don't need anyone to make you happy ... you don't ...

SIELSKI:	And your needs? Well? You're welcome to my peaceful home, don't you see ... I keep on inviting you ... don't you feel it ... have you never felt it? Not with words, but I wait. I look at you and I wait ... and whenever you want to ...
WANDA:	*(Pale, enormously moved but with a smile, touches, as if with fear, his arm)* Hush ... dear sir ... please be quiet!
SIELSKI:	*(Presses her hand, swept away by emotion, in spite of himself)* I ... am waiting.
WANDA:	*(Tears herself away and runs towards the window, where she leans on her hands, her back turned to* SIELSKI, *after a while, as if after tears, drily, shortly)* Go, sir ... would you? Please go?
SIELSKI:	*(Standing fixed to the spot, quietly, helplessly)* What? I should go? Hmm. Where to?
WANDA:	*(Almost brattishly)* Wherever you like ... to the garden ... to the woods? *(Suddenly, without moving, in an altered voice)* Anyway, someone's coming ... *(Looks through the window)* Ah! The Judge ... with Lolek ... they're coming here ... really ...
SIELSKI:	*(With agitation)* The Judge ... has found out ... from his wife ... yes, probably from her ... Pardon me ... I'm going outside ... *(He approaches the door)* I'm leaving.
WANDA:	And how does she know?
SIELSKI:	I told her ... I'm sorry ... just slipped out ... good bye ... I'm very sorry ... *(He trips on the doorstep)* It slipped out. *(Exits,* WANDA *looks after him for a while, eventually exits left. For a while the stage is empty)*

Scene Five

JUDGE, DOCTOR

JUDGE:	*(Enters first, through the garden doorway, and behind him follows the* DOCTOR. *The* JUDGE *is apparently under the impression of his initial meeting with the* DOCTOR *but naturally is trying to be relaxed and friendly. Entering, he says, as if continuing an earlier conversation)* Of course of course, an enormous surprise, my wife arrived out of breath.
DOCTOR:	And the hospital? Some vodka, perhaps? What's new at the hospital?
JUDGE:	Vodka! Perish the thought! Not my habit ... any more ...
DOCTOR:	Please ... sit down, dearest Judge ... tell me ... what's new, at the hospital, for instance?

JUDGE:	*(Rather troubled)* Aha! Of course … naturally … certain changes … of course … at the hospital … so much time … it happens …
DOCTOR:	*(Eagerly)* Any changes? Well?
JUDGE:	*(As above)* Certain trivial, completely meaningless … it happens … not my area … everyone knows, except my household … you must realize … so much work … dawn to dusk … I speak to no one … a man learns, you know, like a young student. Not like my wife at all …
DOCTOR:	*(As above)* But nothing major … no fundamental changes?
JUDGE:	Where? Oh, you still mean the hospital? Of course, each to his own … he, he! Nothing major … dear me! Nothing that would, hm … Besides, you'll find out … go and see for yourself … naturally … as if … still on the cigars? He … he … I've given up.
DOCTOR:	*(With a distracted smile)* Really? You don't smoke?
JUDGE:	Travesty! … not a puff … nothing … hygiene, you might say. Vodka and tobacco, strictly forbidden … the whole lot … I know you mock such regimes … he … he … what's to be done? Various opinions … new chap forbids it …
DOCTOR:	What new chap? Who?
JUDGE:	Who? *(Momentarily confused, doesn't know what to say)* Well a … certain doctor, certain doctor.
DOCTOR:	Aha!
JUDGE:	Exactly! Certain acquaintance … you don't know him … yes, it happens … *(Pondering)* Dear sir … dear sir … I wanted to ask … *(Suddenly, quickly, lightly)* How long shall we be entertaining you?
DOCTOR:	What do you mean? *(Bursting out with artificial laughter)* What? Entertaining me? Ha, ha! You're good, merciful Judge! I've come back … haven't I … to hell with it! I've come back at last and I'm not thinking of going anywhere … what for? Where to?
JUDGE:	I was only … he, he! … thinking … *(Delicately, carefully)* … perhaps you'd like to take on something bigger … more rewarding, less demanding job … somewhere …
DOCTOR:	*(Furrowing his brow)* What? What? Make boots? Shave beards? What?
JUDGE:	He, he! Always the same … He, he! Shave beards … *(Suddenly becoming serious)* No, I simply thought you might stick to the original plan.
DOCTOR:	*(Expectantly)* What plan?

JUDGE:	Well, move to a bigger town, completely enormous one … it happens … for example, Lwów … professorship … some such … wider arena … task … greater magnitude …
DOCTOR:	*(As above)* Forget it, I'm staying put. If I can't manage to live here then that's that. Ha, tough luck! You must endure me! I'll start work at the hospital shortly.
JUDGE:	*(Fearfully)* Where?
DOCTOR:	At the hospital … I must work … This inactivity … so wearing … I loathe it! Oh! *(Rising)* I'll live again … why not? Huh … all I need is work! That's it … I'm starting work at the hospital.
JUDGE:	*(As above)* Yes … hmm … it's just, at the hospital …
DOCTOR:	What?
JUDGE:	There's someone different now … temporarily …
DOCTOR:	*(Strangely calm)* Ah! Yes … temporarily …
JUDGE:	Exactly … the post of Chief Physician is currently filled … one could wait …
DOCTOR:	*(As above)* Naturally … one could …
JUDGE:	But there's more to life than hospital jobs, eh?
DOCTOR:	Hmm … yes …
JUDGE:	As already pointed out, the original plan should not be forgotten. Lwów … how about that? Our spiritual aristocracy … all that is best … cream of the crop …
DOCTOR:	Eh. No need …
JUDGE:	No need? What do you mean? No need? I don't understand.
DOCTOR:	It strikes me that I've lost any inclination to work …
JUDGE:	Lost the inclination? *(After a while)* Hmm! You're put out that there's someone else? Honestly! You need to … hmm! It happens.
DOCTOR:	*(Sitting quietly, lights his cigar slowly and only later says)* No, not upset … *(He smokes)* … not remotely … even I'm surprised. Clearly I'm not so dependent on work … that's not why I'm back.
JUDGE:	It's not?
DOCTOR:	No … and it's not inactivity that I find so wearing.
JUDGE:	But what?
DOCTOR:	The fact that I killed my wife.
JUDGE:	Sir … honestly … Tut!
DOCTOR:	Yes, I killed my wife and no one did anything to me.
JUDGE:	Sir … really … tut!
DOCTOR:	And that … that is unbearable … I came back to get rid of it …
JUDGE:	Really, sir … what's your …

DOCTOR:	That's the only reason I can't live, do you hear? The only one! I practically sleepwalked here … it just drew me … drew me … and now I know …
JUDGE:	*(Covering his ears)* Quiet! Be quiet! What do you want? It's finished … the jury reached a verdict …
DOCTOR:	They didn't know what happened … I'll tell them everything …
JUDGE:	Oh! You mustn't touch it … that's not good … it's not!
DOCTOR:	The jury didn't know I killed a child … not a woman …
JUDGE:	Be quiet! Have mercy … leave it alone … there's a verdict … give thanks to God.
DOCTOR:	There's a verdict … good! But I can't live. Those jurors were strangers … they had no idea. I want justice.
JUDGE:	Justice? Alright … everything was carried out in perfect accordance with the law … and with what people feel … what everyone feels.
DOCTOR:	To hell with that! What's everyone to me, when I don't feel the same … when I'm terminally ill. And it hurts, gnaws away. I want to recover – I come to you as my physician … just as they came to me for medication. I helped people, didn't I, as much as I could, you must all admit that. And now I come to you.
JUDGE:	Hmm … yes … I understand. You must collect yourself … You must believe I did everything … but what can I say? They've already judged you … You want something different because you're suffering … it happens. And where will I find alternative justice? We are all human. I am very sorry for you … but we are human. They come to you for a cure, you say … alright – and what do you do? You give them a phial with Latin on the label and you wait and see – the remedy is in there. And they take the phial and believe and sometimes they even get better … it happens … and often it doesn't … and you never know which way it'll go because you feel that good health isn't in that phial but out there, somewhere … what do I know? In the hands of God, say some … what do I know? We are human. What advice can I offer? Thirty years a Judge … and believe me, I feel … I feel that human justice is … like that remedy … it has its limits … like your education. It stretches as far as you believe and beyond that …
DOCTOR:	*(In a hoarse voice)* Well?
JUDGE:	That is a private matter. What do I know? Each individual is his own judge … yes … hmm … it happens.
DOCTOR:	*(As above)* Ah … yes …
JUDGE:	Hmm. Must be going … the wife's waiting … night is falling … hmm.

DOCTOR:	*(As above)* His ... own ... judge ...
JUDGE:	*(Giving him his hand)* Good night ... must be going.
DOCTOR:	*(Distractedly)* Ah yes ... goodnight. *(Suddenly approaches the JUDGE with a strange smile, patting him on the shoulder, quietly)* You're a terrible man ...
JUDGE:	Hmm?
DOCTOR:	A dreadful man ... ha, ha! You know everything!
JUDGE:	How's that? What, for example?
DOCTOR:	For example, one thought I have right now ... ha, ha!
JUDGE:	What do you ... What thought?
DOCTOR:	Ah, I brought it with me from my travels ... I hadn't realized ...
JUDGE:	What?
DOCTOR:	The thing you said just now.
JUDGE:	I don't understand ... *(Silence; the JUDGE looks at him then repeats)* I must be going.
DOCTOR:	Yes, you must ... and I'll be left alone. Ha, ha! Alone with myself!
JUDGE:	Never mind ... we'll see each other soon.
DOCTOR:	*(In a strange voice)* You think so, Judge?
JUDGE:	I don't understand.
DOCTOR:	No? *(In an unconscious tone)* No? *(Suddenly embraces him and kisses him on both cheeks)* Goodnight!
JUDGE:	*(Gives him a prolonged look – slowly)* Goodnight! *(After a while, leaves)*
DOCTOR:	*(When the JUDGE is in the doorway)* Judge!
JUDGE:	*(Looking around)* What?
DOCTOR:	You are a terrible man.
JUDGE:	*(Shrugging his shoulders)* Oh, doctor, honestly ...
DOCTOR :	Goodnight! *(The JUDGE departs. The DOCTOR sits lost in thought for some time, then repeats quietly)* His ... own ... judge ... *(He goes to the bureau, takes out the revolver, moves away on tiptoe, looking around in all directions)*

Scene Six

WANDA, SIELSKI *enter from the garden*

SIELSKI:	Tell me, dear lady ...
WANDA:	*(With a smile, pale, with a trembling voice, moving her hands to her heart)* Wait ... wait ...

SIELSKI:	You were calling … I heard it plainly … I was walking home slowly … past the garden and I thought the garden was empty … when all of a sudden I heard your voice … ah, I surely heard it once, twice, you called me … And when I entered the garden I found you so pale and strange … tell me, please!
WANDA:	*(Suddenly, directly)* Yes, I was calling.
SIELSKI:	And … what's the matter?
WANDA:	I'm frightened.
SIELSKI:	*(Quietly)* Of what?
WANDA:	It's getting dark … and … I'm all alone … and … everything …
SIELSKI:	And you called me …
WANDA:	Ah! My God … try to understand … what a child you are … try to understand.
SIELSKI:	Miss Wanda, say it … because now I am frightened … because I have a thought and I'm afraid to believe it …
WANDA:	*(Sobbing, with laughter, quietly)* Oh, so your invitation no longer stands?
SIELSKI:	What …? Louder … what?
WANDA:	*(Bursting out)* Invite me in, won't you … invite me to your home at last, where there is always light and peace … won't you invite me in!
SIELSKI:	Wanda! Wanda!
WANDA:	*(Throwing herself into his embrace)* Oh you … great big child! My love! Take me, take me to your home!
SIELSKI:	*(Holding her close)* Wanda. *(Pause, they embrace)*
WANDA:	*(As though waking from a dream, her voice half hoarse, through tears, quietly)* Only now …
SIELSKI:	Now you are mine.
WANDA:	My God! Now he …
SIELSKI:	Who? Say it!
WANDA:	How shall we tell him?
SIELSKI:	Ah, where is he? Come on!
WANDA:	I don't have the courage! Now he'll be alone …
SIELSKI:	Come on …
WANDA:	Quiet … he's there.
SIELSKI:	*(Indicating the door)* In here? *(They approach the door, at that moment a shot is heard)*
WANDA:	Oh God! *(SIELSKI quickly opens the door and enters first)*
SIELSKI:	What is this? *(Suddenly)* Help!
WANDA:	*(Entering behind him)* What? What? *(Piercingly)* Ah! …
SIELSKI:	Help us! … He's dead. *(The curtain falls)*

Snow (1902)

Stanisław Przybyszewski

Śnieg (1902)

Stanisław Przybyszewski

Dramatis Personae

TADEUSZ (TADEK)
KAZIMIERZ (KAZIO), his brother
BRONKA, TADEK's wife
EWA, BRONKA's friend
MANSERVANT
MAKRYNA, BRONKA's old nurse

Act 1

Scene One

KAZIMIERZ, BRONKA

The audience looks onto a fashionable dining room, from which – through large high windows and a glassed winter orangery – are visible bare, frosted trees in the garden and large flakes of snow. In the corner is a great, old-fashioned fireplace, next to it a stack of pine firewood that KAZIMIERZ *now and again throws onto the fire with a nervous gesture.* BRONKA *stands by the window anxiously, her eyes fixed on the blizzard*

KAZIMIERZ:	Why so restless? Don't be a child. What do you fear?
BRONKA:	For God's sake Kazio – the relentless blizzard? All day long! Those snow drifts. Beyond the town that treeless road runs for at least a kilometre. The driver might lose his way! The sleigh overturn into a ditch …
KAZIMIERZ:	*(Interrupts her)* Well? In goes our Tadek, headfirst. Soft landing.

BRONKA:	Ugh – insensitive.
KAZIMIERZ:	Calm down, Bronka. How infantile! Married a whole year, yet still so infatuated one would think you'd met yesterday.
BRONKA:	That's right. And life is beautiful.
KAZIMIERZ:	Indeed. How many love letters did he send this week?
BRONKA:	One more! How precious! Cherished as always! Beautiful words, beyond compare!
KAZIMIERZ:	Mm – words are overused. Still, Tadek does love you. *(Thoughtful)* A lot. I envy that, your love and happiness. *(Pause)* My resistance crumbles – I see a peaceful haven – that's me, working freely, my companion a beloved, affectionate woman. The old bohemian life. Theatre, museums, the circus, galleries, Italy, Paris. All the same – I'm so jaded …
BRONKA:	Kazio, Kazio – so unhappy. A well of sadness.
KAZIMIERZ:	Ah yes.
BRONKA:	Suppose you fell in love, Kazio – what then?
KAZIMIERZ:	With you, perhaps. Try me.
BRONKA:	*(Joking)* Silly boy. A simple, virtuous girl? What would you do? Not your type.
KAZIMIERZ:	*(Ironically)* On the contrary. I've had my fill of brainless performing peahens – tedious, vulgar high spirits and fake arousal. Be gone, oh tepid, insipid angels of provocation! And death to all withered crones who dash themselves to pieces on the bald mountain of learning and social activism! Believe me, sirens make me sick *(Rubs his forehead and nervously throws a couple of logs onto the fire, paces the room)* I need – a simple girl – pure, noble creature – yes – for evenings spent together by the fire – unsullied, amoral. Unconventional, to serve beside me – instinctive, passionate, pure of heart. Ha! Then, the tedium – simply evaporates!
BRONKA:	Hm. Be honest. You, with such a paragon … I'd give … two days … and then? Consult your inner muse.
KAZIMIERZ:	Really? Strange that I should spend a whole day conversing freely with a simple girl (like you), share all my thoughts and, instead of feeling bored, feel better than ever – here at my brother's – with you … *(Lightly)* Truly Bronka, I'll fall in love.
BRONKA:	*(Copying his tone)* If you spent less time moping and said what you thought, I might accuse you of flirting.
KAZIMIERZ:	*(Laughing)* Why not, fair sister-in-law? Seduction is an art … like drinking fiery Amontillado.
BRONKA:	Not my tipple. *(Unsettled)* Where's Tadek? I mean it, Kazio, that sleigh is in a ditch.

Snow (1902)

KAZIMIERZ:	Patience! The sleigh is overburdened, well, the snow is deep – one can't drive horses to death.
BRONKA:	You're right. Your moping, Kazio, it's so wearing and oppressive, it … *(She breaks off)*
KAZIMIERZ:	Well …?
BRONKA:	… it makes me want to run and wake Ewa … Why is she constantly asleep?
KAZIMIERZ:	She may not be.
BRONKA:	So she's avoiding us.
KAZIMIERZ:	No – she feels we're better off without her.
BRONKA:	You're so insensitive. My dear, old friend, finally here! Imagine my joy! Kazio – she's changed completely. I'd no idea it could happen in two years!
KAZIMIERZ:	How?
BRONKA:	*(A little troubled)* Well … I'm blushing … I suppose – I can tell you anything – like you're not really a man.
KAZIMIERZ:	Aha. About Miss Ewa – I'm curious.
BRONKA:	Well, she's an orphan – terribly rich. That's her misfortune – spoilt … That sounded wrong. We boarded together at school – a strange relationship. Her love was difficult, obsessive – a torment, sometimes. Now she'd be timid, like a lamb, craving affection – then overwhelmed by empathy, second-guessing me, then a whimsical tyrant, jealous of my thoughts – every beat of my heart.
KAZIMIERZ:	And then?
BRONKA:	After his wife died, Ewa's guardian withdrew her from school. She became mistress of her fate, her own fortune, and her melancholy – even perhaps her own boredom … you see, Kazio – the perfect wife.
KAZIMIERZ:	Mmm. You've said little of the sudden transformation.
BRONKA:	Ah yes – I'm distracted. *(Thoughtfully)* Despite her whims and violent tantrums, she was terribly happy, life and soul of the party. But now, she's – I'm not sure, Kazio – I feel – I'm ashamed to admit – like a stranger. I'm uneasy, this vague fear and – she's – how beautiful – you saw. Didn't you?
KAZIMIERZ:	Hadn't noticed.
BRONKA:	Are you blind? A proper man?
KAZIMIERZ:	Alright but still your guest intrigues me. Why the change? Broken heart? Unrequited love?
BRONKA:	Her? No, Kazio, no.
KAZIMIERZ:	So certain?
BRONKA:	I knew them, her young acolytes – a closed circle – someone held her attention – Tadek – though – they didn't get close.

KAZIMIERZ:	Tadek knew her?
BRONKA:	Of course – before me.
KAZIMIERZ:	*(Lightly)* They were in love?
BRONKA:	*(Backs away, seems upset by something)* You think I'd invite her if they'd never met?
KAZIMIERZ:	Yes – you're right – theoretically – limited knowledge of the female heart.
BRONKA:	I'm worried I'll upset Tadek. He may have wanted us to be alone … She's dearer than a sister – I love her more than anything – to Tadek she remains unknown *(Sleigh bells are heard outside the window –* BRONKA *with a joyful cry)* Tadek! He's here! Oh at last *(Runs through the left-hand door)*

Scene Two

KAZIO

KAZIMIERZ:	*(Sits and regards her with inexpressible sorrow, twists his moustache agitatedly, adds firewood to the grate, paces the length and breadth of the room, stops, seizes his head in his hands and utters in a quiet whisper)* Yes, yes – too late, too late. *(Sits, smokes a cigarette, apathetic, lost in thought. In the hall* BRONKA's *voice is heard, 'Tadek, my love, my own Tadek!'.* KAZIMIERZ *shudders violently –* TADEK's *voice 'How I've missed you!',* KAZIO's *face contorts in a painful, bitter smile)*

Scene Three

BRONKA, TADEK, KAZIO

BRONKA:	Come, enter, my love – how cold you are – warm yourself by the fire.
TADEUSZ:	Not remotely cold, my sweet. *(Greets* KAZIO*)* Well, Kazio dear, been guarding the house? Haven't annoyed Bronka, with talk of art, metaphysics?
KAZIMIERZ:	Absolutely not! Mainly I've tried to acclimatize her to my long-term presence.
TADEUSZ:	So – you like it here?
BRONKA:	Tadek – come, to the fire – you're frozen.
TADEUSZ:	Very enticing – I'd prefer a hot meal – I'm ravenous.
BRONKA:	Yes, yes, of course. *(Runs out)*

Snow (1902)

Scene Four

TADEK, KAZIO, BRONKA

TADEUSZ:	*(Contented)* So Kazio. I've found peace and happiness. I never dared to dream, a paradise. I'd lost the will to live, so I thought, before I met Bronka. My heart had dried to a husk; my soul was aching and the thick fog of boredom descended.
KAZIMIERZ:	I know, it's appalling. All your letters disturbed me – I was terrified you'd write, 'Farewell, dear brother, I am bored to death and pass into the womb of Eternity …' In fact, fear would have been tedious, so I wasn't really. Always highly unsettling, though, to receive such letters from one's brother … *(Suddenly)* Why would a boisterous, youthful man, held in affection, plunge into hellish despair? Me, alright – I was always hopeless, but you, you?
TADEUSZ:	Long story; you'd get frightfully bored. I'd be gone, if it wasn't for Bronka.
KAZIMIERZ:	*(Off the cuff)* A woman?
TADEUSZ:	Yes and no … not sure … Indescribable longing, for someone or something … don't know.
KAZIMIERZ:	Was she bad? Damaged goods?
TADEUSZ:	No, the opposite. Lost the will to live, that's all. Torments herself and others. Destructive type. I really did suffer!
KAZIMIERZ:	And then?
TADEUSZ:	Then. Hm … She wanted to be a slave but had to be a mistress. I was too scared of losing her, couldn't push her away. I blamed myself. I hated both of us. It went nowhere.
KAZIMIERZ:	And so?
TADEUSZ:	The mournful ballad concludes.
KAZIMIERZ:	Seen her since?
TADEUSZ:	Last sign of life – my wedding day. A very sincere, expressive letter, my pain vanished.
KAZIMIERZ:	Or else, hell hath no fury …?
TADEUSZ:	Oh no. She was Bronka's friend, she loved her passionately and was genuinely pleased that Bronka was marrying someone she herself would have made unhappy – her words.
KAZIMIERZ:	*(Probingly)* After that, you didn't see her?
TADEUSZ:	No.
KAZIMIERZ:	You never think of her?
TADEUSZ:	No. Bronka fills my head and heart.
KAZIMIERZ:	If you happened to see her?

TADEUSZ:	*(Thoughtful)* See her? No impression. Stone dead. Besides, was it love? Could have been the juvenile ambition of a man who'd known no opposition, then lost his mind when he failed to conquer the woman he wanted. And I felt ashamed, uncertain, dissatisfied, you get the picture. *(Rises, paces the room)* To see her … out of the blue … hm … something deeper might stir …
KAZIMIERZ:	You don't seem entirely sure.
TADEUSZ:	If I didn't have Bronka. I'm such an extrovert, I could never relax with her – those cold, medieval walls. It was haunted. Bad dreams, hallucinations came at you, repeatedly. Energy melted like wax in a flame. Morbidity sucked the marrow from your bones. Look – I do best in full sunlight, these fists can tackle someone bigger and stronger, if necessary. *(He straightens up, powerful and strong, and suddenly with a cheerful laugh claps his hands loudly)* Come on Bronka, come here!
BRONKA:	*(Offstage)* Wait – one minute!
KAZIMIERZ:	Where did you meet Bronka?
TADEUSZ:	Oh, at uncle's. In the woods: she was out riding, her horse bolted. This frenzied galloping startled me, but alas, the Amazonian rider lacked control, though she held on very bravely. How I managed to stop that horse I have no idea. Laid up for a few weeks, my reward – Bronka, peace and joy.
KAZIMIERZ:	*(With an ironic smile)* Strange adventure.
TADEUSZ:	Ah, yes. I used to read romantic fiction, through sheer boredom – I'd no idea these strange events do happen.

Scene Five

BRONKA, TADEK, KAZIO

BRONKA *enters, behind her a servant with a tray filled with snacks and drinks.*

BRONKA:	*(Embracing* TADEK *friskily, stroking his face with her hand)* So impatient. I only wanted to prepare it myself.
TADEUSZ:	Why so much?
BRONKA:	Supper's a long way off – eat – help yourself.
TADEUSZ:	*(Pours vodka and lifts his glass to* KAZIO, *eats the snacks and speaks whilst eating)* Some blizzard, can't see a thing. Those snowdrifts are waist deep.
BRONKA:	I was so anxious.

Snow (1902)

KAZIMIERZ:	*(Jokingly)* Yes, your terrible suffering beneath the overturned sleigh replayed constantly before her eyes.
TADEUSZ:	*(Holds her head)* You feckless child, I can't take one step.
BRONKA:	Because next to you nothing bad can touch me, I'm certain.
TADEUSZ:	*(Suddenly rising)* How odd! Completely forgot. One minute. *(He goes towards the door)*
BRONKA:	Where are you going?
TADEUSZ:	One minute, dear ... surprise ... *(He disappears into the hall; offstage,* TADEK's *strong voice is heard):*
TADEK:	*(Offstage)* Paweł!...

Scene Six

BRONKA, KAZIO

BRONKA:	*(Cheerful as a child)* Another costly surprise I expect. I must get annoyed, too many reels of expensive fabric – velvet, silk.
KAZIMIERZ:	He loves you, it's his pleasure. Listen, Bronka, you've prepared your own surprise. Will it be nice, I wonder. Tadek's so happy, a couple's happiness is usually possessive. I get worried sometimes that I'm in the way. Never mind a woman, unknown ... as you said ... to Tadek ...
BRONKA:	*(Forcefully)* No ... that's not right. The number one rule. You want to keep a man's love, push him away, now and again, release him. I've done the right thing, I have. Me and Ewa will entertain each other, read, and he can hunt, visit neighbours, bargain over the price of wheat with the local Jews, then each day return wanting more.
KAZIMIERZ:	*(With sad irony)* I wasn't prepared for such refined tactics.
BRONKA:	*(Laughing)* No, they're tried and tested by our female ancestors.
KAZIMIERZ:	Very well, I'm merely concerned that Tadek's good humour will be spoilt. I love to see his strength and zest for life, his calm stability around you.
BRONKA:	Not to worry about him. Now don't mope around all evening, spoiling my mood. Say you're sorry, kiss my hand. *(KAZIO holds her hand, but doesn't kiss it, and looks into her eyes)*
BRONKA:	What's this?
KAZIMIERZ:	Nothing, it's a luxury holding your warm, delicate hand. It seems my heart has a secret. *(He kisses her hand.* BRONKA *eyes him thoughtfully)*
BRONKA:	Kazio, you really are depressed.
KAZIMIERZ:	When you're not born under a lucky star, like Tadek, that's what happens.

Scene Seven

TADEK, BRONKA, KAZIO

Enter TADEK, *who unrolls an expensive silk shawl at* BRONKA'*s feet.*

TADEUSZ:	When you ran out to meet me, I should have unfurled this beautiful shawl beneath your feet. Instead I packed it away under the seat and forgot completely.
BRONKA:	*(Throwing her arms around his neck)* My darling, my sweet, terrible spendthrift!
KAZIMIERZ:	*(Looks at them for a while then rises)* I'll leave you to it, I'll write some letters. *(To* BRONKA*)* And for supper, that great celebration, I should probably don my tailcoat.
BRONKA:	Otherwise I shan't even deign to look at you!
KAZIMIERZ:	And so farewell! *(He exits, pausing by the window a while and muttering)* When the hell will it stop snowing! *(He turns to* TADEK*)* You're so lucky, Tadek, that snow doesn't make you sad. *(He exits)*

Scene Eight

BRONKA, TADEK

BRONKA:	*(Looking at* KAZIO*)* What's wrong with Kazio? Seems strangely preoccupied.
TADEUSZ:	Wrong? Still not used to him?
BRONKA:	Oh, you must know I'm very happy. He's like mild autumn sunshine. It's a little sad to be with him, but peaceful.
TADEUSZ:	Yes, yes. Our family tree declines. We're the weak, autumn shoots on a formerly vigorous ancestral trunk.
BRONKA:	Kazio, yes, but not you. You're strong, your face gleams with joy and energy.
TADEUSZ:	*(Embraces her, leads her to the fireplace and seats her beside him)* It's your love – your love has given me strength.
BRONKA:	Your eyes are glowing like two hot coals, greedy things, and yet so sweet, so good. *(She takes his head, holds it to her breast and kisses his eyes)* I could kiss – kiss them endlessly – into forgetfulness …
TADEUSZ:	*(Laying his head on her breast)* Your love is my only joy.
BRONKA:	*(Playing with his hair)* Strange. Doesn't really feel like hair, such soft tendrils … In my father's courtyard there was a clump of delicate grasses … such pleasure, lying there, freely. To bury my face in your hair … *(She kisses his hair)*

Snow (1902)

TADEUSZ:	Remember when your horse bolted?
BRONKA:	Terrifying, I nearly fainted, borne by that fierce creature – and yet this strange delight.
TADEUSZ:	Remember, when I swept you off your feet and carried you around the room? *(He clasps her about the knees; she puts her arms around his neck)*
BRONKA:	Tadek, my darling. They say young girls should weep at the altar, not me – I wanted to shout, shout for joy, that soon our sleigh would be whisked along by two wild steeds … to your home …
TADEUSZ:	Remember the January sunset, the sky was ablaze, the frosted snow was ablaze, the horses thundered along, foaming with sweat. *(He embraces her more tightly)*
BRONKA:	Hold me close, as you did then, wrapped in the wolf skin. *(She moves away from him suddenly)* Tell me, as we entered the house, why did your eyes glint with cold steel?
TADEUSZ:	I was burying my past.
BRONKA:	What was your past?
TADEUSZ:	What … oh … complex, terribly sad … messianic suffering, inner torment, despair, contempt for myself and the world at large …
BRONKA:	Were you ever in love?
TADEUSZ:	Was it love? I may have thought so. I wouldn't want to propose a theory of love, but the key must surely be pride, complete confidence in oneself and the beloved – I've felt that certainty only with you.
BRONKA:	*(Stroking him)* Tadek, be honest. I spoke to Kazio today at length, about Ewa.
TADEUSZ:	*(Surprised, a little annoyed)* Ewa?
BRONKA:	Yes, Ewa. Why the look?
TADEUSZ:	No, I recall that soon after our wedding, you wanted to boast to her about our happiness, and all I want is to live with you, you alone, because happiness in love is very fragile and easily tarnished.
BRONKA:	By?
TADEUSZ:	Bad atmosphere, third party. Ewa's changed a lot, you know. Kazio's quiet and mournful, you were right, he's calming, like autumn sunshine, but she's a dormant volcano, waiting to spew fire.
BRONKA:	How do you know?
TADEUSZ:	How? I'd see her sometimes, you know that. She interested me, like Kazio with some rare painting or exotic object, an animal or flower …

BRONKA:	*(Fearfully)* Tadzio! Tadzio!
TADEUSZ:	*(Surprised)* What's the matter?
BRONKA:	Well, I've heard that love wanes, when people spend all their time together, that sometimes they need to be apart, to keep the love fresh, and return with increased longing. I don't know, why I thought of it, but I wanted you to go hunting, visit the neighbours … and I couldn't just stay here all day, on my own, waiting …

Scene Nine

BRONKA, TADEK, EWA

The heavy portieres leading to the adjacent room part and in the doorway stands EWA. *She looks ghostly white, with a gaze of terrible sorrow at* TADZIO *and* BRONKA, *who, turned towards the fireplace, do not see her.*

BRONKA:	Am I right Tadzio? I am, aren't I?
TADEUSZ:	Darling, where did you get those ideas? Could any man love a woman more than I love you? After a whole year's marriage? And miss her more than I miss you?
BRONKA:	Tadzio, your last letter, your dear, sweet letter … so beautiful, I still carry it close. *(She takes the letter from inside her corset and kisses it passionately)*
EWA:	*(Who has for a moment withdrawn behind the portiere into the adjacent room, which is a winter orangery, and is walking back and forth in nervous discomfort, suddenly)* I hear voices in the room. Your soft rugs deaden my footsteps.
TADEUSZ:	*(Rising up)* What's this? Who is that?
EWA:	May I enter?
BRONKA:	Tadek, what's the matter? *(She looks at him for a while and goes towards the door)* Do come in, Ewa, come inside. Oh, Tadek will be so pleased *(She opens the portieres fully.* TADEK *looks on as if in a dream.* EWA *enters and simultaneously the curtain falls)*

Act 2

Scene One

EWA, TADEK

The same room. Wintry afternoon dusk. Through the window a white mass of snow glitters, fire in the grate. For a while the stage is empty. After a while, enter TADEK *and* EWA.

Snow (1902)

EWA:	*(Runs up to the fireplace and warms her hands)* Ha, I'm chilled to the bone. Should've warmed up by now, near you.
TADEUSZ:	Nothing will warm you up.
EWA:	Really? But that's what I came for, to heat the cockles of my heart on your happiness.
TADEUSZ:	*(Ironically)* You'd need to have one in the first place.
EWA:	*(Stretching it out)* Re-e-e-ally? …
TADEUSZ:	Oh … alright. We've paid each other enough compliments during our … *(Looks at his watch)* … three-hour walk, perhaps we should talk about something else.
EWA:	You start … but first, ask for some light … it's dusk, a melancholy flicker in the grate … the snow glimmering outside, these soft rugs, portieres … phew … it's dangerous, unsettling, it breeds desire … *(Lost in thought, she looks around)* You arranged this place yourself?
TADEUSZ:	I did.
EWA:	Fully aware?
TADEUSZ:	Fully.
EWA:	So you do know that your house is a copy of mine?
TADEUSZ:	I do.
EWA:	And you did that why?
TADEUSZ:	Test of strength, to convince myself I'd broken away, overcome, forgotten …
EWA:	*(Smiling)* And you also hung a picture, which I gave you, painted by me, in your study, for the same reason?
TADEUSZ:	You've been in my study?
EWA:	For a whole night before you arrived.
TADEUSZ:	And what did you do there?
EWA:	What did I do? I felt happy, that you love and long for me.
TADEUSZ:	You're gravely mistaken.
EWA:	Indeed I am not. In fact your study seems rather like a haven, where, having torn yourself away from bliss, security, Bronka's coral lips, you remain for hours on end, breaking your heart, longing desperately for the source of that strange pleasure that sets your blood racing, oh, the naked desire …
TADEUSZ:	For what?
EWA:	The thing that causes you insatiable pain. You're built for war – once you longed to become a leader, to create new worlds … Oh to stand in those trenches, amidst the corpses, to remove your helmet, wipe your brow … quiet corners, soft rugs, happy hearths, they're not for you. For your brother, whose soul has turned to ash …

TADEUSZ:	*(Looks at her with seriousness)* Just tell me why you're here. Surely your instincts aren't so criminal as to intentionally destroy the happiness of two people, one of whom you nearly ruined already.
EWA:	*(With a hollow laugh)* Hardly … Shame I released you so soon.
TADEUSZ:	You didn't release me, I tore myself away.
EWA:	*(Thoughtfully, looks unmoving into the fire)* Yes, that's true. I admired your strength, only then did I love you …
TADEUSZ:	*(Laughs, mockingly)* Yes, I know, really. Let me speak – stop interrupting. Why did you come?
EWA:	So you don't know, that Bronka invited me, insisted? That she may even have resorted to certain white lies to get me here: the letter said she was ill.
TADEUSZ:	You shouldn't have come.
EWA:	*(Surprised)* Why not? You invoked me, didn't you, and longed for me.
TADEUSZ:	I longed for you, invoked you!? I forgot you completely.
EWA:	*(Sadly)* You forgot me. I saturate your entire house. I only had to cross your threshold to feel that it was mine, that here I reign supreme, that everything is imbued with me.
TADEUSZ:	Ha, ha … you mean the furnishings. Well, I did consciously attempt to model these rooms on yours – if for example a drunkard gives up vodka and wants to ensure he's no longer addicted, barring his disgust, he'll drink a couple of glasses. If he doesn't feel like downing the whole bottle, that's a sign, of his release. You see? All calculated to remind me of you …
EWA:	*(Crossly)* And yet …
TADEUSZ:	And yet I never once thought of you; you didn't feature in my dreams.
EWA:	*(Throws sticks onto the fire, as though she hasn't heard what TADEK has said)* You really have suffered, you poor, poor man. You must have experienced terrible inner conflict and distress. To have all the conditions for happiness, wealth, security, a wife who loves you and whom you love … You do genuinely love her? Or can you gain full satisfaction only through struggle and pain? Have you paused in a trench surrounded by corpses, to remove your helmet and wipe your brow?
TADEUSZ:	*(Mockingly)* Hyperbole was once the order of the day; now its passé.
EWA:	*(Paying no attention)* You're content to rest, in the greenest of valleys, before you storm the peaks. *(She turns towards the fireplace again lost in thought)* How that would make me love you.

Snow (1902)

TADEUSZ:	Listen, Ewa, you have to leave. Let's not play guessing games or make insinuations. You know I loved you. A scattering of snow, soft snow has covered all my memories, of pain, struggle, suffering and when the snow disappears …
EWA:	Yes?
TADEUSZ:	Detrimental.
EWA:	For whom?
TADEUSZ:	For you, for me, and most of all for Bronka.
EWA:	*(Wiping her forehead)* For Bronka, Bronka. Oh, I love her so much … *(After a while)* She'll be very unhappy …
TADEUSZ:	*(Approaches her and sits beside her)* Listen – carefully and try to understand. Your habit of pretending not to hear, lose that, please, it's pointless.
EWA:	*(Nonchalantly)* I'm listening and will try to understand.
TADEUSZ:	I'll admit, I'm very tense. Also, I have thought about you quite a lot, even longed for the suffering you caused. It's possible that I missed the agony, but now, leave me alone. I love Bronka, I will stay with her.
EWA:	If you stay, you'll finish her. Your wounds have been reopened, you're fluttering into the flame, like a moth; the moment you heard my voice behind that curtain, this elaborate house of cards – your happiness – collapsed. *(With irony)* Ha, ha … you can't fool me. This snug corner is a cage. You're straining at the leash, to conquer! You are the last conquistador, great and beautiful – that noble race would never make do with some pathetic little corner of Europe.
TADEUSZ:	*(Bitterly)* New worlds – no thanks – conquest through mass slaughter.
EWA:	Not quite. First, you need to enslave them, then level mountains, experience the torment and pleasure of this new world's conception. And supposing the conquistador should accidentally crush a delicate flower beneath his iron foot – well? *(Drawn out and as though sleepy)* Anything to enable a miracle …
TADEUSZ:	And then … what then …
EWA:	Slowly … slow down … *(Laughing suddenly)* Ha … ha … the conquistador's blood burns within you. *(She looks at him and then drops her gaze)* First, you must command the waves, level mountains, trample a flower beneath your iron foot.
TADEUSZ:	*(Threateningly)* Bronka? *(EWA is silent; she kindles the fire with the poker and throws in fresh firewood)*
TADEUSZ:	*(Secretively)* Bronka?

EWA:	*(Nonchalantly)* That's right. *(Silence, during which* TADEK, *annoyed, paces the room)*
TADEUSZ:	*(Approaches her)* Ewa, I beg you, leave us in peace.
EWA:	No more peace for you.
TADEUSZ:	I know that, I do, but for Bronka at least.
EWA:	Tadek, you're blind. Didn't you see her wide eyes alighting nervously on you, then me, like frightened birds? How I love her ... Did you not see her artificial excitement, how resolutely she turned to Kazio, for assistance ... *(Silence,* TADEK *moves determinedly from one side of the room to the other)*
TADEUSZ:	So ... I'm to conquer new worlds? To what end?
EWA:	To live beautifully and be beautiful.
TADEUSZ:	And if one lacks the skills to conquer?
EWA:	Then one submits, and that is beautiful.
TADEUSZ:	And if it's just a lot of pointless flailing about? Thoughtless destruction of oneself and all around?
EWA:	That too is beautiful. Someone who flails about, wracked by desire, without ever achieving his goal, is also beautiful.
TADEUSZ:	And if all he should long for is a peaceful haven, a warm hearth?
EWA:	That's Kazio's territory.
TADEUSZ:	And mine?
EWA:	*(She gives him a prolonged look and smile)* Yours? Me – me – me.
TADEUSZ:	*(Stops before her, in a strangled voice)* Why, why, why, when I laid everything at your feet, when, with you and through you, I could have conquered these new worlds, did you reject me?
EWA:	Because you didn't know how to be my master.
TADEUSZ:	And now?
EWA:	Now I love you, love you because you wanted to forget me, you wanted to break through it, because only the strong can break through. I love you completely, longing, fearing, that you don't want to be mine.
TADEUSZ:	*(Laughing nervously)* I need to light a lamp. Bronka's due back. Just in time to participate in this performance of yours and accuse me of making unseemly advances. *(He lights a lamp, silence)*
EWA:	*(Nonchalantly)* You travelled the world?
TADEUSZ:	*(Looks at her surprised, then reverts to the same tone)* Oh yes, nearly two years.
EWA:	Africa, I believe?
TADEUSZ:	*(Mockingly)* Yes, but Stanley got there before me, so I amused myself by hunting tigers ... You're right ... ha ... ha ... conquistador

	potential ... When a tiger disemboweled two natives in front of me, I felt no sense of triumph ...
EWA:	*(Mockingly)* And?
TADEUSZ:	And ... I had the simplest thought – my turn next.
EWA:	*(Tauntingly)* No weapons then?
TADEUSZ:	*(In the same tone)* The ammunition was damp.
EWA:	You didn't fear death?
TADEUSZ:	I desired it. So beautiful – to be mauled by a magnificent creature.
EWA:	Yes, it is ... there's Bronka. *(The door to the hallway is heard opening; a loud conversation between BRONKA and KAZIO)*

Scene Two

BRONKA, KAZIO, EWA, TADEK

BRONKA *and* KAZIO *enter.*

BRONKA:	*(Overly excited)* What a wonderful ride! The sparkling snow on the frozen water, the moon, the moon ... oh, how wonderful. Well, Kazio – you said so too ... *(Turning towards EWA)* You must come tomorrow – like it was all created for you – the snow, the moon and Kazio – Kazio. Ha ... ha ... ha ... look, he's bored – but no one skates so beautifully.
KAZIMIERZ:	Bronka exaggerates, as usual. The mere isn't entirely free of snow and my dear sister-in-law amused herself by lunging in knee-deep.
BRONKA:	*(Distracted)* Oh ... untrue ... you bad man ... *(Suddenly to TADEK)* Tadek, you're not annoyed that I took such prolonged advantage of my freedom? I knew that you, my love, and dear Ewa were together – you could at last throw off the shackles of wedded bliss, and fly to those places where I cannot follow. *(She embraces EWA)* Oh Ewa, how lucky you are, you're completely different. I remember clearly when I saw you after our engagement. Well, Tadek? Your room was the same, exactly the same as this ... *(As if waking from a dream)* Ewa, how strange that the room was designed in exactly the same way as ours.
EWA:	Nothing strange there, Bronka – merely coincidence.
TADEUSZ:	*(Coldly)* The same designer probably worked on both houses.
BRONKA:	Hm ... of course. Remember Ewa, how we sat by the fire? You gazed into the flames, and I talked endlessly, endlessly, I don't

	even know what I said, you were so good, so patient. *(Suddenly bursts out laughing,* TADEK *approaches her fondly)*
TADEUSZ:	What's the matter, dear, why so uneasy?
BRONKA:	I'd like to fly. Up there, like a bird. I'm on the ground flapping my wings, yearning to gain height, but they're like lead … *(To* EWA*)* Oh Ewa, how lucky you are.
KAZIMIERZ:	Didn't I say that too much exertion is bad for you? I begged, I pleaded, you wouldn't listen, and now you'll have to pay for all that romantic ice skating.
BRONKA:	*(Stubbornly)* No, you're wrong, enough hysteria, I'm a stupid, spoilt child *(She suddenly bursts into tears, runs into the adjoining room.* EWA *rises and wants to follow her)*
TADEUSZ:	Stay here, I'll soon calm her down. *(He follows* BRONKA *out)*

Scene Three

KAZIMIERZ, EWA

KAZIMIERZ:	*(Uneasy)* She's sick, surely. All day she's been unsettled, hyperactive or something …
EWA:	I'm surprised, I've never seen her like this.
KAZIMIERZ:	*(Suddenly)* You have noticed that since yesterday she's changed?
EWA:	That's just what I said to your brother.
KAZIMIERZ:	Did you notice her unease during supper yesterday and the whole of today?
EWA:	Indeed, I am surprised.
KAZIMIERZ:	You've no idea, I suppose, what could have caused this sudden change?
EWA:	No.
KAZIMIERZ:	Hm … Presumably you've also noticed that Tadek isn't quite himself, pensive, unsettled …
EWA:	I've never known him otherwise.
KAZIMIERZ:	I'd say he arrived happy, missing Bronka, haven't seen him so full of strength, faith and hope for a long time.
EWA:	Your point?
KAZIMIERZ:	*(Looking sharply at her)* This sudden alteration is beyond me.
EWA:	You are, I take it, blaming me.
KAZIMIERZ:	Did you notice that when Bronka came down to breakfast this morning, her eyes were red? I could have sworn she'd spent the whole night crying.

Snow (1902)

EWA:	You think that's my fault?
KAZIMIERZ:	Oh hardly, on the contrary … don't think for a second that I plan to cross-examine you, but since yesterday things seem to have changed so overtly and radically … there's the conundrum, I'd like to solve … I'm highly strung, you see, and we neurotics don't like closeness before a storm …
EWA:	Closeness?
KAZIMIERZ:	Yes, well, call it what you will, there's something in the air, and a sensitive soul like Bronka feels that instinctively … Can you hear the sobbing? *(In the adjoining room TADEK is visible, as he holds BRONKA to him and tries to settle her. Silence. KAZIO strains to hear with increasing trepidation. EWA rises and walks with equal trepidation about the room)*
KAZIMIERZ:	*(Walks behind her)* Can you?
EWA:	Quiet … be quiet …
KAZIMIERZ:	*(Takes her by the hand and leads her towards the window)* Let's be honest, I don't know you, but what I've heard from Bronka and Tadek gives me enough insight.
EWA:	*(Nonchalantly)* Sir, enough needling. I know it, alright – what you want to say.
KAZIMIERZ:	No, you really don't … I've never got mixed up in anyone's affairs, even my family's, which includes Bronka and Tadek …
EWA:	So let's be open: you know from Tadek that we're very close. I know that he frequently wrote you letters, three or four years ago, in which he obviously appraised you of his emotional state. You know he loved me and that this kind of love can be incubated – and will intensify – beneath a light scattering of snow.
KAZIMIERZ:	That's exactly it.
EWA:	Bronka told you that I love her deeply, that at school we were inseparable. Is that all she said?
KAZIMIERZ:	Yesterday, at length.
EWA:	You're honest, I'll reciprocate. Before two years were out, she paid me a visit, as his fiancée, so ecstatically happy, that although my heart was broken, I accepted her betrothal to the man I loved most passionately.
KAZIMIERZ:	You loved him?
EWA:	Yes – when I'd lost him … *(They look at each other for a while)* And now you want to ask why I've come here to destroy my friend's happiness?
KAZIMIERZ:	That question may have occurred to me, but of course it's entirely irrelevant … Frankly, I have little sympathy for you. No, no,

that sounded wrong. We don't have much in common, but that won't sway me … *(Suddenly)* Did you yearn constantly? *(EWA has rested her head against the window pane and is silent)* You were in constant pursuit of something beyond your reach and you always knew it? *(EWA turns towards him and is silent)* Your main objective – to hold a man captive, following you blindly, bound by unquenchable desire.

EWA: *(Hotly)* Yes.
KAZIMIERZ: *(Sharply)* And that's Tadek?
EWA: *(Forcefully)* Yes.
KAZIMIERZ: *(Sharply)* And Bronka?
EWA: Can't you hear the cheerful laughter … You know what'll happen next?
KAZIMIERZ: Well?
EWA: Bronka will enter, she'll throw her arms around my neck and apologize, so passionately, for having made a scene … Sir … the moon is bright – pass me my furs … let's take a walk … perhaps our confessions will increase in their sincerity. *(She looks at him for a long time)* Is it beyond your control?
KAZIMIERZ: What?
EWA: You love Bronka!
KAZIMIERZ: *(Gives her a long look)* I do.
EWA: Her laughter, can you hear? That beautiful, silvery girlish laughter.
KAZIMIERZ: Alright, let's go.

Scene Four

BRONKA, EWA, TADEK, KAZIO

BRONKA *and* TADEK *enter, their arms linked, cheerful and contented – on the outside.*

BRONKA: *(To EWA)* My dear, darling Ewa. You've known me so long. You've all been too good. Ewa spoilt me with her kindness and Tadek has finished the job. Ewa, you know I am mad, I have moments, when I'm completely inscrutable.
EWA: Why so sad, why apologize to me? *(She strokes her face)* My delicate mimosa, how oversensitive, how anxious you are …
BRONKA: A child unable to control her impulses might be excused, but not me. *(Nervously, quickly, blurting out)* Sometimes these

	heavy thoughts oppress me. It's not that. It's like … not a sense of misfortune exactly … only a distant, distant memory of those childhood hours, when I searched the whole farm to no avail for my sister. I knew that something bad had happened. I felt it, I felt. I scoured the woods, the entire stretch of riverbank, returned home breathless and distraught. *(Increasingly distraught she draws closer and closer to* EWA*)* Ewa! Ewa! As if something was in pursuit, something tore at my hair … I fell on the grass in front of the veranda. I hid my entire face in my hands, so I couldn't see, and then they came … they came …
EWA:	Who did?
BRONKA:	The workmen, and beside them my nurse, and they bore my beloved sister on a stretcher … she had drowned in the mere …
EWA:	*(In spite of herself)* In the mere?
BRONKA:	Yes – yes – in the mere. *(To* TADEK*)* Tell them to fill it in. Its black formlessness reminds me of the one at home …
TADEUSZ:	Calm down, Bronka, stay calm. I'll do anything you want. If you like, I'll level everything. *(Suddenly irritated, looking sharply at* EWA, *which* BRONKA, *holding* EWA, *cannot see)* Yes, I'll do it. I'll fill the mere with earth, I'll chop down all the trees …
EWA:	And I suppose you'll command them to sweep away the snow? Oh children, children … Now it's Tadek's turn to be upset.
BRONKA:	Tadek, how have I upset you?
TADEUSZ:	Bronka, my love, you haven't upset me at all, you know I get sad when your painful childhood memories resurface.
EWA:	*(Stroking her head)* Forget, just forget. Leave us, gentlemen, for a while, she'll settle down.
KAZIMIERZ:	You're right, come on Tadek.
TADEUSZ:	It's alright, it's alright, Bronka.
BRONKA:	Look, I'm calm already, do go, I'll be fine with Ewa, she's the only one who's ever known how to comfort me. *(*KAZIO *and* TADEK *exit)*
KAZIMIERZ:	*(Turning at the door)* Ewa, you wanted to walk in the park!
EWA:	Later on, when Bronka's completely settled.
BRONKA:	Then we'll all go together.
EWA:	Oh, no, my love, I want to be a nice guest; one that doesn't get under a young married couple's feet. They shouldn't feel the slightest pressure to entertain. *(She continues to stroke her)* The black formlessness of the mere frightens you and here it's so cozy with your husband. *(*KAZIO *exits after her first words)*

Scene Five

BRONKA, EWA

BRONKA:	Ewa, am I insufferable?
EWA:	*(Thoughtful)* No, no, your outburst surprised me, that's all.
BRONKA:	Don't take it to heart, Ewa.
EWA:	No. Even if …
BRONKA:	*(As though guessing her thoughts)* If what?
EWA:	Even if this change in you … *(She breaks off)* Be honest, you're afraid … or perhaps not, but you don't trust me anymore.
BRONKA:	*(After a while)* I'm honest, I'll tell you everything … You've really changed …
EWA:	*(Smiling)* I've changed?
BRONKA:	I'm struggling to rediscover my beloved Ewa. There are times when I think that a whole eternity has passed since you embraced me so warmly and shared my joy about Tadek's proposal.
EWA:	*(In spite of herself)* Yes, a whole eternity has passed.
BRONKA:	Faced with that I am helpless. It reminds me of the deep black mere. *(EWA strokes her hair)* I may have caught a slight chill, I'm not fully present, perhaps, but your touch doesn't feel the same. Once you wanted your love to brand me, there's a kind of touch that burns, like hot steel, but now so strange and distant … you know, you do. As though autumn's quivering desire had finally shaken all the yellow leaves from her chestnut lined alleyways …
EWA:	Desire?
BRONKA:	Yes, yours! It's offensive! At school, you remember, I shrank from your sudden, possessive love, now your desire frightens me. Tell me, Ewa, why this constant unease around you?
EWA:	Listen, you're upset, but I understand. Consciously, I don't feel the slightest change towards you, but maybe it's true … you're no longer mine, exclusively … you love your husband. Unconsciously, perhaps you fear something unnamed … Do I know? *(Laughing suddenly)* Perhaps you're jealous? Well? Tell me straight.
BRONKA:	No, no, I'm not jealous, but I really am afraid …
EWA:	Of what?
BRONKA:	Your beauty …
EWA:	Meaning?
BRONKA:	Meaning? Well, you could be stunningly beautiful, ha, the most beautiful woman in the whole world and I would never be

	afraid because I know that Tadek won't look twice at that. Your beauty is different. You can bind someone to you and drag them after you without realizing, without their knowing where this infatuation will lead them ... yet still they follow blindly ... on and on ...
EWA:	Where to?
BRONKA:	I don't know. I can't understand any of it – I only know how to feel. Something is prizing my soul open, who knows ... *(Lost in thought)* Today Kazio told me that there's a certain point at which all contradictions merge ... something like a sphere of limitless size becomes a plane and I thought, the black slick of the mere can deepen into infinity, so the bottom merges with the sky ... *(Thoughtful)* Which direction? The gaping black mere or the majestic sky ...
EWA:	Whence these thoughts?
BRONKA:	*(She looks sharply at her suddenly and then smiles)* That's right, Ewa, we won't find each other again ... *(Suddenly tender)* But now a small chink has opened up to reveal what's lurking deep within me, the thing that cannot surface on its own, and I'm so grateful ... again you seem closer ... how strange ... unnamed desire awakens ... perhaps I'm just too weak? To bear the pain of desire?
EWA:	What? Haven't your longings been satisfied?
BRONKA:	One remains.
EWA:	Which? Do you know it?
BRONKA:	No, not yet! *(Silence)*

Scene Six

KAZIO, BRONKA, EWA

KAZIMIERZ:	*(Enters, uneasy; to* BRONKA*)* Has my dear sister-in-law calmed down?
BRONKA:	*(Jumping suddenly into cheeriness)* Alright, don't unsettle me again. No more theories of inevitably merging contradictions.
KAZIMIERZ:	*(Jokingly)* ... Not a precise description but you're a case in point – once sad, moody, now cheerful ...
BRONKA:	No thanks to you. That bored expression triggers despair.
KAZIMIERZ:	Just wait, by tomorrow it will have intensified.
BRONKA:	How delightful.

KAZIMIERZ:	*(To* EWA*)* Shall we take that walk? I've arranged Tadek in front of some paperwork, estate management, completely beyond me, I'm afraid.
EWA:	And you, Bronka, forget your worries, relax, just relax … *(She embraces* BRONKA, *lays her down on the chaise longue and covers her with a shawl)*
BRONKA:	Oh, how lovely, how well I feel. *(*EWA *and* KAZIO *exit)*

Scene Seven

BRONKA

BRONKA:	*(Lies still for a while, then slowly lifts herself up on the chaise longue, listens anxiously, then takes a letter from her bodice, looks at it, kisses it, covers her face with the letter and weeps quietly)* Tadek! My only Tadek!

Act 3

Scene One

BRONKA, TADEK

Through the brightly lit window, they are visible walking slowly through the glass orangery into the salon. Early morning. The sun's rays redden the snow beneath the windows. BRONKA *enters first and leans against the chaise longue.*

BRONKA:	No peace, none to be found … anywhere … No, not even a little … I wanted to be close to you, that's all, to find relief … Tadek – Tadek … What's happened to us?
TADEUSZ:	My sweet love … can't you understand, you're unsettled? Remember how you cried, when I left you alone for a week?
BRONKA:	Oh no, no. That was different … A spoilt madam unable to cope with the thought of your being away for seven whole days, can you imagine!
TADEUSZ:	And now? I'm here, beside you, aren't I, day and night.
BRONKA:	But where does your spirit wander?
TADEUSZ:	My spirit? *(Gravely)* It's beside you, always.
BRONKA:	*(Abruptly)* Beside me? Tell me again, your spirit is beside me, always.

Snow (1902)

TADEUSZ: *(Forcefully)* All the time! *(He walks the length and breadth of the room, deep in thought, BRONKA tracks his movements)*

BRONKA: Always beside me?

TADEUSZ: I'll be honest, I have felt it, more than once, in the past, a terrible desire that inflamed my heart and tore at my mind …

BRONKA: *(Interrupts him abruptly)* Desire!? You've felt it too. For what, what did you long for?

TADEUSZ: Calm down, Bronka, you know very well, how much I love you. I could feel desire for no one except …

BRONKA: *(Shouting)* Except … tell me!

TADEUSZ: *(Stroking her)* Except … for longing …

BRONKA: *(Rises)* What? Desire for longing!! What's that supposed to mean?

TADEUSZ: Don't be so touchy. Give rational conversation a chance. Sit down, Bronka, my love, sit. I'll tell you everything … a desire for longing … hm … hm … well … when I was young, I practically tore up the ground through excessive desire. I didn't know what to do. I yearned to achieve something so great, powerful and beautiful, unlike anybody else …

BRONKA: Perhaps I've been an obstacle?

TADEUSZ: No, no, Bronka, no. It was a long, long time ago … I felt such a surfeit of strength, thought I could manifest the whole world … ha … ha … ha … I studied, scrabbled about in the vast rubbish heap of human knowledge, I traversed the globe in order to honour the vow encrypted in my soul – accomplish a great deed …

BRONKA: And I, a mere woman, was an obstruction?

TADEUSZ: Oh no, absolutely not – that's different. Me and Kazio – we're the last of our line … Kazio didn't know desire, or perhaps he did … I know nothing about Kazio. *(Pause)*

BRONKA: Carry on.

TADEUSZ: I've nothing left to say.

BRONKA: Tadek! Was that desire lost at my side?

TADEUSZ: You see – how can I respond? I … *(Muddling)* … suddenly felt so vulnerable, I was overwhelmed – I felt this intense longing for peace, relief …

BRONKA: I was a mute cushion beneath your troubled head?

TADEUSZ: *(Sadly)* Bronka, why are you being so aggressive?

BRONKA: I'm not being aggressive, I'm reacting to the notion that I've been your plaything, your companion, ideal for conversations in that bloody inglenook …

TADEUSZ: Calm down, Bronka, calm down. Why can't you listen quietly? All I wanted to say was that with you I have found peace and

	happiness. I've forgotten how to long for anything, because you have satisfied me.
BRONKA:	*(Looks at him and grasps his hands)* But why have you now started to long for your desire?
TADEUSZ:	*(With a quiet smile)* Why are you now longing for the time when you didn't feel any desire? *(Silence)*
BRONKA:	*(Thoughtful)* You're right. *(Pause)* You did ask, why am I sad and aggravated, precisely now, when you've returned, so strong, so happy, so devilishly full of desire … for your Ewa!
TADEUSZ:	*(Taken aback)* Ewa?
BRONKA:	*(No longer restraining herself)* Ewa! Ewa! Yes, Ewa! You think I didn't see how you trembled, how astonished you were, as she stood there by the door? You think I'm only here as your plaything, a cushion beneath your weary head, and not to feel, feel the terrible longing, that's tearing you away from me!? *(She tears at him, then suddenly falls helplessly and looks at him astonished and almost unconscious)* Tadzio, forgive me, I think I have accused you of desire … that's unfair, because my own has far outstripped yours.
TADEUSZ:	*(Mysteriously)* Bronka, for what?
BRONKA:	*(In a forceful outburst)* For Ewa, for Ewa, for Ewa!
TADEUSZ :	*(Mysteriously)* So, she has infected you as well?
BRONKA:	*(Falling)* Yes, that's right …

Scene Two

KAZIO, TADEK, BRONKA

KAZIO enters, looks surprised.

KAZIMIERZ:	Up already? Why so early?
TADEUSZ:	*(Mustering himself)* Same questions to you!
KAZIMIERZ:	Hm, I've been up all night reading, needed some air, went for a stroll in the grounds. Coming back, spied a light in the salon windows – unexpected – came in to see what's happened and now I'm off to bed.
BRONKA:	Nothing, nothing's happened. What could have happened? Your speculations about the purpose of life, stepping beyond one's boundaries, constantly seeking something that eludes you, if it

	even exists – it knocked me firmly out of my slumber and wound me up. I didn't let Tadek get a wink of sleep.
TADEUSZ:	*(With concern)* Maybe you should lie down for a bit, Bronka? *(He kisses her hand)* Go on, Bronka, lie down; look, I'll have a rest too.
BRONKA:	*(Lively)* No, no … and you Kazio, stay, stay here. We feel so good around you …
KAZIMIERZ:	*(Forces a laugh)* Did you hear that, Tadek? Bronka feels good with me, now you're back, I'm a comfy little couch or equivalent, I can be removed discretely into the wings, I know my cue …
BRONKA:	You, how ungracious.
KAZIMIERZ:	*(To* TADEK*)* And when you weren't around, she told me I'm intolerable, that I've imported an atmosphere of weariness and boredom into your home, that any moment she'd be running off to wake Ewa …
BRONKA:	*(Suddenly with feigned surprise)* You know, Tadek, it's puzzling. The whole time you were away, Ewa definitely suffered from fatigue, she slept all day.
TADEUSZ:	*(Aggravated)* She slept? … She slept all day? Hm … *(He rises, and paces the width of the room)* Listen Kazio, this business with the inheritance, it's really very tangled. I've been thinking – either some papers have gone missing or else the sums don't add up. *(Cheerfully)* Listen, Bronka, get dressed, order breakfast, call for the sleigh, the horse will dash through the meadow, the woods …
BRONKA:	Yes, yes … through the meadow – through the woods – how lovely … *(With a sudden gesture, she undoes her hair)* … and in the wind, in the rush, look, my hair, like this, and this … *(She lets her hair loose, ties it up again quickly, rises)* And so to fill our lungs, inhale that blue expanse … *(She breathes deeply and stretches out her arms … suddenly with a flirtatious smile to* TADEK*)* Oh look, Kazio's amazed, he'd no idea I could yearn for a storm, a blue expanse …
KAZIMIERZ:	On the contrary, I am dumbfounded. I envy people who still know how to yearn for anything.
BRONKA:	Tadek, ah, how naïve, he envies those who yearn. Go on, Tadek, go and deal with the matter, it shouldn't take long.
TADEUSZ:	Half an hour at most.
BRONKA:	*(Artificially)* And I in the meantime will teach Kazio to yearn.
TADEUSZ:	Good idea, excellent. *(Exits)*

Scene Three

BRONKA, KAZIO

BRONKA: *(She approaches the portieres, through which* TADEK *has exited, looks around, and then approaches* KAZIO *and grasps his hand)* You know, where he's gone?

KAZIMIERZ: Yes.

BRONKA: You do? How can you. Do you suppose he's gone to deal with your affairs?

KAZIMIERZ: I know he hasn't.

BRONKA: *(Forcefully)* He's gone to Ewa, to Ewa, to Ewa! *(Silence)* Must it be so?

KAZIMIERZ: Ha, that's your fate, when you're tormented by terrible yearning, to outstrip yourself and everything else, when no pleasure fulfills you – he's in no fit state to control the motion that compels, compels someone forward, blindly, forever onwards, over corpses, the victims of one's crimes ...

BRONKA: *(Frightened)* It's stronger than the hurricane that uproots towering oaks?

KAZIMIERZ: Stronger.

BRONKA: Invincible?

KAZIMIERZ: No.

BRONKA: *(Secretively)* But stronger than Ewa, isn't that right?

KAZIMIERZ: *(Shaking his head)* Unfortunately, no.

BRONKA: *(Rises)* No, you say, no. *(Despairing)* Tell me, why not, why not?

KAZIMIERZ: Because Ewa is that desire. Not its object. He may not even see her, he knows nothing about her, but it's as though she's inside him, tormenting him, whipping him into some infernal chase.

BRONKA: But why, tell me, why?

KAZIMIERZ: No one knows, or understands, and never will.

BRONKA: What can I do, I'm lost. I desire, I really do, but it's about him. My God, I've been so blind – in all this madness – I only now comprehend that he's never belonged to me.

KAZIMIERZ: *(Sadly)* Listen, Bronka, I really didn't want to make you see this. I've always known he was never yours – that's what saddened me. I hid my sorrow behind a mask of boredom and nonchalance, which seemed to work, I had hoped things might clear up.

BRONKA: Why didn't you tell me, straight away? There's time to recover; this is like a sudden storm. My soul is like the willow, cloven in two by

	lightning, its roots poking through the earth, splinters scattered all around. Why didn't you tell me? Why didn't you open my eyes?
KAZIMIERZ:	Listen, Bronka, calmly, and you'll understand why.
BRONKA:	Kazio, you seem different, what's the matter?
KAZIMIERZ:	What's the matter? You've just noticed what's been staring you in the face for a whole week? (BRONKA *looks at him tentatively and wide-eyed*) Bronka, don't be afraid, it's alright … I'll tell you. As the weeks have passed I've fallen in love with you. You're my first love. I had a cold soul, white and pure, like that snow, out there in the field. Why you? Why does my love deepen, hour by hour? Perhaps this makes more sense of my recent behaviour. Never mind … (*He looks at her with a quiet smile*) Don't take offence. Then storm out. I don't expect or want you to return my feelings. If I knew you did, I'd reject you without hesitation. Not because you're my sister-in-law – but because your soul has been touched by another – stronger than mine.
BRONKA:	Kazio, stop it, I don't understand.
KAZIMIERZ:	(*Tired*) Never mind. In my thoughts, I can love you, caress you, day and night, pretending you're not my brother's wife. But the mistress of this, my ancestors' house, and wife of my brother – whom we love equally – her dignity I could never sully with even the most fleeting thought.
BRONKA:	(*Approaches him and strokes his hair quietly*) Stop, don't talk.
KAZIMIERZ:	Alright. You can see, though, how someone who's been stuck in an emotional hinterland, a swamp, would want to follow those elusive lights that hover above it. To feel the pleasure of saying 'I love you'. (*Silence. They hold hands and sit beside each other, after a long while*) It's been a pleasure to present this attractive résumé of my life … My only concern, it causes me acute pain – how will you bear it?
BRONKA:	(*Alarmed*) How will I bear what?
KAZIMIERZ:	Listen, Bronka, over recent days I've watched with genuine pleasure how you've empowered yourself, how you've grown, how you've fought, struggled to take responsibility and become conscious of everything that lies deep within you. Not as a man in love, but as an artist, I've delighted in your search for a new vocabulary to describe these manifestations, enabled through suffering … Bronka, be strong and beautiful, arrest the blow that's been aimed at your skull.
BRONKA:	(*Aggravated*) What can crush me?
KAZIMIERZ:	(*Harshly*) Tadek did not belong to you and he never will. His spirit will fly from you. You want to sleep with a corpse, go ahead.
BRONKA:	That's not true.

KAZIMIERZ:	(*Sadly*) If I depended on your loving me back, I might resort to lies. If I didn't love you, if this blood didn't flow through me, I might be glad to wound your heart. But I told you nothing, though I knew, and now, when it's irreversible, I want to mobilize your inner resources …
BRONKA:	(*Looks in an unfocused way at* KAZIO) Alright! I'll be strong, I'll be beautiful. And you, will you help me?
KAZIMIERZ:	How?
BRONKA:	(*With a muffled cry*) I will kill her, kill, kill her! And you will assist me!
KAZIMIERZ:	Me – no.
BRONKA:	(*Laughs mockingly*) You love me, so you said? I got the impression you'd do anything for me, endure any sacrifice, and now you're backing down.
KAZIMIERZ:	I am not. Why would I want to put my hand to such a pointless, thoughtless crime in cahoots with some cruel little bitch – these aren't the actions of a strong, beautiful woman.
BRONKA:	(*With growing urgency*) What are you talking about? You … heartless, bloodless, gutless. What exactly do you love with? Your love amounts to liking the sound of nice words, what a pipe dream.
KAZIMIERZ:	(*Regards her at length*) That's your damage speaking, but you're right, I'm unfit – maybe even too strong for your co-dependent love, vampiric mind-set, vampiric crimes … (*He rises and slowly goes towards the exit.* BRONKA *looks after him, then runs up to him, grasps his hand and pulls him back into the room*)
BRONKA:	No, dear brother, don't go. I've come to my senses and it's down to you. I do have a soul as well Kazio – damaged maybe, but expansive enough to encompass the beauty and goodness of your words, if only a small portion of your sadness and longing. Be honest – don't you feel desire as well.
KAZIMIERZ:	No, not now … Whatever there was inside me has been resolved through you.
BRONKA:	(*She repeats thoughtlessly*) Through me … through me … through me … (*Suddenly moves into happiness*) Kazio, did you really say, you love me?
KAZIMIERZ:	(*Thoughtfully*) Yes.
BRONKA:	That you'd reject me, if I loved you back?
KAZIMIERZ:	I did.
BRONKA:	And you said you're too proud, too pure, to let the slightest thought of desire sully the mistress of your ancestors' house, your brother's wife?
KAZIMIERZ:	Yes – and that is the sum of my soul.

BRONKA:	*(Grasping him suddenly by the hand)* Dearest brother. *(She puts her arms suddenly around his neck, holds his head to her breast, then leans against his shoulder half sleepily)* I'm worn out, so drowsy, would you rock me, rock me endlessly, into eternal rest, you're so endlessly good, endlessly … *(Suddenly rouses herself)* Kazio, do you know, what I am?
KAZIMIERZ:	I do.
BRONKA:	Tell me, say it, what am I?
KAZIMIERZ:	Clean, white snow falling on the dormant, frozen earth. Womb-like it shrouds the corpse until, from that once-dead husk, now warm and quick, the new shoots spring …
BRONKA:	*(Thoughtful)* I was sure the seeds had withered.
KAZIMIERZ:	They grew cold, rotted in the mud …
BRONKA:	And now they're pushing upwards, for the snow is melting … You're right – I am the snow … *(Suddenly roused)* Why is Ewa not asleep? Can you hear? *(KAZIO listens)* Can you hear? And now, she's walking down the stairs … any moment, she'll arrive. *(She passes suddenly to forced cheerfulness)* Kazio, how strangely cheerful I am. *(She puts her arm around him, tried to sway him from one side to the other)* Lullaby, my little one, lullaby … Well, go to sleep now, you naughty boy. *(EWA stands in the doorway and appears amused by the scene)*

Scene Four

BRONKA, KAZIO, EWA,

BRONKA:	*(Looks at her)* Lullaby, my little one, lullaby. Well, if you don't want to sleep, at least say hello to Miss Ewa!
KAZIMIERZ:	*(With forced cheerfulness)* Good day Miss!
BRONKA:	*(Greets EWA)* Just think, Ewa, everyone's up so early this morning. Just like Christmas Day … We'd this tradition at home; the children were beaten with switches, if they didn't rise early, so we leapt out of bed.
EWA:	For God's sake, that was Good Friday or Good Saturday.
BRONKA:	Oh, never mind … Just look at my big, soft, gentle bear. Ah, naughty Kazio …
KAZIMIERZ:	Bronka got out of the right side of bed this morning.
BRONKA:	That's true … I feel like a child again, when I used to climb the poplars, right to the top, next to that cursed black mere.
EWA:	Not the black mere again?

BRONKA:	*(Bats her hand)* Oh – it's all the same. Mere, or no mere, razor or guillotine, wheels of a train or textbook demise in one's cosy little bed ... Death is death. All the same, when and how ... *(Suddenly breaking off)* Ewa, look, this naughty Kazio, he's just like a tall poplar; no, he's like a towering uncle of mine who used to give me gut-wrenching shoulder-rides.
EWA:	Why so cheerful?
BRONKA:	*(Seizes her by the hands, cheekily)* Oh Ewa, I often have these silly mood-swings, irrational desires, I poison my own life and everyone else's, but it goes away, and then I'm doubly happy ... *(Rather tired)* Kazio, look, you're just useless, huh, you're boring, really, really boring ... Ewa, what if we two just ran to the garden, right now, the snow is waist deep ... The sheer pleasure of getting right down there, send it flying, legs and chest, like bellows, quicken the dormant, frozen earth, blow the embers into life again ...
EWA:	*(Pretends she is paying no attention, jestingly)* Bronka's lost her head. Into the snow, now, in my morning dress, and house shoes?
BRONKA:	Well, my dear, I'm hardened to it. You're dressed, aren't you ...? Come on, Ewa, so icy, you've caught a chill, I'll warm you up in the snow. I'll rub whole fistfuls in your face, I'll wash your hair. Oh, if you only knew, the snow's capacity for warmth, revival, frozen hands and cold hearts ...
EWA:	No, Bronka ... *(Always with the same secretive smile)* I don't need the snow, I do very well with my frozen hands and cold heart. My soul does not require a dusting of snowfall to warm it up.
BRONKA:	*(Looks at her for a long time)* No? Really, it doesn't? Come on then, Kazio, let's lunge in the snow together, let me roll you around? You'll make a capital snowman ... *(She illustrates with her gestures)* Two coals just here, for eyes, a little mud, here, for a nose, and here I'll do this for your lips, a pipe in your mouth like so ... Ewa, you'll miss out. Come along, Kazio *(She drags KAZIO along with her)* Ewa, Tadek will be here shortly. *(She runs into the hallway with KAZIO, her voice can be heard)* Tadek! Tadek! Ewa's on her own, we need some breakfast.

Scene Five

EWA

EWA *alone – she approaches the window, looks out for a while, tapping her fingers against the pane, cold and severe. She approaches the fireplace, kindles the embers with a poker, then sits motionless, gazing into the fire.*

Snow (1902)

Scene Six

TADEK, EWA

TADEUSZ:	*(Enters, looks about the room, approaches* EWA, *moves the armchair and sits next to her)* Is a 'good morning' in order? *(*EWA *remains silent)* Who called? Or shouldn't I ask?
EWA:	*(Raises her head drowsily)* Bronka. She's run out into the snow in her morning dress and house shoes to play with Kazio … It's beautiful to lunge in waist deep, she said, breaking waves of snow … Are you not worried she'll catch a chill?
TADEUSZ:	*(As though in his sleep)* Never mind.
EWA:	You're not jealous of Kazio? *(*TADEK *looks at her but does not reply)* Where have you been?
TADEUSZ:	Keeping to myself.
EWA:	Beside me, with me?
TADEUSZ:	*(Livid)* No, I told you: keeping to myself.
EWA:	*(Strokes his hands)* Why so angry, that now you must stay with me, forever?
TADEUSZ:	With you? Stay with you? Death is infinitely preferable.
EWA:	*(Lost in thought)* When I entered your home – no, no, that's it … that precise moment … exactly … The time you came back, I stood in that room, over there, I didn't hear your conversation, but I felt your happiness, just for a moment, I hesitated, before interrupting.
TADEUSZ:	*(As if waking from his sleep)* Where's Bronka?
EWA:	Bronka has freely chosen to plough into a snowdrift so that the icy shard planted in your frozen soul can germinate more quickly.
TADEUSZ:	*(Hesitates, looks at her, looks into the fire, and then suddenly)* What do you want?
EWA:	*(Harshly)* Pardon me? You still don't know? *(Pause)*
TADEUSZ:	It'll never happen! *(Livid)* I'd sooner crush your skull, trample you underfoot, you stupid bitch – I'll brain you with my bare hands before I let that happen.
EWA:	*(Looks at him with admiration)* The force of your love for me, it's very beautiful.
TADEUSZ:	*(Grasping her by the hands)* I detest you.
EWA:	I know – so your love is valued more highly.
TADEUSZ:	I can't deny my love, I can't deny my horrible, horrible desire for you, but I won't make this sacrifice, I swear, it'll never happen, never.
EWA:	It must.
TADEUSZ:	*(Startled, with a muffled cry)* I'll tell you once again, never. Never.

EWA:	*(Motionless, with widened eyes)* Yes, it will, today. *(Noise and chatter is heard in the corridor, a pair of quarrelling voices)*
TADEUSZ:	*(Listening)* What's going on? *(He rings; after a while, the* SERVANT *enters)*

Scene Seven

TADEK, SERVANT

TADEUSZ:	What's that noise, who's quarrelling?
SERVANT:	Sir, there's a woman, insists on seeing you.
TADEUSZ:	Why didn't you show her to the kitchen?
SERVANT:	I did, but she won't go, has as much right to see the mistress, she says, as her own birth mother.
TADEUSZ:	*(Wiping his forehead)* Show her in. *(The* SERVANT *exits – pause)*

Scene Eight

MAKRYNA, TADEK

A strange woman enters, serious; she looks around, and then speaks quietly, without a shade of self-deprecation.

MAKRYNA:	They didn't want to let me in, go through to the kitchen, they said. But I've every right to use the same door, as all the ladies and gentlemen, even the world's grandest.
TADEUSZ:	*(Approaches her alarmed)* What do you mean? *(*EWA *has her back turned to* TADEK *and* MAKRYNA*; she suddenly bursts out laughing;* TADEUSZ*, not hearing* EWA*'s laughter, grabs* MAKRYNA*'s hand with increasing trepidation)* Well, what do you mean?
MAKRYNA:	*(Points to* EWA *and says very quietly and seriously)* I know that lady and she knows me. *(*EWA *stops laughing, turns suddenly to look and they measure each other with their gaze)* You'll permit me to sit here in this corner and await my mistress, your wife – my beloved child, sir, cherished and raised by me … *(She sits in the corner, by the door;* TADEK *moves back towards* EWA*, but* EWA*, again turned towards the fireplace, does not see him. Suddenly,* BRONKA *rushes in, covered in snow, launches herself at* TADEK *and wraps her arms around him very tightly)*

Snow (1902)

Scene Nine

BRONKA, TADEK

BRONKA:	Tadek, warm me. Put me in the fire, my whole body is shaking. Tadek, make me warm.
TADEUSZ:	*(Loosening her grip)* Your old nurse is here.
BRONKA:	*(Jumps away from TADEK startled, looks around, suddenly sees the woman who has risen from her seat, launches herself towards her)* You, it's you, my dearest mother! How good to see you! How kind of you to come!

Act 4

Scene One

BRONKA

Beyond the windows, the snow whitens in the dusk of late winter, BRONKA *enters the stage space slowly and painfully, as though overcome by suffering. She holds a crumpled letter in her hand. She approaches the window, looks for a long time onto the park, and then unfolds the letter, smoothing it with her hands and reads, with her back turned to the audience.*

BRONKA:	*(Reading in a quiet whisper)* 'My dear Bronka' *(She lowers the letter and sobs)* 'You alone', – oh God … That's it. I'm alone. *(She turns)* I really am … Ah! Makryna, Makryna! *(She rings, looks confusedly in front of her)* Makryna, our wet-nurse – who laid my sister to rest … the black, black mere …

Scene Two

SERVANT, BRONKA

SERVANT:	*(Enters)* Madam, you rang?
BRONKA:	Yes. Tell them to sweep the snow from the mere.
	(SERVANT stands in silence; BRONKA *impatiently)* Well?
SERVANT:	Madam, not two hours ago, there was heavy snowfall, two metres deep, it will take two hours.
BRONKA:	*(Impatiently)* Impertinence! Assemble the whole village, the mere must be clear, as glass, arrange everything – the ice cutting, fishermen, torches, we shall have fishing today.

SERVANT:	Yes, Madam.
BRONKA:	*(Very annoyed)* It must be now, now, now! *(The servant bows and wants to leave)* Where's Kazio?
SERVANT:	Locked in his room, he told me to say …
BRONKA:	Well?
SERVANT:	That he won't be down today after all, he has to work.
BRONKA:	*(Drawing it out)* In-dee-d? You go and ask him to get up the urge right now. *(The servant bows and wants to leave again;* BRONKA *suddenly confused)* You saw your master?
SERVANT:	He just went out, into the woods.
BRONKA:	*(Uneasily)* Alone?
SERVANT:	No, with that lady who's staying.
BRONKA:	*(Looks at him)* Ah, alright … *(Thoughtful)* Call Makryna, and remember, the snow should be swept at once from the mere, arrange the ice cutting, torches, and Makryna straight away. *(The* SERVANT *exits)*

Scene Three

BRONKA

BRONKA:	*(Alone, seizes her head in her hands and walks about the room)* Alone, all alone … With Ewa, he did go … Kazio's locked himself in … me and Makryna rattle about the house … ha … ha … ha *(She walks about the room)* Two days ago, I was the one, and now … *(Again she unfolds the letter and reads quietly)* 'Barely a week has passed and I long, I thirst for you …' *(She throws the letter down onto the ground)* Lies! All lies! *(After a moment of contemplation, she bends down and picks up the letter, kisses it)* No, no, it's not a lie *(She cradles the letter, sits on the ottoman)* It was God's will, it was …

Scene Four

MAKRYNA, BRONKA

MAKRYNA *enters and stands quietly by the door.*

BRONKA:	*(Not seeing* MAKRYNA, *she droops more and more)* It was God's will. *(Silence; she rouses herself suddenly startled)* Who is it? *(She suddenly sees* MAKRYNA*)* Ah, it's you, Makryna. *(She approaches her, takes her by the hand and seats her down next to her)* How lovely you're

Snow (1902)

	here, so nice … *(She suddenly looks sharply at* MAKRYNA*)* But really, Makryna, what possessed you to walk through a blizzard for two whole days, such bitter frost, to visit your former motherless charge … *(She breaks off and looks astounded at* MAKRYNA*)*
MAKRYNA:	*(Thoughtful)* It wasn't sudden. I protected you, apple of my eye, more than any birth mother.
BRONKA:	You raised me … and when I was tiny – breast-fed me – you know, Makryna, you haven't aged, still so calm, quiet and good.
MAKRYNA:	*(Shakes her head)* Calm, quiet and good.
BRONKA:	Makryna, remember when I was fretful, how gently you'd lift me from the cradle, how you'd pace the room, hold me close, comfort me.
MAKRYNA:	I remember you before, before I laid you in any cradle.
BRONKA:	*(Suddenly)* What do you mean?
MAKRYNA:	*(Calmly)* Before you came into the world. I held you close, nursed you, brought you to life … *(Thoughtfully)* Now, I've come to close the eyelids I once kissed open … with my own fingers …
BRONKA:	*(Rouses herself)* Am I dreaming?
MAKRYNA:	Dreaming? What is life? A dream within a dream. Passing starlight bathes, awakens you without motive or intention, only to return years later and withdraw the life it sparked … *(*BRONKA *moves slowly towards the bell;* MAKRYNA *with a smile)* Why do you fear me? You want to call your servants? Perhaps you'd care to drive me out? *(She grasps* BRONKA *by the hand)*
BRONKA:	*(Startled)* Your hand, so terribly cold …
MAKRYNA:	*(Looks at her tenderly)* Bronka, you remind me of your father. He was seated in his workroom. Suddenly, he stood bolt upright.
BRONKA:	But why?
MAKRYNA:	Your sister had drowned herself …
BRONKA:	What? What? What?
MAKRYNA:	Your sister had drowned herself. I personally fished her out of that mere, just like the one beyond this window. I took her in my arms, the pitiful corpse – huffed and puffed, I warmed and held her – little use. Once, I had kissed her into being, and now these fingers closed her lifeless eyes … As I passed by the veranda, bearing my dear burden, your father stood within, as if turned to stone, and you lay buried face-down in the grass …
BRONKA:	*(She looks at* MAKRYNA *half conscious)* Makryna, I must be ill. I can't take it in. You kissed my sister and me into being only to close our eyelids with your cold fingers? Is that right? Yes? And there are stars that awaken life, they're fated to pass by, then

return as destroyers? You said that? You tell such beautiful tales. Tell me the one … wait, wait … I am so drowsy … It's true! These stars, they tear, pull, rend people, you have to go, high into the sky, down into the pit, across the oceans, you are compelled, you are … *(She snuggles close to MAKRYNA)* He followed his star, and I, Makryna, I … am alone; so pick me up and take me in your arms then lay me at my father's feet. I will see my sister … my mother … Makryna, calm, quiet, good … Oh, how drowsy … Sit beside me … *(She is overcome by drowsiness, and stretches out onto the ottoman, closes her eyes* MAKRYNA *rises quietly, looks at her, and then leaves the room solemnly. A moment of deep silence,* BRONKA *appears to be asleep;* KAZIO *enters, approaches* BRONKA*)*

Scene Five

KAZIMIERZ, BRONKA

KAZIMIERZ:	Bronka, what's the matter?
BRONKA:	*(As though woken from sleep)* Oh, Kazio, Kazio, what a relief.
KAZIMIERZ:	Bronka, were you asleep?
BRONKA:	I don't know, I don't. My head is so heavy, and I am completely alone. Tadek's gone to the woods with Ewa, as you see I'm alone. Kazio, why is that?
KAZIMIERZ:	*(Fearfully)* But Makryna was with you?
BRONKA:	*(Wiping her eyes and temple)* What do you mean? Makryna? I dreamt of her, of my father, my mother … Kazio, I dreamt about mother! I walked and walked along a steep, barren hilltop. Crosses loomed in the grey dusk. Suddenly, there's a woman, sitting in the road – I see nothing, I hear nothing, but I feel it's my mother sitting there, clutching a dead child to her womb. Ha, ha, ha! Kazio, why so startled? Listen – she watches, as the other child wanders barefoot along the winding pathways, lined with thorn bushes … upwards, upwards, and relentlessly. I'm walking on as if compelled by someone tracking me and then mother abandons the child she's holding and opens her arms, I am deathly tired and fall onto her breast … then suddenly, a gust of wind unveils the fog, and there I lie in the terrible iron grip of skulls and bones … oh!
KAZIMIERZ:	Bronka, Bronka, you are sick.
BRONKA:	Ha … ha … ha … sick, sick. What does that mean?! *(She gives* KAZIO *a long look, and then says secretively)* Kazio, this morning, you said you loved me. Or was it a dream?

Snow (1902)

KAZIMIERZ:	Yes, yes, I did and say again, I love you.
BRONKA:	That's good. You won't leave me, Kazio? Will you?
KAZIMIERZ:	No.
BRONKA:	And you know why Tadek left me?
KAZIMIERZ:	Yes.
BRONKA:	I know as well. It is true, Kazio?
KAZIMIERZ:	What?
BRONKA:	I was the snow, the good, white snow holding the poor earth and warming it, yes, Kazio?
KAZIMIERZ:	*(Thoughtful)* Yes ... Or else the healing hand, that shields a wounded bird ... he was so comfortable with you, while he was sick, but now he has grown new feathers, his sinews strengthened, he prepares for flight ... no need, his wings are fully spread ...
BRONKA:	*(Alarmed)* Don't, don't say that!
KAZIMIERZ:	*(Aggravated)* I must. Tadek will fly from you, with Ewa.
BRONKA:	With Ewa? With her? Who is Ewa? What is she?
KAZIMIERZ:	Who or what? My fantasy, your nemesis, and Tadek's hellish desire. That is Ewa. *(He smiles)* No? Then listen, Ewa is my fantasy, I needed her to highlight your strength and beauty. To you, she is fear, distress. You sense she'll lead you into dark despair; you feel she's abducting Tadek, compelling him beyond you with insatiable hunger for a greater power ...
BRONKA:	*(Rises and straightens herself)* Look, I am strong, I am powerful and cold enough, to destroy her! I am stronger than all of them. I'll tear her apart and kill her for I am his only desire!
KAZIMIERZ:	Its scope has exceeded you.
BRONKA:	*(Incensed)* Kazio, look at me! Look! I too am young and beautiful ... he told me so, repeatedly. Why should its scope exceed me?
KAZIMIERZ:	*(Takes her hands and says quietly and gently)* You are my soothing balm.
BRONKA:	*(Looks at him, then suddenly)* Are you tempting me?
KAZIMIERZ:	No, Bronka, I said I'd reject you, if you reciprocated, but I love your helpless despair. Something terrible is happening and I want to be your brother, your friend, whatever you need ...
BRONKA:	Is this true?
KAZIMIERZ:	Don't you know me?
BRONKA:	*(Strokes him)* Yes, Kazio. I am alone and so are you ... I don't love you, only your pure, beautiful affection. Why am I so drowsy, so depleted?

KAZIMIERZ:	*(Tenderly)* You didn't sleep.
BRONKA:	How we tormented each other.
KAZIMIERZ:	What did he say?
BRONKA:	Oh, nothing. He was good, sweet, loving, I understood, that the limit of his desire had fallen far, far beyond me. *(Suddenly with a shout)* Kazio, where is Tadek?
KAZIMIERZ:	In the woods with Ewa.
BRONKA:	*(Suddenly, thoughtful)* Over the mountains, over the waves, through the woods … and beyond Bronka … to where? What destination?
KAZIMIERZ:	*(Stroking her hands)* I don't know.
BRONKA:	Was Makryna a dream, Kazio?
KAZIMIERZ:	I brushed past her in the corridor.
BRONKA:	Brushed past her? What are you?
KAZIMIERZ:	*(Smiles secretively)* Ha … Perhaps Makryna's brother, for we two love you more than anyone.
BRONKA:	That's right, it's true.
KAZIMIERZ:	Makryna travelled far, as did I, to express my love … *(Silence)*
BRONKA:	Yes, yes, you and Makryna.

Scene Six

SERVANT, BRONKA

The SERVANT enters.

SERVANT:	Madam, the snow has been cleared.
BRONKA:	Oh, thank you … Has the ice been cut?
SERVANT:	It has.
BRONKA:	The fishermen summoned?
SERVANT:	Yes.
BRONKA:	The torches prepared?
SERVANT:	Yes, Madam.
BRONKA:	Thank you. You may go. *(The SERVANT exits)*

Scene Seven

KAZIO, BRONKA

KAZIMIERZ:	What's all this?
BRONKA:	Nothing, I'm going fishing … *(Searchingly)* Will you come too?

KAZIMIERZ:	Wherever you like. *(Silence)*
BRONKA:	*(Suddenly cheerful)* You remember our wonderful drive yesterday, the day before, through the orchard?
KAZIMIERZ:	*(Thoughtful and gazing into the distance)* Yes I do.
BRONKA:	*(Quickly, then increasingly slower)* Suddenly, you're lost in thought, gazing into the white distance, at those black hills that will be verdant when the snow disappears …
KAZIMIERZ:	*(Like an echo)* When the snow disappears …
BRONKA:	Kazio, do you love me, truly?
KAZIMIERZ:	Yes!
BRONKA:	Knowing that I love Tadek?
KAZIMIERZ:	Yes.
BRONKA:	You're fine enough to reject me, if I loved you back?
KAZIMIERZ:	At the slightest provocation.
BRONKA:	And if I were to ask a genuine favour?
KAZIMIERZ:	What?
BRONKA:	*(Searchingly)* Even that? *(A moment of silence, they look at each other for a long time)*
KAZIMIERZ:	*(Thoughtful)* Anything, everything.
BRONKA:	*(Suddenly)* The ice-skates, where are they?
KAZIMIERZ:	Ice skates, what for?
BRONKA:	Appearances …
KAZIMIERZ:	Very well. As you wish.
BRONKA:	Let it happen.
KAZIMIERZ:	Hm. Let it happen.
BRONKA:	*(With the greatest offence)* Will it happen?
KAZIMIERZ:	Yes! *(Smiles)* But why summon fishermen? Why people? Torches?
BRONKA:	*(Looks at KAZIO)* You're right! It can happen out of sight! Ha, ha, ha! No attempts to resuscitate! Ha, ha, ha! What a farce my sorrowful heart dictates … *(Rings)*

Scene Eight

SERVANT, BRONKA, KAZIO,

The SERVANT enters.

SERVANT:	Madam, what is your wish?
BRONKA:	No fishing today – announce it. Tomorrow – in the morning – understand?

SERVANT:	*(Surprised)* But everything's prepared.
BRONKA:	Excellent. But its tomorrow morning now – ha, ha – strange fish …
SERVANT:	No need for torches then?
BRONKA:	You haven't understood?
SERVANT:	Yes, Madam, but the mere has been cleared.
BRONKA:	Excellent.
SERVANT:	The ice cut.
BRONKA:	Even better.
SERVANT:	I should still call it off?
BRONKA:	For the hundredth time. *(Servant bows and exits)*
KAZIMIERZ:	Alright, let's go!
BRONKA:	Yes, let's! Boredom is just the same, everywhere. *(She laughs hysterically)*
KAZIMIERZ:	Indeed – my presence will be undeniable proof that there's more than one fish in the mere. *(They laugh)* We don't have to write a will …
BRONKA:	*(Gathers herself nervously)* Ha, ha, ha – no last will and testament … Are you ready?
KAZIMIERZ:	Long since.
BRONKA:	Alright then, come with me … *(she looks around, bids farewell to the room with her glance – they exit)*

Scene Ten

MAKRYNA

The stage is empty for a while. MAKRYNA *enters, looks to all corners.*

MAKRYNA:	No more … fruits of my labour … One, I bore in my arms, now this. *(She approaches the ottoman, circling the room slowly)* Here sat Bronka … only this morning … beckoned by her mother's ghost … I loved her best of all … *(she continues to circle the room, touching items of furniture one by one)* … my little white dove … her fair hawk … they have flown. Now I … remain … *(She sits motionless and remains)*

All the Same (1912)

Leopold Staff

To Samo (1912)

Leopold Staff

Dramatis Personae

TOMASZ KORZECKI
ANNA KORZECKA, his wife
JULJA (JULA, JULKA), their daughter
STEFAN GROŃSKI
STANISŁAW STOPA (STACH)

Act 1

An apartment room, very sparsely furnished. In the upstage wall, a door to the landing and a window. In the right-hand wall, a door to STANISŁAW's *room. In the left-hand wall, two doors; upstage to* JULJA's *room; downstage to the kitchen and* KORZECKI's *bedroom. Countless objects and items of furniture line the walls – an old piano, a cupboard, a chest of drawers piled with papers. On the window sill stands a bunch of flowers in a glass. In the centre, a table, on it a lighted lamp. An early autumn evening.*

Scene One

KORZECKI, KORZECKA

KORZECKI, *a tall beardless man, sits at the table shuffling through papers.* KORZECKA, *a short overweight woman, with traces of powder and rouge on her face, sits in an old armchair, back turned to her husband, so lamplight can fall on the newspaper cuttings that she is reading, which are tacked together.*

KORZECKI:	*(Raises his head, looks round at the door, looks at his watch and shakes his head)* She's late.
KORZECKA:	*(In a subdued voice, a shade disheartened and superior, still fixed on her reading)* She won't be long.
KORZECKI:	*(Rises, with poorly concealed impatience)* I want to go out …

KORZECKA:	*(As above)* Then go.
KORZECKI:	*(Sits, forcing himself to be silent)* I'll wait.
KORZECKA:	*(Raspingly)* Wait, then. *(KORZECKI goes to the cupboard, takes down a bottle and glass, pours; KORZECKA looks round)* Drinking, again?
KORZECKI:	A drop.
KORZECKA:	We've both said, me and Julja …
KORZECKI:	Just the dregs. Can't deny a man everything.
KORZECKA:	Please yourself.
KORZECKI:	Anyway it's empty. *(He sets the bottle aside, disappointed, strolls around the room, casts an eye over the calendar hanging on the wall)* Month's not been changed.
KORZECKA:	You again.
KORZECKI:	But it's the first. *(He rips off a page)* No one bothers … Do everything yourself.
KORZECKA:	Who cares about the calendar?
KORZECKI:	Yes, I know. You don't care. About anything, ever. *(KORZECKA shrugs her shoulders, remains silent; KORZECKI hesitantly, in a different tone)* Got any change?
KORZECKA:	From where? Don't manage the house do I.
KORZECKI:	Pin money then, from Julja.
KORZECKA:	*(Dismissively)* Hardly. You get your own.
KORZECKI:	You know it's not the right day.
KORZECKA:	*(Touchily)* Or for me.
KORZECKI:	*(Takes offence)* Oh, yes, I know. I'm saying nothing. No-thing.
KORZECKA:	Good idea. *(Silence)*
KORZECKI:	*(Sits again)* Half past six. How odd.
KORZECKA:	*(Angry)* Can't see it myself.
KORZECKI:	Why's she not back?
KORZECKA:	*(She turns suddenly with a brusque movement, in fact she controls herself and returns to her work)* Who knows.
KORZECKI:	She ought to be.
KORZECKA:	*(In an irritated voice)* She dashes from one lesson to another! Three in one afternoon.
KORZECKI:	Never this late …
KORZECKA:	*(Explodes)* Darling. What a bore. Round and round, half an hour, same questions, bothering me. Can't you see …
KORZECKI:	*(Leaping up angrily)* See what? Hermetically sealed. Don't care, no empathy, your own flesh and blood.
KORZECKA:	Can't I have one solitary hour, one minute?
KORZECKI:	Solitary hour! Days, weeks, years on end, morn 'til midnight, pinned to those bloody cuttings …

KORZECKA:	*(Offended)* What's it to you? Salt in your eye? Drag me into your countless petty affairs? No privacy or escape? Into the clear, fresh air …
KORZECKI:	Stale, more like. Inhale.
KORZECKA:	Stale to you. Of course.
KORZECKI:	Stuck with tabloids, I'm afraid – can't afford books. That's your fault.
KORZECKA:	*(With disdainful superiority)* How infantile.
KORZECKI:	*(In a taunting voice)* Glass houses. You've seen a different me, so hold your tongue. An unfortunate man, deposed, he falls, overcome, beneath life's heavy yoke, respect him. You should know …
KORZECKA:	*(Offended)* And I'm to blame how, exactly? That you should raise your voice?
KORZECKI:	Raise my voice?
KORZECKA:	Yes you do!
KORZECKI:	Only asking. How touchy. No questions allowed … *(Bitterly)* Go ahead – use your anger to poison my life. Death by neglect for a poor old man; thus ends his long, bitter struggle against adversity. Butt of mockery and contempt, he fell from the heights …
KORZECKA:	Blame yourself.
KORZECKI:	Myself? Victim of fate! Indiscriminate, the invader, and you collaborate, humiliate, my tormentor.
KORZECKA:	Fate? Was it fate that stuck its fingers in some grubby little deal?
KORZECKI:	*(With hurt pride)* Don't say that.
KORZECKA:	Ah. Who started? Alright – that's enough. With no means of escape, to a different plane, higher emotions, refined thoughts … what would I do …
KORZECKI:	Yes, yes, quack, quack.
KORZECKA:	*(With contempt)* Typical.
KORZECKI:	Ah yes, infantile. Not some superior creature whose poetic strains echo within this vale of prose.
KORZECKA:	The cycle of poverty – I might say, deprivation, were I not ashamed. I wasn't born for this and you …
KORZECKI:	Know it by rote. *(Making light of it)* We're hardly talking lords and ladies.
KORZECKA:	Landowner's daughter! Landed gentry!
KORZECKI:	Two glorified tenants tied the knot.
KORZECKA:	Same to you, you waste of space. *(She approaches the chest of drawers and looks for something among the papers)*
KORZECKI:	*(Jumps up as though he's been burnt)* What are you looking for? Hands off, what a mess!

KORZECKA:	My cuttings, they're in here.
KORZECKI:	Put them somewhere else.
KORZECKA:	Where? One of your other luxury apartments?
KORZECKI:	Try the fire. Don't care. *(Arranges his papers, finds books among them)* What's this?
KORZECKA:	Stefan's books, of course.
KORZECKI:	No room. My documents go there.
KORZECKA:	Stefan can't come to lessons like a child, carrying books and a chalkboard. Jula puts them here.
KORZECKI:	She does? Alright. But not your clutter. No room. Just my very tricky documents. Most solicitors would be stumped …
KORZECKA:	*(With irony)* Don't you pretend to be a solicitor. *(With a sigh)* I once held that popular profession in utter contempt, now I endure a fate far worse …
KORZECKI:	What! How is it worse! Don't denigrate work, a profession. It's all sacred! Noble! I'm a legal adviser – I have no shame.
KORZECKA:	Don't forget to add 'junior'. Wife of a junior advisor, working in some dive. It's horrible !
KORZECKI:	I never give up, I work, last shred of strength, for my family, tears of sweat …
KORZECKA:	You? You? You? If it wasn't for Jula, giving tuition …
KORZECKI:	She supports her over-worked, toiling father.
KORZECKA:	When did you ever contribute to the housekeeping? God knows how you melt the cash!
KORZECKI:	Don't point the finger, you skinflint. Slovenly cow, rotting away – you've no right.
KORZECKA:	Oh yes, I do. 'For richer', I agreed, not 'poorer'. I've been cheated. Living in this hole, surrounded by junk. Moment of madness, shackling myself to misery, to you – squandered both our fortunes. I could have had luxury!
KORZECKI:	Your little whims! That's what did it. Never enough money, I could never get enough.
KORZECKA:	You dare accuse me? I sacrificed my heart. *(With emphasis)* To this day, in my breast, a broken heart. And in return …
KORZECKI:	Not again. Broken where? When? Who was he?
KORZECKA:	You question me?
KORZECKI:	You never do answer.
KORZECKA:	Disbelieve at your peril!
KORZECKI:	Perish the thought! *(Dismissively)* No-one wanted you, did they? You were on the heap.
KORZECKA:	The heap!

All the Same (1912)

KORZECKI:	Now faint! For romantic effect. I shan't dab your brow. My God, I'd rather beat my own.
KORZECKA:	I made an offering, a sacrifice, for you. To this day, the spectre of strangled happiness haunts my heart. I broke his spirit and mine.
KORZECKI:	Blah di blah. Romantic fiction, gossip columns – you read it somewhere.
KORZECKA:	*(Tearfully)* I read it! Gossip columns! On my mother's life …
KORZECKI:	You believe your own stories. Convinced yourself, that's all.
KORZECKA:	*(Pathetically)* I swear. I hold love's relic in my heart. Balm of my mean existence. Memory does endure in this soulless corpse.
KORZECKI:	Anyway, it's out of fashion. Passé.
KORZECKA:	Heartbreak? Passé!
KORZECKI:	Bloody pointless! A relic? Rubbish!
KORZECKA:	*(Sternly)* Rubbish to you, sacred to me.
KORZECKI:	Honestly. You're getting on. Grown-up daughter. Grandchildren soon, who knows? And in the moonlight, beneath the cypress trees, you lament Sir Knight, your lover, slain by a dragon.
KORZECKA:	So harsh, block of ice, inhuman! No respect for bleeding hearts, their sanctity …
KORZECKI:	Humph! (STANISŁAW *enters by the upstage door*)

Scene Two

KORZECKI, KORZECKA, STANISŁAW

STANISŁAW *stands in the doorway, hat in hand, and soaked through. He regards those present. Tense atmosphere.*

KORZECKA:	Knock before entering.
STANISŁAW:	*(With a smile and a bow)* Point taken. (KORZECKA *exits left, slamming the door*)

Scene Three

KORZECKI, STANISŁAW

STANISŁAW:	*(Looks after her with a half-ironic, half-pitying glance, then makes for the door on the right. In front of the door he stops and addresses* KORZECKI*)* Hello and good bye.

KORZECKI:	Hello. (*STANISŁAW opens the door*)
KORZECKI:	Stach!
STANISŁAW:	(*Stops and speaks with his back turned*) What?
KORZECKI:	Off to your room?
STANISŁAW:	You noticed!
KORZECKI:	One minute.
STANISŁAW:	(*Still with his back turned, looks at his watch*) Your fine friend's due at seven. Piece of work.
KORZECKI:	Highly respectable man.
STANISŁAW:	Like a hole in the head.
KORZECKI:	Not your decision. Julka's pupil, he pays.
STANISŁAW:	(*Turns to face KORZECKI, looks him in the eye, with emphasis*) That's why he's moved to this tenement block. I suppose.
KORZECKI:	One empty apartment, he moves in. When you own the block, turn him away. In the meantime, someone else's property.
STANISŁAW:	Go to hell, his lordship!
KORZECKI:	Bother you, does it, his class? Your objection?
STANISŁAW:	Nothing.
KORZECKI:	Alright.
STANISŁAW:	English lessons.
KORZECKI:	What's it to you!
STANISŁAW:	Don't like him. That's all. Right, I'm off.
KORZECKI:	Wait.
STANISŁAW:	I'm waiting.
KORZECKI:	(*Uncertainly*) How are you?
STANISŁAW:	(*Annoyed*) Anything useful to say?
KORZECKI:	Oh get out, you cracked misanthrope.
STANISŁAW:	Cracked or not. My business.
KORZECKI:	I need to talk.
STANISŁAW:	Keep it brief.
KORZECKI:	Like some cactus. Don't touch.
STANISŁAW:	Not here to be touched. Sublet a room, pay for it; my own master.
KORZECKI:	Enter the stranger. 'I sub-let a room, I pay for it.' To me, to us, you're more than a man who sub-lets a room.
STANISŁAW:	How kind. Is that all?
KORZECKI:	What's the hurry?
STANISŁAW:	(*Measuring him with his gaze*) Clearly, I dislike clean-shaven old men with beer bellies, shiny bald patches and red cheeks …
KORZECKI:	(*Offended*) Show some gratitude. You'll never learn.
STANISŁAW:	(*Provocatively*) Gratitude? Why?
KORZECKI:	You grew up in my house. I raised you in my house.

All the Same (1912)

STANISŁAW:	Big favour. *(Tapping each word out on the table with his finger)* A nugget of capital in mother's will, on condition, that you drag me up. *(Pointedly)* Fully covered.
KORZECKI:	I replaced your father. Money doesn't buy heart. Common decency.
STANISŁAW:	Drop the paternal tone. I was denied the honour of having a father, so spare me that as well. *(After a while with passion)* And your smirk.
KORZECKI:	Who's smirking? You think I'm tactless …
STANISŁAW:	*(Growing louder)* No point! Tact is offensive. Alright? Instead of saying 'he's a bastard', we say 'father unknown'. I spit on fathers unknown.
KORZECKI:	You're paranoid. Think anyone cares? Hardly a scandal these days. Sins of the fathers, modern society, passé.
STANISŁAW:	Don't give me society or parental absolution. Conventionally, the girl is stupid or the man a rogue. Alright?
KORZECKI:	A father is always a father.
STANISŁAW:	Albeit unknown. Mister Blank. Nice ring. A blood relationship with mystery. Many walk the streets. Mister Blanks. You never know, which one …
KORZECKI:	Surely you can't assume that any old man …
STANISŁAW:	*(With bitter humour)* Spot on. It's appalling. Bump into someone. Could be him, could be him. Jostle your man in the street and you may have jostled your father. *(Clenching his fists)* And I hate them, all. Equally. My Mr Blank, each one. A rogue.
KORZECKI:	As you wish.
STANISŁAW:	Consensus. *(Wants to leave)*
KORZECKI:	Just bloody wait …
STANISŁAW:	What now?
KORZECKI:	A serious conversation, this once.
STANISŁAW:	I'm listening.
KORZECKI:	*(With hesitation)* It didn't work. Again. Placed a bet, nothing came of it.
STANISŁAW:	What can I do? I'm not the Holy Ghost of Lottery.
KORZECKI:	Remove your coat and hat.
STANISŁAW:	Prefer to stand, more respectful. Well?
KORZECKI:	You do know.
STANISŁAW:	I do not.
KORZECKI:	Have you got any?
STANISŁAW:	What?
KORZECKI:	Stop bloody pretending. It's the first. Did you get any?

STANISŁAW:	And did you get any, sir?
KORZECKI:	Stop messing around. Jula's not back. And you know how much she'll give me. Cigarette money.
STANISŁAW:	And one drink.
KORZECKI:	Never mind. Basically nothing.
STANISŁAW:	She's right. She keeps the house. You let it go.
KORZECKI:	Dear boy. Spare me the sermon. Whichever way you turn it, zero. I ask you.
STANISŁAW:	Nothing myself to speak of. Not likely, is it? Creditors swallow half my wage-packet. *(Bats his hand)* Anyway, who cares?
KORZECKI:	Alright …
STANISŁAW:	*(Mockingly)* Out the till? No way. Creamed off enough.
KORZECKI:	Didn't mean that.
STANISŁAW:	Shame. 'Course, it won't climb back on its own.
KORZECKI:	No one willing?
STANISŁAW:	Like who? Tried all the pawnbrokers. My legs worn to stumps just looking. No lenders.
KORZECKI:	What's to be done?
STANISŁAW:	Well's run dry.
KORZECKI:	And that's your advice.
STANISŁAW:	*(Assertively)* Oh, I'm through. Stopped running anyway. If they catch me, that's fine. I took money, but our deadline's gone now. You promised you'd win. Yes? Enticed me. And now? *(Nonchalantly)* Worst case – sacked from accounts.
KORZECKI:	Hardly! Locked up more like …
STANISŁAW:	I'll serve my time. I'm tired. But you'll go down with me.
KORZECKI:	*(Looks round at the door)* Not so loud. Keep calm.
STANISŁAW:	How can I? You sit there, arms folded, telling me to 'get money'. But how to pay it back? You forged the bill, and the cash needs to go back because they're about to realise, so then *I* have to run ragged with my tongue out like some dog!
KORZECKI:	I forged it. Saw me, did you?
STANISŁAW:	I didn't see but I know. Else you wouldn't squirm, or invoke the saints. Why don't those people who vouched for you pay up? Oh right, didn't actually sign, did they? Who really would vouch for you? Think I was born yesterday? Can't unearth a document? Would I have raided the safe otherwise? I knew very well who'd be shamed if the fraud came to light. To save you, I wouldn't lift one finger. But scandal would taint her. And because she feeds and clothes you with money got by her last breath, teaching, why shouldn't she bear the shame for her fraudster-papa. I did it for

	her, not you bloody parasites. Alright? And now, it's all gone to pot, you can fend for yourself.
KORZECKI:	You'd sell my soul.
STANISŁAW:	Alongside my own. Oh well! For those who die in poverty, sooner's better than later. Has to end some time. A dog's life.
KORZECKI:	No sacrifice, thank you. As for the money you supposedly took at my behest, how much …
STANISŁAW:	I make no excuses. I'm just as much a rogue. Isn't that what you wanted? Makes sense. At your invitation I drank. Bottle by bottle. Together we gambled and lost, sharing our hope and guilt. And the devil knew. I'd never played before. Nor drank beyond my means. But you did. Beyond hers. Then on the fruits of forgery. You're the one who asked me to save you. That's one way to fall. Easy enough, at the start. Besides, I'd every right to get embroiled but you'd no right to implicate your daughter. Me? I'm nothing, wasted, sullied, unloved. Romantic, you'll say, and it's true. Damn that as well; I fall to my knees, head bowed.
KORZECKI:	Listen, wait. If not for me, then for her. You said that for her …
STANISŁAW:	*(Laughing)* Yes, let's say we commit crimes for her: you forge signatures and I plunder the cash box. What's one more theft: for her. Honourable sacrifice.
KORZECKI:	Think it over …
STANISŁAW:	For her, it's all for her. Your opinion of me! Deep down, you're laughing. You think your little serenade, 'For Her', will make me your instrument? 'Delusional – thinks he's in with a chance'. And you as go-between. Basically, she resents you. If she knew what you'd said in her name. You're not worthy to be a father. I'm not worthy to think of her. I'm a bloody scoundrel. It's over.
KORZECKI:	Solves nothing.
STANISŁAW:	*(With a bitter smile)* Rogue with a Heart *(Seriously and sadly)* So be it. All done now. No illusions at least. Clear cut – it's over. Broken cycle. Vicious circle. Really was. What made me this way? She doesn't love me, probably. Why's that, why can't she? Because I'm like this.
KORZECKI:	She's very fond, she loves you, like a brother.
STANISŁAW:	Too close to home. Spare the 'brotherly' or 'fatherly', thanks. Family to you means cash cow. We know that. And don't pull her down. Mix her up. She thinks I'm an idiot. She's perfectly right. Always have been, and lazy, good time boy, drunkard. Not on purpose. Might have moderated myself, if she'd been friendlier, warmer. I stumbled through despair, instead of pulling myself up,

	realizing that I had to earn her love, become worthy of it. No use talking. If I could shift a few years back! Pipe-dream! Well? You must long for that sometimes. Save you doing a few bad things. Too late! Can't be fixed.
KORZECKI:	It must be!
STANISŁAW:	Doesn't matter any more.
KORZECKI:	Have mercy!
STANISŁAW:	*(With a sudden gesture, he empties all his pockets)* I'll be merciful and turn out my pockets. Take everything. The leftovers. Not enough?
KORZECKI:	Won't dent it.
STANISŁAW:	Tough. Can't give with one hand and take with the other. You're on your own. If they investigate me, drink my health.
KORZECKI:	No, not enough – where can we get some!
STANISŁAW:	You'll manage. You'll squeeze your daughter dry …
KORZECKI:	Not enough …
STANISŁAW:	Damn you! You'd even sell her to the devil! Own up!
KORZECKI:	Rubbish.
STANISŁAW:	To that smart ass, then. Shame she's so different from the rest of you.
KORZECKI:	Mind your tongue.
STANISŁAW:	*(Pats him on the shoulder)* I've earned the right. It wasn't cheap. With you, money talks. I paid cash. Well, old chap, deal? We deserve each other.
KORZECKI:	*(Offended)* Words fail me …
STANISŁAW:	Pity. Zero on all fronts. All the best, take care. *(Julja enters through the upstage door)*

Scene Four

KORZECKI, STANISŁAW, JULJA

JULJA:	*(Throwing off her coat, gloves, hat)* Here I am, father dear, I'm home. *(She looks around, cheerfully)* My mature student hasn't arrived?
KORZECKI:	Not yet.
JULJA:	Good, that's good. Hello, Stach.
STANISŁAW:	*(Drily)* Hello.
JULJA:	*(To STANISŁAW)* Gloomy and overcast, as usual – like foul autumn weather.

All the Same (1912)

STANISŁAW:	*(Muttering)* Sun doesn't shine on me. I'll clear the air. *(Gets ready to leave)*
JULJA:	*(Stopping him)* What now? I didn't mean that.
STANISŁAW:	I know what you meant. I'll clear off.
JULJA:	No sense of humour.
STANISŁAW:	I never intrude. *(Exits)*

Scene Five

KORZECKI, JULJA

JULJA:	What's rattled his cage?
KORZECKI:	*(Batting his hand)* You know him.
JULJA:	Where's mother?
KORZECKI:	Pressed between sheets of paper like a dried flower.
JULJA:	*(With mild accusation)* Father, no sympathy? Its innocent enthusiasm! Everyone has a passion.
KORZECKI:	Well, yes. But always the same …
JULJA:	What can she do, poor thing? She's bored. Can't go out. Terrible time. I'm drenched. *(Looks at her watch)* And running late.
KORZECKI:	Forty-five whole minutes.
JULJA:	It's the first, though. I had to run a few errands, pay off some debts, only small. Try as I might, tying up loose ends every month seems impossible. Always a bit owed here and there. Luckily, it's nothing good intentions and resilience can't solve. There's even a bit left for you, father.
KORZECKI:	No rush, none at all. Handy for minor expenses, though.
JULJA:	I'm due at the landlord's with rent.
KORZECKI:	No hurry.
JULJA:	I don't like being in arrears: keeps things under control.
KORZECKI:	You got that from me, child. Proceed modestly, with your chin up, frugally, yet with pride.
JULJA:	I'll rest a bit first. *(Sits)* Been all over town.
KORZECKI:	Washed out.
JULJA:	Yes, I'm sleepy. Just a little. *(With a sigh)* My God. No bed of roses, life.
KORZECKI:	That's it. And to think we saw better days …
JULJA:	*(Energetically shaking off negative thoughts)* No regrets, none – that's best.
KORZECKI:	Easy to say.

JULJA:	I'm learning to accept my fate with good humour. I want to be strong, father. Believe me, sometimes it's hard, really hard. My spirit fails me often. I drag myself up. Don't like to complain, even to myself. It doubles the misery. It might get better, easier.
KORZECKI:	God willing. We've earned it by patiently enduring fate's hard knocks.
JULJA:	I'm not afraid of work or hardship. I just want us to have enough money to live on and to stay positive.
KORZECKI:	*(Shrugging his shoulders)* Seems reasonable.
JULJA:	We'll manage somehow. We mustn't despair.
KORZECKI:	If it wasn't for anxiety. Constant anxiety.
JULJA:	Everyone has that. You get nothing without some worry. It would just be good if things were a little easier. I don't ask for much, do I? I've learned to have modest dreams.
KORZECKI:	You never know what's around the corner. Blue skies, why not? I don't mean for us. For you, my child, you. I think only of you and your happiness, since one … One single wish from you and our lives could be better.
JULJA:	*(Surprised)* From me? Don't I wish it?
KORZECKI:	*(Soothing)* Well, yes, yes.
JULJA:	I enjoy my work. I want you to be happy. That's my reward. Even after a hard day's work, when I'm worn out. I always long for these quiet walls, the lamplight, stacks of books, the old piano, flowers … *(She casts an eye over the flowers)* Oh, no one's changed the water. Look how they've wilted.
KORZECKI:	*(With feigned concern)* I can't believe it … Really … Let me …
JULJA:	It's alright, father. I'll do it myself. I pity the wilted flowers. So pretty, cheerful. *(She busies herself with the flowers)*
KORZECKI:	Where does he get such lovely blooms this time of year? They must be so expensive. I like that about him, you know. Refined sensibility – it's proof. Man of our sphere, no question. Former sphere, I should say, but ours. And that he sees you as a woman of that sphere. A woman, not a teacher. A woman who belongs …
JULJA:	Oh, I've no time for that.
KORZECKI:	I understand, really. But a woman, honoured, as a woman, in that way …
JULJA:	Basic expression of politeness. You can't stop or prevent that.
KORZECKI:	Who said you should? On the contrary. I like it, I said. *(With a half-sly smile)* Seems he's not entirely oblivious.
JULJA:	*(Evasively)* Oh …

All the Same (1912)

KORZECKI: Now, now. Nothing wrong with that. No one buys flowers ...
JULJA: Don't read the bouquet for intentions, father, you might be wrong.
KORZECKI: Might. You said it, child. And if I'm not? Surely ... who knows, dear? Whether you've made an impression. *(Patting her on the shoulder with delight)* I'm pretty sure you have. I promise. That bouquet ... I know people.
JULJA: You're being silly, father.
KORZECKI: Why not? Beautiful, aren't you? Education, refinement, breeding, whole package ...
JULJA: Let's not discuss this.
KORZECKI: Why not, I repeat. You're from a respectable, slightly impoverished family, it's true, but haven't poor women married rich and returned to their former station? He might be fate's instrument, who knows, and raise us up again. *(Secretively)* Cunning. That's it. Get under his skin. When a woman wants ...
JULJA: Father, stop it. I don't look at people and calculate. It's not me. I don't want to have this conversation. It's humiliating. I don't see life as a hunt, or people, who approach me, as prey. Stefan's approached me as a student. That's what defines our relationship; please stick to it, no subversion.
KORZECKI: Dear child. Did I mean to offend or humiliate you? I was referring to opportunities presented by fate. Nothing wrong with that. All relationships are to some degree formed through fateful encounters.
JULJA: *(Quietly)* No opportunities here.
KORZECKI: *(Cheerfully)* Fate will decide.
JULJA: So we can stop.
KORZECKI: Of course, if you prefer not to talk ... But why not admit the thought. I know you're proud. But if he makes the first move ... You can count on that.
JULJA: I don't want to count on anything or anyone. The situation makes it impossible. Self-reliance, contentment, spiritual freedom, no question – complete moral independence. I don't want my emotional life to be governed by thoughts of what I can get. My life's already full of petty troubles, mundane tasks, so it's crucial that I feel unfettered, inside, bright and free of all humiliation, blame. Anything I feel for Stefan must be free of calculation.
KORZECKI: These things aren't mutually exclusive.
JULJA: Please, can we leave this now? Anything that casts doubt on my way of thinking really pains me.

KORZECKI:	I appreciate your concern. Though to regard his wealth as an obstacle to mutual affection would be … *(Triumphantly)* … well, trivial, unsophisticated … it …
JULJA:	You're right. But we're friends, no more.
KORZECKI:	No question. But that's often how love begins. What's in a name? I have a knack for these things. I know people. And nothing should stop you from marrying him, if …
JULJA:	*(Numbly)* I will never be his wife.
KORZECKI:	*(Uneasy)* You love someone else?
JULJA:	No.
KORZECKI:	Alright then.
JULJA:	I cannot be his wife.
KORZECKI:	Don't love him then? Worked it through in your mind? Sure you don't love him? That doesn't necessarily rule anything out, so long as …
JULJA:	I believe in his sincere friendship. Beyond that, I've no right …
KORZECKI:	*(With relief)* No right? You'll gain it. Based on hard facts. That's the least of your worries.
JULJA:	Let's leave it there, as I said.
KORZECKI:	Very well, we'll bide our time. He's a fine man, no question, and a faithful friend – his eyes say it. Great gift, friend you can trust, and should, unreservedly. Someone to lean on when things get tough, for better or worse, he'll never fail to … well … repay you …
JULJA:	I value his friendship and am pleased to repay it with equal sincerity.
KORZECKI:	*(Rubbing his hands together)* Right then. Lovely. A great strength, friendship. Support in hard times. Because it's tricky. No question. Look, how we live. Your mother and I sleep in the kitchen. You're in a tiny windowless cage, barely space for a bed. And a room for lessons, you really need that.
JULJA:	I'm not complaining.
KORZECKI:	But I can see you're stretched. Lots of lessons, poorly paid. It's not easy. These people are hardly rich. Except for him. *(After a while)* Charge him enough?
JULJA:	Same as everyone.
KORZECKI:	Not enough. You could raise the fee. He can afford it.
JULJA:	It wouldn't be right.
KORZECKI:	Dear child. In life, you have to be practical, capitalise, capitalise on every opportunity. Money doesn't grow on trees.
JULJA:	But it's not fair …
KORZECKI:	This isn't about fairness, it's about means.

All the Same (1912)

JULJA:	Leave it to me, please, father.
KORZECKI:	I'm sure he wouldn't mind if you raised his fee. You'll see. He likes you.
JULJA:	Father!
KORZECKI:	You should make the most of it. Beauty is God's gift, same as diligence, talent, a good memory, strength …
JULJA:	Ask someone to pay for my beauty … have you any idea …
KORZECKI:	Don't be oversensitive. He'll be very pleased. I'm telling you, those lessons … think they're all he cares about?
JULJA:	*(Sternly)* If that were the case, father, you wouldn't object?
KORZECKI:	I know life. I've been through a lot. I don't dwell on trifles.
JULJA:	But that's …
KORZECKI:	Child, it's absolutely harmless.
JULJA:	*(Turning briefly)* Enough about this.
KORZECKI:	If someone wants to be ideal, an angel, they're lost to the world.
JULJA:	Alright. Our opinions differ.
KORZECKI:	That's all they are – opinions.
JULJA:	Do you seriously think that?
KORZECKI:	*(Impatiently)* I always take life very seriously.
JULJA:	But you did say …
KORZECKI:	Absolutely.
JULJA:	Then you should know …
KORZECKI:	What?
JULJA:	Well … *(She blurts out)* Oh, I don't want to hide anything … best to speak out, once, clearly and openly …
KORZECKI:	What?
JULJA:	I feel something more than friendship … I can't deny it … so I can't let you exploit him …
KORZECKI:	Who said that? I agree with you … completely …
JULJA:	I had to say something …
KORZECKI:	You love him then?
JULJA:	Listen father. It's not that sort of love.
KORZECKI:	Never mind labels … An attachment, then …
JULJA:	Yes, deep attachment, sisterly love …
KORZECKI:	You're a free agent … And him? Does he know?
JULJA:	I've not concealed it. Well, I may have tried but it's impossible …
KORZECKI:	Of course it is. You haven't noticed … well … is the feeling … mutual …
JULJA:	I think so.
KORZECKI:	What did I say …
JULJA:	What did you say, father?

KORZECKI:	Nothing … nothing … it's just …
JULJA:	*(As though suddenly remembering herself)* No, father, forget this … It's not true! It isn't! *(As though reproaching herself)* We're just friends … Nothing more … I imagined … that's all …
KORZECKI:	I don't object … you're old enough … If it's meant to be, why not?
JULJA :	We're just friends, father. *(As if hurrying herself)* How thoughtless! Forget everything … The conversation never happened …
KORZECKI:	*(Surprised)* Why?
JULJA:	*(After consideration, composing herself)* Never mind. *(She moves away from him and looks at the clock)* Is that the time. He'll be here soon. I'll just pop downstairs. If Stefan appears, ask him to wait, please, father. I'll be right back … *(She exits)*

Scene Six

KORZECKI, KORZECKA

KORZECKI:	*(Goes to the downstage door on the left and opens it)* Sweetie pie! *(Batting his hand, he shrugs his shoulders and returns)* Tut.
KORZECKA:	*(Entering)* What do you want?
KORZECKI:	*(With irritation)* Oh, nothing, didn't realize … don't let me disturb … you'll only complain …
KORZECKA:	Well, what is it?
KORZECKI:	*(Strolling)* Oh, nothing, carry on … can't ever talk … always busy.
KORZECKA:	Standing here, aren't I …?
KORZECKI:	*(More mildly)* Well, yes. Family affairs do sometimes require attention. Flesh and blood. Talk it through, together.
KORZECKA:	Is there a problem?
KORZECKI:	Poor little me. Shouldering the lot. Solidarity! Responsibility! You can't conjure happiness out of thin air. It's my job, as a father and ours, as parents – to ensure our daughter's happiness.
KORZECKA:	*(In a dreary, monotonous voice)* What's the story?
KORZECKI:	You know. Have a guess? I said our daughter's happiness. You've never thought she can, or should, get married? Successfully? You women better understand these things.
KORZECKA:	I'll have none of it! No part! Marriage – the daily grind! I never want to hear she's unhappy, like her mother.
KORZECKI:	Here we go, from your perch. Give it a rest.

KORZECKA:	She must heed my plight. The modern world shuns true, spiritual love …
KORZECKI:	If we all billowed about in the clouds, the human race would die out.
KORZECKA:	No less than it deserves.
KORZECKI:	And yet, you see, it thrives. Worth noting. Be realistic. If Julja were to make a good marriage … which could happen … her fate would be secured, as would ours.
KORZECKA:	For money! The marriage of true minds, trodden into dirt … I won't be an accomplice to this crime!
KORZECKI:	They can still love each other, can't they? That happens to be the case. Good plan. You want to wash your hands and keep the soap.
KORZECKA:	Things will happen without my intervention.
KORZECKI:	Could be. But trust this nose. Something's in the air.
KORZECKA:	I know nothing; I've no desire to know.
KORZECKI:	You know nothing because you're not looking. I'll stake my neck, he's hooked.
KORZECKA:	Pardon me?
KORZECKA:	Stefan, our Julja.
KORZECKA:	Hooked! The expression! Profanes true love.
KORZECKI:	What? I'm just saying.
KORZECKA:	These matters are sacred, other-worldly, beyond reach. The unanointed should keep their distance.
KORZECKI:	I have a barge pole. *(Cunningly)* Oh I know, we should ignore them, turn a blind eye. If a thing's bound to happen, oil the wheels, why not. The politics of love. Ho, ho! Wasn't I young, once? What? Well, go on … *(Jovially)* I certainly knew how to cut the mustard? You'll have some stories.
KORZECKA:	Your word choice! Can't listen. *(Knocking)* Someone at the door. *(Exits)*
KORZECKI:	Two short planks. *(Renewed knocking)*
KORZECKI:	Please, come through. (STEFAN *enters through the upstage door*)

Scene Seven

KORZECKI, STEFAN

KORZECKI:	Oh, sir, it's you. You may have passed our daughter on the stairs.
STEFAN:	Miss Julja's gone out?

KORZECKI: Back in a tick. She asked me to admit you and beg your patience. She's just popped downstairs with the rent. No urgency but we don't like being in arrears. *(With a smile)* Chip off the old block. Inherited my pride. Two peas in a pod …
STEFAN: I'm happy to wait. I have time.
KORZECKI: In your case, the saying goes.
STEFAN: Saying?
KORZECKI: *(With a smile)* Time is money.
STEFAN: *(Coldly)* Ah, yes.
KORZECKI: *(Admiringly)* You probably have some anecdotes.
STEFAN: Permit me. *(Sits)*
KORZECKI: *(Hospitably)* But of course. Don't stand on ceremony.
STEFAN: Good to be indoors at a time like this.
KORZECKI: Haven't you been home? *(Tapping his forehead with laughter)* Silly question! You didn't get soaked in the stairwell.
STEFAN: Just back from my place in the country.
KORZECKI: Horrible in town when it pours. One enormous puddle.
STEFAN: *(In a nonchalant voice, as though killing time)* The country's no different. In weather like this, I prefer the town to flooded villages. All you can see is fog and the rain beating down.
KORZECKI: You often take advantage of the town's proximity.
STEFAN: A great luxury, under an hour on horseback. Life on a country estate isn't always engaging. Nor does it satisfy every need. Besides, one doesn't always feel like working and sometimes it's not practical.
KORZECKI: Why bother if you don't need to. Ho, ho, country ways, my old life! I'm still not used to the town. I adore the country.
STEFAN: *(As above)* Personally, I prefer some balance. After a few days in the country, I long for the town and vice versa. That's the reason – for spending a few in each.
KORZECKI: Two homes. Ha, the means to own two properties! Variety is the spice of life. Country fare tastes better when you've been in town.
STEFAN: I don't deny it. Even wise men acknowledge that youth has its rights.
KORZECKI: Especially such a well-endowed youth.
STEFAN: Rather lacklustre, I'm afraid.
KORZECKI: What on earth's the matter?
STEFAN: You can only sustain it so long.
KORZECKI: You can afford to, in your position. Carpe diem, so they say. Seize life.

All the Same (1912)

STEFAN: A fairly useful maxim. When it's adopted by men of privilege, they sometimes feel guilty; give it a bad name, as if dwelling in misery were the natural order. That should be the preserve of slaves, who've never possessed their own souls, orchards and granaries. Whereas I am an heir to life and welcome its bounty. But, there are still moments, when doubts arise, unbidden.

KORZECKI: What's stopping you?

STEFAN: *(Settling into the armchair and looking at the ceiling, measuredly, as if bored)* Difficult to say. Sign of the times, perhaps, that all things, even the best, dissolve in melancholic vapour. Each passing moment, bittersweet. Who can be sure, it's not the onset of winter? To love each moment is a blessing and a curse. On late spring afternoons, rose petals seem made of light, translucent crepe, a fragile premonition of November clouds. Country life in November! Every day inspect the farms, drag yourself through fields with your gun and dog, through woods and ditches, repetitive and somewhat dull.

KORZECKI: *(Cajoling)* Even chickens get unhappy in their barn.

STEFAN: Even you would get fed up in an empty old country house.

KORZECKI: People it with guests. You've lots of neighbours. *(With a sparkling glance)* Gatherings, suppers, card tables, wine …

STEFAN: It happens. Not always entertaining. And troublesome.

KORZECKI: Honestly?

STEFAN: My housekeeper, formerly my nurse, has died – the owner made her mistress of the house – and no replacement can be found. I'm at my wits end.

KORZECKI: *(Sympathetically)* That shouldn't be difficult at your age. The house will burst into life when a young, grateful person moves in. Hymen's torch will be lit.

STEFAN: Lots of people get their fingers burnt.

KORZECKI: Exceptions do not prove the rule. What could be lovelier than joining sweetness with affluence?

STEFAN: Complex task, best left to others.

KORZECKI: Self-denial? Why? Life will be generous and may even bless you. Youth and solitude are sorry bedfellows. There's no surprise. Thirty year old men aren't made to be hermits. Look around, reach out, that's all. *(Meaningfully)* Sometimes you don't realize that joy has brushed your elbow. Before donning love's blindfold, youth should open wide its eyes.

STEFAN: *(Rising)* You exalt the golden handcuffs, I see.

KORZECKI: Freedom isn't always best.

STEFAN:	Sometimes that's not very obvious.
KORZECKI:	You can always change your mind at the last minute. Your watch … yes … Julja is rather slow …
STEFAN:	*(Hiding his watch)* Oh no, just habit.
KORZECKI:	Any minute … now … Returning to our conversation …
STEFAN:	*(Taking out his cigarette case)* Do you smoke? *(He offers)*
KORZECKI:	*(Accepting)* Oh thank you … *(Sniffing)* Lovely … *(Lights it)* There you are.
STEFAN:	*(Declining)* Thanks … not now …
KORZECKI:	But returning to our conversation … I, for example … married young … and now after many years, please believe me, if I regret anything, it's that I didn't do it sooner …
STEFAN:	*(Approaching the wall)* Beautiful painting … very beautiful … garden at dawn …
KORZECKI:	Yes, a garden … Wasted years, all alone … a travesty …
STEFAN:	*(Looking closely at the painting)* A garden at dawn, or dusk? Couldn't say for sure … How odd. Living close to nature, you'd think I could tell. But I can't distinguish … Sometimes painters treat light in a very ambiguous way, don't you think?
KORZECKI:	Yes … a little ambiguous … you're right … what I mean is …
STEFAN:	Because apart from that it's a very good picture … lots of charm … atmosphere, poetry … Art's all about poetry, of course …
KORZECKI:	Yes, in life as in art …. what is life without poetry? And as I say the poetry of life is …
STEFAN:	Do you know the painter's name? Sadly I can't see a signature.
KORZECKI:	Signature? … No … no … I don't know … It's a picture … Nothing special …
STEFAN:	*(Gesturing towards the door)* I can hear footsteps I think on the stairs …
KORZECKI:	Yes … Julja. *(JULJA enters through the upstage door)*

Scene Eight

KORZECKI, STEFAN, JULJA

JULJA:	Sorry I asked you to wait. Good evening *(She gives STEFAN her hand)*
STEFAN:	The sight of you looking well is my reward.
KORZECKI:	I tried to keep him entertained. I won't disturb you *(Exits)*

All the Same (1912)

Scene Nine

STEFAN, JULJA

STEFAN:	Three days we haven't seen each other – it's been like three centuries.
JULJA:	So keen to learn? I'd no idea you'd prove such a diligent pupil.
STEFAN:	Have I ever missed a lesson?
JULJA:	You're right. The hardship. A long journey from the country.
STEFAN:	Barely two miles.
JULJA:	If it wasn't for the town: theatre, music, I might believe I'd instilled a love of learning.
STEFAN:	Truly, you have. A model pupil, I think.
JULJA:	For sure. And yet …
STEFAN:	You have concerns?
JULJA:	I don't know.
STEFAN:	Then why the note of caution?
JULJA:	*(Seriously)* Alright. Perhaps I should raise it.
STEFAN:	Why the serious tone, almost stern?
JULJA:	I need to touch on a certain issue …
STEFAN:	What do you mean?
JULJA:	It requires explanation.
STEFAN:	Have I done something wrong?
JULJA:	Maybe.
STEFAN:	You're frightening me.
JULJA:	*(Troubled)* I am? The matter's more peculiar, really.
STEFAN:	Peculiar?
JULJA:	*(Trying to stay positive)* It even seems quite amusing, sometimes.
STEFAN:	Amusing as well?
JULJA:	Of course. All of a sudden a grown man is overcome with enthusiasm for learning a language in which he's had no interest. He regularly saddles his horses, rain or shine, and makes a long journey into town, for lessons. Is not this urge peculiar? What will you gain by learning a language? Are you planning a trip to England?
STEFAN:	I dislike travel.
JULJA:	Are you thinking of studying English literature?
STEFAN:	No, native literature is enough for me.
JULJA:	A hobby, then?
STEFAN:	Not quite.

JULJA:	That doesn't tell me much.
STEFAN:	Don't you believe in learning for its own sake?
JULJA:	Not in your case. I think you're someone who acts with clearly defined purpose. Really I shouldn't be asking. I'm a teacher and I teach whoever answers the ad. That ought to be enough. Though admittedly I've been wondering …
STEFAN:	We may have moved beyond that so the conversation could be pointless.
JULJA:	How do you mean?
STEFAN:	We've become friends. Isn't that right?
JULJA:	Yes.
STEFAN:	Close friends?
JULJA:	I don't know how it happened, but yes.
STEFAN:	So, even if my original reasons don't pass muster, we can now see and speak to each other because we're friends.
JULJA:	The student/teacher relationship as a trial ground for friendship?
STEFAN:	If it were?
JULJA:	*(Determinedly)* Lessons, as a pretext, would have to stop.
STEFAN:	My punishment?
JULJA:	This does affect me you know and I'm offended.
STEFAN:	As a teacher. Doesn't my friend forgive?
JULJA:	You think she can?
STEFAN:	She must. The grace of friendship, that's all I ask. Shouldn't it pass its first test?
JULJA:	Was this in your initial plan?
STEFAN:	If I say yes?
JULJA:	You'll admit to a ruse I've already forgiven.
STEFAN:	Has the plan worked?
JULJA:	I'm angry but I forgive you – the best possible proof.
STEFAN:	In that case, mutual friendship.
JULJA:	And the teacher who fell for it all?
STEFAN:	You don't need a foreign language to find words of friendship.
JULJA:	So let us speak the language of friendship. Heart to heart.
STEFAN:	Openly and without constraints.
JULJA:	So the lessons were a decoy.
STEFAN:	A ruse you've already forgiven.
JULJA:	What took you there?
STEFAN:	How to say this.
JULJA:	Clearly.
STEFAN:	Will you pick faults?

All the Same (1912)

JULJA: As long as we remain outside the shadow of deception.
STEFAN: Doesn't bright light make soft contours seem excessively sharp?
JULJA: It also eliminates ambiguity. That's all I'm afraid of. Light sanctifies even the darkest things. My courage shrinks away in darkness, it even goes blind.
STEFAN: Light is also blinding.
JULJA: Being dazzled by the sun is better than not seeing in the dark.
STEFAN: Are you a sun worshipper?
JULJA: A lover of clarity. And so, what took you there?
STEFAN: Basically, sympathy. I met you at my relatives' several times, I felt the need to get closer. It took a long time. I looked out for you; I'd see you in the street, but always from afar.
JULJA: No coincidence, your apartment here?
STEFAN: Partly, yes. It could have been taken. But its proximity made all the difference. The mere thought of living close to you …
JULJA: As for the tuition …
STEFAN: Can I tell you everything?
JULJA: You absolutely must. For honesty's sake.
STEFAN: Won't I regret being honest?
JULJA: Friendship requires it.
STEFAN: I count on friendship.
JULJA: Yes, and so the tuition …
STEFAN: As someone who doesn't live with his child's mother …
JULJA: Wife.
STEFAN: As a man who is attached, which you knew about …
JULJA: Yes …
STEFAN: My ability to visit you at home was hampered by the fact that we aren't closely acquainted …
JULJA: I understand – nor is this a formally managed household.
STEFAN: A relative of mine, praising your personal qualities, was struck by your talent as a teacher. She waxed lyrical about the progress of her daughters. That's when I seized upon the plan. It was my first clumsy step …
JULJA: I didn't think it was clumsy. Instinctive, I believed.
STEFAN: I was terribly grateful to you for not spotting my pathetic strategy, or rather for the generosity, which you at once showed me.
JULJA: I have never concealed that nor will I. You took me in. I decided you're a good man. That's perhaps why I suspected nothing.
STEFAN: Thank you. If we didn't live in a world of accepted forms, prejudgements, what could be simpler, than saying 'We feel a sympathy towards each other, we won't deny ourselves the joy of

	occasional meeting.' Today it seems straightforward, natural. Your experience may be different, of course.
JULJA:	Indeed.
STEFAN:	And rightly so. That's probably best ... *(JULJA is silent; STEFAN at once more freely)* You've no idea how I treasure this friendship. I couldn't do without it now. The thought of its loss frightens me. *(With increasing warmth)* These brief moments spent in your company are all I really count as living. I long for them, they please me. In the emptiness of my days, the silence of my lonely house, closed even to my friends, so that none can disturb my silent thoughts of you, I live with memories, of your face, and a hundred echoes of your voice.
JULJA:	I believe your feelings are sincere. I want to be honest as well. I don't know, I'm no longer sure, but I think I sensed, guessed your friendship, straight away. It was dear to me.
STEFAN:	This makes me very happy.
JULJA:	I needed friendship. So very much! I don't complain about my life, I bear it. But I felt this strange void, loneliness. It may surprise you, when I have parents. But that's how it is. I can admit it, to a friend. I love them. And yet, perhaps our differing views, ways of thinking, the atmosphere in which they and I grew up, something divides us.
STEFAN:	They don't understand you.
JULJA:	I may be at fault, unable to fully understand. But the fact is, there's poor communication. And sometimes I get so irritated ... No, no I shouldn't feel or think like that ...
STEFAN:	Tell me everything that's on your mind.
JULJA:	Something's pressing on me, wearing me down. It seems so close in here, sometimes, and dark ... it repels me ... then I feel ungrateful ... a bad daughter, because of these emotions ... it gnaws away, suffocates, I don't know ...
STEFAN:	You're not well ...
JULJA:	The walls appear cold, and the view through that window onto the courtyard, too grey for an entire lifetime. Surely it's not a curse? But why? Whose crime? It's sad that I'm sentenced to nothing, for no reason.
STEFAN:	You bear so much sadness and keep silent ...
JULJA:	Sometimes, not always. I control myself. I know how to suppress it. I don't give in, I fight. And yet ...
STEFAN:	Your lips speak of desire ...
JULJA:	Desire?

All the Same (1912)

STEFAN:	A dream of happiness …
JULJA:	*(With a sad smile)* Oh, happiness! Who dreams of that! A golden bird far beyond reach. It dwells in distant skies.
STEFAN:	In our hearts. It lives and sings. Listen to your heart and perhaps it will tell you …
JULJA:	What?
STEFAN:	*(Quietly)* Of my love.
JULJA:	*(Fearfully)* No! Don't say that word! It frightens me. Its sound, an echo. Whispered, it resounds too loudly in my empty life.
STEFAN:	The word I uttered and the feeling that inspired it are both true.
JULJA:	I don't want to hear, it frightens me. *(Pleadingly)* Stay as my friend, just a loyal friend …
STEFAN:	That word is dearer to me than life, than the whole world. Believe in it, say you do.
JULJA:	Only those at liberty can speak it.
STEFAN:	*(Bowing his head, in a hollow voice)* No, I'm not free. *(After a while)* But all the same I love you.
JULJA:	*(Rising)* I can't listen. I feel like a thief, stealing from another woman …
STEFAN:	Those bonds were severed long ago, for good.
JULJA:	Conventionally that's not possible …
STEFAN:	A noose around my neck. I tried hard to regain my freedom, no stone was left unturned. Today, I must admit, I've failed.
JULJA:	*(In a hollow voice)* I knew it.
STEFAN:	I can never call you my wife. I must be open. But I'm here, in the light, as you wanted. I've never denied it, a woman stands between us – legally my wife – nor do I wish to deny my love. Don't tell me to hide my feelings. Let's stand together in sadness and sincerity, looking truth in the eye …
JULJA:	*(Aghast)* The truth …
STEFAN:	Yes. It's inescapable now.
JULJA:	Why think about it, why!
STEFAN:	You mean ignore it, shrink away, say it's quite usual? Or does that frighten you as well?
JULJA:	Perhaps, yes …
STEFAN:	We are the unlucky exception, we should therefore prove the rule?
JULJA:	We must both forget …
STEFAN:	That's impossible. For me, forgetting would be a hundred times worse than suffering for my love.
JULJA:	There's no other way!

STEFAN:	Julja, if I were free, I would ask for your hand in marriage. Would you turn me down?
JULJA:	No.
STEFAN:	Do you love me?
JULJA:	Don't ask, in our position.
STEFAN:	But if that were the case, would you love me?
JULJA:	Yes.
STEFAN:	And so the obstacle is greater than your love?
JULJA:	We should suppress it.
STEFAN:	So we must kill memory, thought, spirit!
JULJA:	We must accept our lot.
STEFAN:	The world is against us. Will we stand against each other too? (*JULJA is silent*) Julja, this is about our lives, not acts of contrition performed for those who will judge us. Should we really play it by the book! We meet, it's an opportunity for happiness, the miracle of life, everything! One life each to spare, that's all! For the sake of happiness, we should reach out ...
JULJA:	Yield to a greater power ...
STEFAN:	Rejection, why? Nothing more serious than life itself! Rules – surely not? They serve lack and suppression. A dead system wants to crush us, the living. Something, not us, decides about us, blind and cruel ...
JULJA:	*(In a whisper)* Cruel, very cruel ...
STEFAN:	Is the world, to which we are oblivious, which doesn't know us or see us, dearer to you than life? By what right should the world, which will give us nothing, pronounce a verdict more terrible than exile – eternal misery, eternal solitude? To deny oneself ... at what cost? Annihilation?
JULJA:	It is true, true, true. My rebellious spirit. But what can I do?
STEFAN:	Love and live! Just think – in our final moments, we'll look back at this irrevocable waste of life ... Overwhelmed by sorrow and sadness. Too late then to curse the fact that we actually willed it ...
JULJA:	We do not will it, no! I want happiness, I summon it, long for it!
STEFAN:	The world can judge, but we can love. Are you afraid of offending opinion? Sacrifice two souls, united, to idle gossip? Must other people's rules determine our emotions?
JULJA:	To stand against everything, alone. But still ...
STEFAN:	The world will still be here. Others will pass through, but not us. A thousand happy people. We have each other for a short time and nothing, nothing, nothing ...
JULJA:	Run towards the void.

STEFAN:	Fear death and die? Become a coward through fear of cowardice?
JULJA:	*(With despairing passion)* I know neither fear nor cowardice. I am myself. Alive. The flame burns within me, sacred, good and beautiful. Love is truth, I hear the voice of profound yearning, of life itself. My thoughts are pure, my desire is pure, my heart is pure because that is brave and true.
STEFAN:	And you don't want to love?
JULJA:	I want to love! I do love!
STEFAN:	Julja! *(Kisses her; long moment of forgetfulness)*
JULJA:	*(Tearing herself free of his embrace)* Let go! Enough! Enough!
STEFAN:	Now there is nothing but you.
JULJA:	Yes, yes … My head is spinning …
STEFAN:	Be mine, Julja!
JULJA:	Leave me alone. I need to collect my thoughts … Leave me alone now.
STEFAN:	Please … do you love me?
JULJA:	Yes … Go now … *(Whispering)* Then … later …
STEFAN:	*(Kisses her in a lengthy, tight embrace)* I am waiting … *(Retreating towards the door)* This evening … *(Exits)*
JULJA:	*(Reaches out her arms towards him)* This evening …

Scene Ten

JULJA, KORZECKI, KORZECKA

JULJA:	*(Alone, stands stock still for a while, then pushes her shoulders back in a gesture of despairing boldness. She collects herself. She goes towards her parents' door, opens it and says in a transformed voice)* The room is free.
KORZECKI:	*(Entering)* I talked to him today. I was rather disappointed. Tricky customer. But everything depends on you.
JULJA:	*(With newly discovered, bold openness)* He isn't free, father …
KORZECKI:	*(Backing away)* What? Isn't free? Isn't … *(Falling into a chair)*
JULJA:	Ask the caretaker to bring up some tea. *(Moves towards the door)*
KORZECKA:	*(Who has entered at her words)* You won't take tea with us?
JULJA:	*(Numbly)* Today, no … I can't … *(She exits left)*
KORZECKI:	*(Angrily to his wife)* Ask the caretaker to fetch the tea … Extraordinary …
KORZECKA:	What now?
KORZECKI:	*(Sits at the table)* Now I'm taking charge. Pen, paper, envelope …

KORZECKA:	*(Shaking her head)* You, taking charge …
KORZECKI:	I said so … That's that. *(Writes; curtain falls)*

Act 2

The same room as in Act 1. Afternoon.

Scene One

KORZECKI, KORZECKA

KORZECKA *is sitting by the table.*

KORZECKI:	*(Walking rapidly about the room)* I can't believe it, unheard of! Strike me down. Anyone would think there's a conspiracy …
KORZECKA:	Don't exaggerate. What's it to us?
KORZECKI:	What do you mean what's it to us? Inspired question! Can't count on anything … Or nurture the smallest hope, make plans! Barely touch a thing, over it topples, pile of dust. Every intention, cursed. Nothing works out!
KORZECKA:	But it's someone else's problem, not ours. Too few of your own worries?
KORZECKI:	Someone else's problem? Not true, no! The whole thing, like clockwork when suddenly … It won't go in … Married … married … he's married … And now, do what you like. All the plans are ruined.
KORZECKA:	Your plans, no one else's …
KORZECKI:	You're so pathetic you are – you're blind … Look at Julja … I knew it was something bad, I could smell it … you could see it in her for a long time, say what you like … she's not been herself … Ho, ho, I'm an old bird … I can spot poor grain …
KORZECKA:	Julja wouldn't dream of it …
KORZECKI:	Don't give me that … What about dinner today, when she told us he'd not been able to divorce, she's completely altered … Strike me down.
KORZECKA:	You imagined it …
KORZECKI:	Don't even try … She was white as a sheet. Did she complain of a headache?
KORZECKA:	She often has headaches …

All the Same (1912)

KORZECKI:	And why now? Why keep it from us that he's married?
KORZECKA:	Because no one asked her. Because she's not remotely bothered. Because she doesn't get mixed up in other people's affairs.
KORZECKI:	You know why? She was hoping things would come right, with the divorce. She waited for the outcome, saying nothing – in the house of a condemned man, don't mention the noose. She waited for that noose to be removed. But now, when hope has gone …
KORZECKA:	All in your head!
KORZECKI:	*(Lights a cigar)* And her tone! Did you hear?
KORZECKA:	What do you mean tone? Her usual.
KORZECKI:	Wrong, unusual! Loud – she never speaks like that. Too loud, determined, as if she didn't care. The way you do when you want to hide your feelings. She wasn't born yesterday …
KORZECKA:	Give it a rest! Even if. It's happened. There's nothing more to say. We can't change anything now.
KORZECKI:	Woe is me, let's give up, like an old crone … This is a wealthy man with a secure income … He likes her. I know it. It was practically arranged, when suddenly, catastrophe. I can't settle. Still, there's enough to go on …
KORZECKA:	*(Quivering)* You'll grant a divorce?
KORZECKI:	Idiot. Missed opportunities! Hope was peeking through the cracks and now – back to square one, this hole, this lack, this … *(Suddenly kicking the table)* … endless bloody madness … *(Rising suddenly)* Old woman!
KORZECKA:	What now!
KORZECKI:	Listen, what do you think? It's more your field. How respectable … is there anything wrong … household manager.
KORZECKA:	What do you mean … manager?
KORZECKI:	Well, housekeeper, keeper of the keys … status, responsibility.
KORZECKA:	Status! What status! A servant, an ordinary, simple servant!
KORZECKI:	Wait – a servant! Simple, ordinary servant! What's the problem? We're all servants. One person serves another; the lower serves the higher, the higher the highest. Ministers, dignitaries, they're all servants. Of the people. Even a king serves his country.
KORZECKA:	Oh a king, some dignitary and a housekeeper. Useful comparison!
KORZECKI:	You don't like the name. That's what it comes down to for women. Titles, etiquette, appearance. Never the essential. Let's just suppose – keeper of the keys, household manager. Even well-born women from impoverished households do those jobs … come across them quite often …

KORZECKA:	Keys, manager – all the same, of course … almost.
KORZECKI:	Almost, yes … That means a lot … Like – look at this – turn it over – upside down – half empty, half full … Your point of view, it depends, everything depends …
KORZECKA:	Of course.
KORZECKI:	Right, so tell me … What's the way … so, you for example, would you become a housekeeper?
KORZECKA:	(Rises) What? Me a housekeeper? How could you even think it? Me a housekeeper!
KORZECKI:	Alright – keeper of the keys.
KORZECKA:	Have you gone mad? Me? Dear man, I wasn't born or raised for that. You offend me.
KORZECKI:	I wasn't born to smoke cheap gross cigars. No choice.
KORZECKA:	You …
KORZECKI:	Yes, an inferior being. Indeed. And this rotten hole is better than …
KORZECKA:	Dear man, it's not for you to decide what's best for me. I know what I owe to myself …
KORZECKI:	I'm also indebted to other people.
KORZECKA:	That's your own fault.
KORZECKI:	Mine!
KORZECKA:	Yes! And for you, I'm expected … unbelievable … a housekeeper!
KORZECKI:	Outdated superstition, don't you see? Scorned by modern, progressive society. Jula would not be ashamed – you listen – being a housekeeper. I say she'd have no shame. She knows a thing or two about what's acceptable … She just wouldn't. I'm telling you. No job is demeaning. Poverty breeds poverty. We deserve something in our old age. Our love and gratitude would be her reward …
KORZECKA:	But a housekeeper! Dear man, it's beyond me, I fail to comprehend, how someone can … sink so very low …
KORZECKI:	(Impatiently) Something must be done! We can't sit here with folded arms. Manna won't just fall from heaven. We need action!
KORZECKA:	You work up these demeaning projects …
KORZECKI:	(With passion) Eat butterfly steak, rose petal salad, drink champagne of morning dew! Old romantic!
KORZECKA:	You foolish, soulless man! You lecture me? You? …
KORZECKI:	(Covering his ears) Don't shout, don't groan, don't lament.
KORZECKA:	Unworthy man, you dare to lecture me!
KORZECKI:	Shush, it's quite alright … (STANISŁAW enters through the door on the right and stands in the doorway)

All the Same (1912)

Scene Two

KORZECKI, KORZECKA, STANISŁAW

STANISŁAW:	Could you please keep the noise down?
KORZECKA:	*(To KORZECKI)* You're not worthy to live beneath the same roof as people like me and Jula …
KORZECKI:	Alright, alright. Unleashed her tongue …
KORZECKA:	Tongue! I've unleashed my tongue! The expression! What bad manners!
STANISŁAW:	I don't want to get involved. Just asking for quiet. Can't take a nap, get some rest from work.
KORZECKI:	It's not night time yet for sleeping.
STANISŁAW:	The day time isn't necessarily for shouting either.
KORZECKA:	*(Suffering offence)* Housekeeper! Me a housekeeper! Jula should become a housekeeper! That man has no trace of respectability … And to mock …
KORZECKI:	Alright you're not a bird brain … go on then, off you go.
KORZECKA:	Jula a housekeeper! *(Exits)*

Scene Three

KORZECKI, STANISŁAW

KORZECKI:	That woman. I despair.
STANISŁAW:	What housekeeper? Why Julja?
KORZECKI:	Housekeeper? Keeper of the keys, I said.
STANISŁAW:	Jula? How? What?
KORZECKI:	*(Evasively)* Oh nothing, nothing at all. A project, plan, a thought.
STANISŁAW:	What's this to do with Julja?
KORZECKI:	Nothing, absolutely nothing. Anyway, you're a sensible man. Work isn't demeaning. Go on tell me, what's wrong with it – household manager.
STANISŁAW:	Wrong with it?
KORZECKI:	You know.
STANISŁAW:	But whose? Where?
KORZECKI:	Nowhere, I said. Theoretically.
STANISŁAW:	*(Carefully)* A plan?
KORZECKI:	Oh sort of.
STANISŁAW:	Castle in the air, or on the moon?

KORZECKI:	Well, alright, a household. Lots of them around.
STANISŁAW:	Not all need a housekeeper …
KORZECKI:	*(Pats him on the shoulder, smiling)* Of course, not all. But an affluent household, established …
STANISŁAW:	*(Looking at him with gravity)* Of course, not a bad idea …
KORZECKI:	*(Livening up)* Don't you think?
STANISŁAW:	*(Strategically)* Excellent, even. And who will it be? Your wife?
KORZECKI:	What? That swollen blister?
STANISŁAW:	*(Slowly)* Julja, then?
KORZECKI:	Actually nothing's certain yet.
STANISŁAW:	But it is Julja. Good idea.
KORZECKI:	You admit it? I've got my head screwed on. You're a thinking man. Such opportunities are rare.
STANISŁAW:	Something's come up, then? An advertisement?
KORZECKI	Advertisement? Oh no. Not yet. Problems with proposing the idea …
STANISŁAW:	Julja wants to propose it?
KORZECKI:	Not at all.
STANISŁAW:	Who thought of it then?
KORZECKI:	*(Evasively)* Just came to me.
STANISŁAW:	*(Admiringly)* Would you look at that.
KORZECKI:	Well, you see.
STANISŁAW:	If it really is an affluent household …
KORZECKI:	Of course.
STANISŁAW:	Whose, though?
KORZECKI:	*(Vacillating)* Well, I …
STANISŁAW:	Go on, whose?
KORZECKI:	Dear boy, you object to people. You've really no grounds.
STANISŁAW:	Object? I know this person?
KORZECKI:	*(Cornered)* Yes, you do …
STANISŁAW:	*(Testing)* Could it be …
KORZECKI:	*(Talking him down)* You did agree that in principle it's a good idea.
STANISŁAW:	That's right. But to whom do I object?
KORZECKI:	Perhaps you don't, I may have misunderstood. So much the better. Because he's actually a fine man, faultless.
STANISŁAW:	Him?
KORZECKI:	Yes, him.
STANISŁAW:	The pupil?
KORZECKI:	That's right.
STANISŁAW:	Julja's supposed to be managing his household?

All the Same (1912)

KORZECKI:	Still in the planning stages.
STANISŁAW:	Your planning stages …
KORZECKI:	*(Reluctantly)* Well … yes … mine …
STANISŁAW:	I see.
KORZECKI:	*(Defending himself)* Nothing wrong with it.
STANISŁAW:	Is she the right age, though, to act as housekeeper for a young, rich, handsome man?
KORZECKI:	Oh, age is no object …
STANISŁAW:	And isn't she too pretty …
KORZECKI:	Dear boy …
STANISŁAW:	I'm casting no aspersions on Julja. The devil, however, does not sleep.
KORZECKI:	One shouldn't assume the worst.
STANISŁAW:	Just a little of the best … You might like to consider …
KORZECKI:	Dear boy. I know her. She's not that sort …
STANISŁAW:	I don't doubt Julja, only the plan.
KORZECKI:	*(Horrified)* As if I would! *(With a broad smile)* You can't buy virtue.
STANISŁAW:	And I suppose you would defend her honour should it …
KORZECKI:	Me!
STANISŁAW:	Blood is thicker than water!
KORZECKI:	He has principles. Besides, no progress yet. Pie in the sky.
STANISŁAW:	Leave it there. That's what I think. I've one point to make. Don't give up your day job – forgery. Killing two birds, with one stone – bad idea. Spoken from the heart, old man. In the end, signatures are far less risky …
KORZECKI:	Than what?
STANISŁAW:	Than the other … you stick with your forgery. To that, I can turn a blind eye *(Slowly)* But the other, that's more dangerous …
KORZECKI:	Spare your threats, dear boy.
STANISŁAW:	*(Quietly)* Stay away from Julja …
KORZECKI:	Her protector! By what right?
STANISŁAW:	I may have one.
KORZECKI:	None whatsoever.
STANISŁAW:	You're in the palm of my hand. Here you sit, on my finger. I bend it, you fall. Wouldn't want that, though I dislike old men. The wily, gifted ones should be kept close. Let's stick with calligraphy, old man … that's best …
KORZECKI:	I resent your tone, I … *(Knocking is heard on the door)*
STANISŁAW:	*(With undisturbed calmness)* There's someone at the door … keep your mind focused … *(Emphatically)* … on Stanisław Stopa's

mantra. Open the door and don't disturb me with any more housekeepers. *(Exits right to his room;* KORZECKI *opens the door; enter* STEFAN*)*

Scene Four

KORZECKI, STEFAN

KORZECKI:	*(Bowing)* Please, come in.
STEFAN:	*(In the doorway, not removing his coat, not setting his hat or his cane aside)* An opportune moment … Julja's not back …
KORZECKI:	No, that's right.
STEFAN:	*(Locking the door)* Very good …
KORZECKI:	Hence my suggestion, the time. I trust my letter didn't surprise you?
STEFAN:	*(With cold calmness)* Its contents, no. Your penetration, yes.
KORZECKI:	*(With a forced smile)* Mm … eyes are made for seeing … my missive shouldn't offend you. Father's duty, that's all … You'll admit that Julja's a refined girl, and refinement, though rare, is the sister of gullibility. Not frivolity, mind. I know my daughter. Good hearts trust easily. Besides, I haven't pried or pressed. I only know what I saw, with my own eyes. No accusations …
STEFAN:	You mentioned options …
KORZECKI:	No accusations; merely a word of caution. My responsibility, that's all. It must be stressed, Julja is independent, self-sufficient. I appealed to your dignity. That will suffice. I have complete faith in you; this alone reassures me …
STEFAN:	*(Coldly)* How very flattering ….
KORZECKI:	One more thing. I care only for my child's peace of mind, you see. I have made suppositions, but expressed them openly, as befits a man of character. I respect matters of the heart, which I know cannot be commanded. It is no slave.
STEFAN:	*(Drily)* That's right. I'm not indifferent to your daughter.
KORZECKI:	Well quite. I don't doubt your intentions. God forbid! But I know that lusty youth can get carried away. Hence my appeal …
STEFAN:	*(Sitting)* I must admit that your letter had a rather unpleasant effect. You've used certain words, which, in light of my feelings, are not entirely appropriate. But I'll ignore that and focus on the content.

All the Same (1912)

KORZECKI: Certain things don't come across on paper, like tone. But still it can smooth the way … That's why I preferred that route, more discrete and clear – to avoid misunderstanding …

STEFAN: That's not the point. I might have preferred to go about things alone, responding in a manner I see fit. Never mind. Well, please be assured my feelings are sincere …

KORZECKI: I am not a man who clings to suspicion. I understand that feelings can be entirely sincere, despite certain obstacles …

STEFAN: Which I've been unable to remove …

KORZECKI: So isn't Julja in danger of getting hurt, swept away by emotions that, as already noted, I only suspect, on both your parts …

STEFAN: We're moving off the subject again …

KORZECKI: I don't wish to appear …

STEFAN: In which case let's focus on the issue, not on suspicion. The letter presents a clear rationale for your pre-emptive strike – your expression – 'just in case'. I don't care to bargain for your blessing; I must admit I would have preferred to meet with disapproval.

KORZECKI: What will be, will be, that's my belief – over-sensitivity can disrupt the outcome.

STEFAN: I suppose your frankness does allow me to speak with relative directness.

KORZECKI: It's about boundaries. I wrote in case things went any further … which they haven't, yet.

STEFAN: *(Somewhat impatiently)* I don't say yes or no. Let's stick strictly to the contents of your letter.

KORZECKI: I should really have the right to appeal for clarity …

STEFAN: In the letter you didn't press for a direct response.

KORZECKI: What could be simpler, than to deny it?

STEFAN: You may have a point.

KORZECKI: My hope rests in you …

STEFAN: I wouldn't want that responsibility. Certainty has its limits …

KORZECKI: But my daughter's peace of mind …

STEFAN: How do you plan to ensure it?

KORZECKI: Difficult to say. It must be considered, I'm her father.

STEFAN: Are you implying that I should stop coming here?

KORZECKI: *(Animatedly)* Oh no. As a student you have certain rights …

STEFAN: And Julja, what does she think? You said she's her own mistress – fiercely guards her freedom. Should she be so inclined, her independence of mind …

KORZECKI: I was talking about the effects of gullibility and sincere emotion combined.

STEFAN: I wouldn't like to throw Julja's emotions into the mix. Will you not trust my sincerity and sense of obligation? That I won't harm Julja, or do anything unless she desires it, and beyond that take responsibility for any consequences, so that she can hold nothing against me. Trust that, in these circumstances, it really would be the best outcome for her and her dearest.

KORZECKI: Yes. One should proceed rationally, sensitive to close bonds, even at risk of appearing calculating.

STEFAN: Hence our meeting. And in reply to your letter just for now accept my assurance that I have no intention of treating this matter lightly, quite the contrary …

KORZECKI: I never doubted that.

STEFAN: Though I may have preferred to go about it in a less disconcerting way. Your letter outlines your difficult circumstances.

KORZECKI: Well you couldn't really call them easy.

STEFAN: May I offer a form of assistance? *(He hands him a cheque)* A cheque.

KORZECKI: I'm in no position to refuse *(He takes it)* Sincere thanks … *(Quickly)* May I take this opportunity to reclaim my letter?

STEFAN: *(Handing him the letter)* Here it is …

KORZECKI: Once again, sincere thanks. I'm in your debt. Don't misunderstand me, please. I accept only because I know it's graciously offered, and no harm done. I trust you and you know I'm forward looking. My opinions differ, even from my wife's. She's terribly superstitious. Even looks down on certain forms of work. Well, when I mentioned, that to make things easier, Julja could become a housekeeper – after you and I spoke, I had this thought – she violently objected. Though Julja begs to differ, I'm sure.

STEFAN: Ah? You think so?

KORZECKI: No question – after you and I spoke I had this thought. No need to exalt Julja. In better times she received a rounded education – housekeeping included.

STEFAN: You're certain Julja would agree?

KORZECKI: All depends on presentation. Her decision will be final. She's free to act. I restrict no one. I respect emotional freedom. *(STEFAN with a hollow silence stops KORZECKI, quickly approaches the door, unlocks it, and at once returns to his former place. After a moment's silence, enter JULJA)*

Scene Five

STEFAN, JULJA, KORZECKI

JULJA:	Oh, sir, it's you. *(STEFAN bows)* Father, I brought the evening paper.
KORZECKI:	You remembered. That's nice. Thank you. I'll go and catch up on the news. My respects. *(Exits)*

Scene Six

STEFAN, JULJA

JULJA:	*(In a quiet, lightly trembling voice)* I'm glad you've come …
STEFAN:	You're very pale.
JULJA:	Pale? *(In a quick whisper)* Uneasy, I'm pursued by doubts. I couldn't settle. But it's alright now …
STEFAN:	Calm down … trust me …
JULJA:	*(Trying to smile)* Now I am calm, I trust you. Can't you see I'm steady?
STEFAN:	Do you believe in my love?
JULJA:	Yes … How could I not?
STEFAN:	I won't let you down. I'll remain as you saw me, in that first moment.
JULJA:	I know that, my dear.
STEFAN:	Your hands are shaking … Your eyes are burning … Your heart beats so quickly …
JULJA:	It's nothing, really. Those feelings have passed. I'm in control now, completely …
STEFAN:	Sit here with me … you're tired …
JULJA:	No, no … it's alright … I'm quiet inside. Peace – the storm has passed; the lake's vast white surface is smooth … but it can't be suppressed … the feeling of humanity … vulnerability.
STEFAN:	Look at me …
JULJA:	You can see I'm at peace … I had these loud voices in my head: it happened! It happened! Like a bell ringing in my ears …
STEFAN:	Do you regret it?
JULJA:	*(Feverishly)* No. I regret nothing. I've no words for this joy. I'm sorry … it's strange to me still, unfamiliar …
STEFAN:	*(In a gentle voice)* Is the thought of our love not sweet to you? Are you not brimming with light and stillness?

JULJA:	*(Looking around fearfully)* I'll learn to feel that way, yes, but I can't collect myself just yet; I'm sleepwalking, different, unfamiliar.
STEFAN:	*(Takes her hands)* I understand your emotions. They translate into my own. I want to help you master them. I want you to be well, because the happiness that we longed for and created yesterday should not be overshadowed. Julja, be strong.
JULJA:	*(Disengages her hands, straightens up)* I am strong. How could I crush shame and foreboding otherwise? *(Passionately)* Not shame! I'm not ashamed of my heart, my blood, my passion! My soul feels pure, because my love is pure! I want to, I must, stand in the light. *(More quietly)* Our secret wearies me …
STEFAN:	*(Slowly, as though explaining)* Our situation makes it impossible to achieve both happiness and absolution at the same time. Haven't we behaved like genuine, sincere people?
JULJA:	*(With pride)* And free! I'm not cowering in the shadows any more. I struggled with myself. I suffered and fought for my own freedom. I stumbled beneath the weight of confused fear yet still I mastered that. I faced things both familiar and unknown.
STEFAN:	*(In joyous agreement)* Love has clarified everything.
JULJA:	*(Raises her palm to her brow and bows her head)* I don't mean that exactly. Only, we project our fears onto other people. *(Becoming impassioned)* The strictest rules! I've trampled underfoot, boldly rejected. Against one law I set another, my own. One life, that's all and I want happiness …
STEFAN:	*(As if wanting to stem her flow of words)* With my heart and soul I'll win your happiness. I'll devote my life to you, each hour …
JULJA:	My grief, hopelessness, struggle – they render my love more precious.
STEFAN:	*(Puts his arm around her and draws her closer)* How can I repay you? You've given me more than love. Your anxiety and tears. Your whole heart, your will. Your struggle with spectres that would strangle our joy in its cradle. *(With emphasis)* To me alone! Me!
JULJA:	One woman, maybe, in a thousand, has the courage to willingly crush her conditioning – follow her heart and overcome obstacles whose importance the world endorses. I have done so knowingly. I don't succumb blindly to suggestion, trickery, deception. I weighed everything up beforehand – all the gossip, mockery, the taunts, everything, that burns, like a slap across the face. All that I set against love …
STEFAN:	*(As though wanting to preempt her and break the flow of her words)* And you said, 'I'm yours' … Julja, this moment will last forever.

All the Same (1912)

JULJA:	I shook myself free! I strode towards happiness. I take pride in my courage. I can face anyone. I love you, there's my self-respect. I listened to my inner voice and aimed for the truth. Self-reliance, self-respect, truth. Whatever they say, I'm a proud and free woman. My love is beyond them, sacred – I neither seek nor need approval.
STEFAN:	*(Wanting through his acknowledgement to calm her)* Now it's my turn. My heart offered itself. It could not do otherwise. It rejoiced in your love without pain or struggle.
JULJA:	Now I have peace and strength. My joy was far too costly for fear and regret.
STEFAN:	When you smile again, no-one will be happier than I.
JULJA:	Now the final test: my family. But I'll survive. Nothing scares me any more. Away with secrets and lies, unworthy of my soul, my pride, our honesty! Oh, give me strength! Delaying may have been a big mistake; I've hidden love beneath a veil of shame. Now let the light be both within us and without.
STEFAN:	*(With light displeasure and discomfort)* Why bother with anyone else when we have each other?
JULJA:	I'm prepared, I'll withstand all accusations.
STEFAN:	*(Assertively)* We're not afraid of them. *(Persuasively)* But why should they be involved? Why spoil the broth?
JULJA:	I'll hurt my parents, I know that, but I won't back down. I've pledged my love and belong to you. I'll bear the heaviest blow, admit to everything. Risk my father's rage, my mother's curse, Stanisław's condemnation.
STEFAN:	Why hurt them? Isn't it better they know nothing? Must we be cruel to others?
JULJA:	Joy is not joy, when it's weighted with lies. I must tell them today.
STEFAN:	*(With concealed impatience)* What's the hurry? Isn't it best to let things evolve?
JULJA:	I must speak. I can't breathe the air of falsehood. Tell the world!
STEFAN:	*(Wishing to more directly lead her away from her intention)* Why is it anyone's business? We're free, aren't we? You said, 'I'm self-sufficient'. We can do what we like.
JULJA:	But of course.
STEFAN:	*(As above)* Should we tell everyone? Isn't that demeaning?
JULJA:	No-one can take away what's our's.
STEFAN:	Dear Julja. We'll spoil it. I'd rather not.
JULJA:	Why should I keep something secret when I'm not ashamed? Even the appearance of untruth pains me.

STEFAN:	*(Hurriedly searching for an answer)* Your free will is questionable if you can't live without the approval of others.
JULJA:	Or their condemnation.
STEFAN:	Even worse. Without others, that's the point …
JULJA:	Don't be afraid. Trust me. Their anger can't change me.
STEFAN:	But why make yourself vulnerable to something that can easily be avoided?
JULJA:	*(With wounded surprise)* I made myself vulnerable to personal difficulty, didn't I? I want to hold my head up.
STEFAN:	Keeping quiet is not a lie.
JULJA:	It's poor conscience, it's evasive.
STEFAN:	I want to spare you any unpleasantness, why broadcast it?
JULJA:	*(Looking at him seriously, as if she has seen something in him for the first time)* Stefan!
STEFAN:	*(Somewhat confused)* You mustn't think I …
JULJA:	*(As though wanting to forget something that's flashed through her mind)* I know it's about my peace of mind. Your concern motivates you. But you don't know me yet. I won't bend. It's through evasion that I deserve the world's contempt.
STEFAN:	The world knows nothing, nor does it need to know. What's the point of all this? Why draw attention to yourself? Listen: we live for each other, don't we … You love me, you're mine … We can be together, always … in my house.
JULJA:	That's precisely why I scorn deception. I want a life that's free.
STEFAN:	*(Hiding his irritation)* We should keep our own counsel. No need to press the creases. Calmly, quietly, no fuss. Being in the public gaze is not pleasant. We can find a way of life that doesn't change us, and won't offend others. Sometimes it's worth feeling those thorns. Certain forms should be preserved. Beyond that, people can say what they like.
JULJA:	*(Her fervour cooling)* Have I misunderstood? It's impossible.
STEFAN:	No it's not. We can actually put up a highly respectable front.
JULJA:	I find that disgusting!
STEFAN:	So not a front, then, if that's the problem. The honest truth.
JULJA:	*(Wiping her brow)* No! I wasn't mistaken … What do you mean?
STEFAN:	The management of my household. It can be arranged. Permit me to come to some agreement with your father.
JULJA:	You and my father?
STEFAN:	Really I wanted to ask if you'd talk to him. Not now. I wanted to obtain your agreement first …
JULJA:	*(Close to tears)* It's choking me, I have to say it!

All the Same (1912)

STEFAN:	Julja, don't do it. I beg you. I trust in your goodness, don't hurt them. What use would it be, to anyone? Be sensible. And your mother! Why? Even Stanisław, a complete stranger …
JULJA:	He's one of the family …
STEFAN:	Remember our love, our happiness.
JULJA:	*(Confused)* Yes, yes … your words shock me.
STEFAN:	Do you think I'm wrong? You know how much I love you, care for your well-being …
JULJA:	I know, I do … *(Looks at him with trepidation, moves closer)* Do I really know? *(Grasps his hands)* No! No!
STEFAN:	What's the matter?
JULJA:	*(Pleadingly)* Say it's not true, this whisper of a terrible thought!
STEFAN:	Julja! What is this?
JULJA:	That you could … *(She throws her arms around his neck and starts sobbing)* No, you cannot be … a liar!
STEFAN:	My darling! Sweetness! What a supposition!
JULJA:	*(Tearing herself away)* No, nothing, nothing … I'm confused, that's all … That's not why you want to hide it! It's my fear that saw deception, not my love!
STEFAN:	My lips will disperse these apparitions. *(Kissing her)* A bad dream, a bad dream.
JULJA:	*(Freeing herself)* Forgive me, please. Don't worry … Leave me alone.
STEFAN:	Calm your fears, abandon all reserve, but first of all collect yourself.
JULJA:	*(With uneasy stubbornness)* Now … Today. I must!
STEFAN:	*(Assertively)* Spare yourself and me … and them …
JULJA:	*(Giving him a sign to leave)* Yes … yes …
STEFAN:	*(Kissing her)* Good bye then. *(Leaves quietly)*
JULJA:	*(Stands for a while, looking ahead, confused. Then seizing her head in her hands, shocked whispering)* No! No! It's impossible!

Scene Seven

JULJA, KORZECKI

JULJA:	*(For a while as though wrestling with herself; then steps deliberately towards her parents' door and says quietly)* Excuse me, father.
KORZECKI:	What is it, child? *(Enters)*
JULJA:	I want to talk to you father.

KORZECKI:	*(Uneasily)* Talk to me?
JULJA:	Yes, and mother. But first to you … something important.
KORZECKI:	Go ahead …
JULJA:	Sit down …
KORZECKI:	So serious … What's happened?
JULJA:	Sit down, father … I've been speaking with Stefan …
KORZECKI:	I'm sitting, child, I'm sitting.
JULJA:	We are a family. Whatever touches one, touches all …
KORZECKI:	Yes, of course. What do you mean? There's nothing is there that could …
JULJA:	Listen, father. We all have our secrets …
KORZECKI:	Very true, my child. I'm all for respecting other people's privacy.
JULJA:	Often though it's not possible …
KORZECKI:	*(Patting his pocket)* Even when no ill can come of it?
JULJA:	It's not possible when others will feel the impact.
KORZECKI:	Child, why make that assumption! Not all secrets are ill-intentioned …
JULJA:	I'm glad you say so, father. You trust our family – that we won't do anything for the wrong reasons, or that will turn out badly.
KORZECKI:	My thoughts exactly …
JULJA:	But there are fronts. Something essentially pure can in the eyes of the world assume a different hue, be seen in a bad light.
KORZECKI:	Who cares about fronts! I am the first to scorn them, if my conscience is clear. And I swear I have a clear conscience.
JULJA:	Yes, father, desire is the true soul of action. Even the basest desire …
KORZECKI:	But when it's positive …
JULJA:	Yes, there's that, but no one has a window on our conscience. The world doesn't analyse our motivation. It judges and condemns on appearance.
KORZECKI:	It acts unjustly, child. Trust me.
JULJA:	That's different. This is there to stay. Sticks and stones do hurt us. The strong can resist pain by knowing that they acted in good conscience.
KORZECKI:	It ought to be enough. Our inner sense of …
JULJA:	I think so too.
KORZECKI:	For instance, all my own actions have flowed from the purest source, love for my family …
JULJA:	Allow me to interrupt you …
KORZECKI:	You're being honest about fronts, you're different, you understand …

All the Same (1912)

JULJA:	They're meaningless. That's why I don't want secrets ...
KORZECKI:	Really it's not important.
JULJA:	No father. You don't completely understand.
KORZECKI:	Everything will be fine.
JULJA:	But what if it's already happened?
KORZECKI:	What do you mean?
JULJA:	And not in the way you wanted ...
KORZECKI:	Has he told you something?
JULJA:	We talked a lot.
KORZECKI:	And he told you?
JULJA:	*(Rising)* There can be no secrets now.
KORZECKI:	Perfectly standard interpersonal matters. One shouldn't attach the slightest importance.
JULJA:	Father, if things had gone further than you'd imagined?
KORZECKI:	I can't see what. Nothing terrible, I assume. People live together, generously, have friendly relations. Support each other materially and morally, it's all the same ...
JULJA:	Your view of things makes it more difficult. I want to spare you, but you'll be upset. Maybe I'm not prepared for this.
KORZECKI:	I repeat it's not a crime.
JULJA:	Please. You know that Stefan and I have a close friendship.
KORZECKI:	That's why we treat him in a friendly way.
JULJA:	I won't hide the fact that I enjoy and need his company. Yes, father.
KORZECKI:	Child, wasn't that obvious?
JULJA:	The lessons were a front, though...
KORZECKI:	I know, I guessed.
JULJA:	You did?
KORZECKI:	I was pleased. Delighted, even.
JULJA:	Your dreams could never be fulfilled.
KORZECKI:	*(With a sigh)* Unfortunately, he's not free.
JULJA:	I knew about that father. I did. He told me himself, as soon as we met. Yet in spite of that my feelings grew, I couldn't stop them ...
KORZECKI:	Into something ...
JULJA:	A deeper emotion, father ...
KORZECKI:	*(With relief)* Is that all? That's it?
JULJA:	I've fallen in love, father.
KORZECKI:	Wasn't I right? Didn't I work it out?
JULJA:	You knew, father?
KORZECKI:	How could I not!

JULJA:	And respected my feeling? Understood? You thought I loved, without knowing … And now you know, there isn't anger in your eyes, you don't berate me?
KORZECKI:	Ah? And who is master of his heart? Am I made of stone? I have a heart, here in my breast, not a hole.
JULJA:	I'm so thankful that you've found these words. You understand a yearning heart. Before I reveal everything, let me say that I didn't expect such generosity. Now I regard my mistrust as a grievous fault. And sometimes, father, I yearned, how I yearned for words like this, from you.
KORZECKI:	You see, we can talk. We understand each other.
JULJA:	Father, no more secrets. This moment is sweet and fresh. It feels good to have a father. To talk, calmly …
KORZECKI:	You've rarely confided in me. You may find it beneficial. But only … only if you want to.
JULJA:	I want to open my heart. I feel peaceful and safe. So many times I've longed to lay my head on your breast, like a child, remember father …
KORZECKI:	Yes, yes … what happened?
JULJA:	I don't know, I stopped being a child, stopped approaching you like this …
KORZECKI:	I can always advise you …
JULJA:	What made us strangers? Perhaps we're both to blame. Never mind. I've been miserable father, so very unhappy.
KORZECKI:	As have we all, my child, in our straitened circumstances, but it could be different.
JULJA:	Promise you'll listen, quietly, like a father and friend. I don't want to beg forgiveness because I don't feel guilty. I want your support. I haven't betrayed or hurt anyone. Not even myself. I want you to listen and judge me with generosity of spirit, as wisdom judges the heart, and old age, life. My confession may at first seem bold, my happiness untamed. Because I'm not miserable any more, father. Does that please you?
KORZECKI:	Truly? It does please me. Very much.
JULJA:	Yes, I mean joy. The sort that's never repeated. Gained through suffering, struggle and tears. The tiniest creature has a right to light and warmth. It would be cruel to claim that a human being is entitled to nothing more than anxiety and loneliness.
KORZECKI:	So I've always maintained, child. Poverty, worry, shackles, millstones, one open grave.

All the Same (1912)

JULJA:	Yes, living in an open grave is terrible, hopeless …
KORZECKI:	Destitution, really … I'm glad you think that way … I had a sense …
JULJA:	You did?
KORZECKI:	Of something.
JULJA:	But you don't know everything. I love him. I know, you'd prefer to see me as his wife but …
KORZECKI:	It's unfortunate, luck of the draw …
JULJA:	I can't give him up, father … I don't want to!
KORZECKI:	I've thought about that too …
JULJA:	You did and …
KORZECKI:	Well … how can I … difficult for me to say.
JULJA:	Please, do.
KORZECKI:	You mustn't ask me …
JULJA:	I'll help you father. If I were to offer myself?
KORZECKI:	Well, there are times, ah … In the worst case … it does happen … but …
JULJA:	You wouldn't disown me?
KORZECKI:	Look, I cannot allow it … but if … you can insure against loss … it's up to you … a woman can become a need, a habit … that's sometimes stronger than convention … a woman can achieve a lot, living with a man, day to day, minor details … with a steady, mild approach, meeting his needs … but you have to be safe … state the matter clearly … terms.
JULJA:	Father, I'm afraid to hear you say that …
KORZECKI:	I can't let my guard down … it would look as if I … you mustn't ask me … The most I can do …
JULJA:	Is what?
KORZECKI:	Well, look through my fingers, turn a blind eye …
JULJA:	Father, that's not what I was thinking …
KORZECKI:	I know you said that if … of course it needn't come to that.
JULJA:	But if it did … if it did …
KORZECKI:	One has to be pragmatic. I won't live forever, I won't leave a fortune, life for a single woman is hard and sooner or later … in our circumstances, who are you likely to get? … At least I'd see you in safe hands …
JULJA:	Father, you don't understand … I can't believe I'm hearing this.
KORZECKI:	Then tell me, child, tell me …
JULJA:	I don't know any more … I can't know, I'm lost.
KORZECKI:	Of course, the first word …

JULJA:	I would do things differently, father … *(Enter STANISŁAW from the right, in a coat and holding a hat)*

Scene Eight

JULJA, KORZECKI, STANISŁAW

STANISŁAW:	*(In the doorway)* Oh, sorry, I'm interrupting … I only …
JULJA:	Come in, please …
STANISŁAW:	Just passing through. On my way out.
JULJA:	It wasn't private, any of it.
STANISŁAW:	Count me out. I'm going. Puff of smoke.
JULJA:	Stach, please, be open. Why do you always talk like that? Puff of smoke?
STANISŁAW:	I know my place, in every space …
JULJA:	Such bitterness, antagonism, towards everyone, including me? Why?
STANISŁAW:	Antagonism? Towards you, miss? What makes you …
JULJA:	So formal. We grew up together; we live under the same roof. I see no reason …
STANISŁAW:	*(Evasively)* Reason … reason …
JULJA:	Did I ever say a bad word to you?
STANISŁAW:	Bad word? No.
JULJA:	Upset you in some way? If I have, believe me, it was unintentional … And I apologize, I ask your forgiveness.
STANISŁAW:	*(Confused)* You apologize, forgiveness? But I … I …
JULJA:	Let's shake hands …
STANISŁAW:	But I didn't … I was never angry …
JULJA:	That's exactly why. And let it be like it used to.
KORZECKI:	Well, give her your hand. She's being kind.
JULJA:	Are you withholding your hand?
STANISŁAW:	What do you care …
JULJA:	Right now I really need to be surrounded by generous hearts and faces … Sometimes I feel I'm making one mistake after another. Bound by terrible uncertainty. I need it so much … Right this moment … you've no idea …
STANISŁAW:	Who am I to …
KORZECKI:	*(Impatiently)* Don't be difficult.
STANISŁAW:	I'm not. I know what I am and you, Julja, know that as well. Or maybe you don't. Good bye, I have to …

All the Same (1912)

JULJA:	Don't leave now, like this …
STANISŁAW:	What's the fuss about shaking hands? You're not doing anyone a favour.
JULJA:	It's not a favour. I don't want favours either!
KORZECKI:	It's not a favour. Stach, I ask you.
STANISŁAW:	Don't look at me like that. Do I see pity? I can't stand it!
KORZECKI:	Lunatic! Deranged boy! Are you worth it? Go on tell me!
STANISŁAW:	No, I am not worth it. Thanks for the reminder.
KORZECKI:	Well, that's not what I …
STANISŁAW:	Alright then. Better be straight. Why say or think otherwise.
JULJA:	You're looking for thoughts that no one has.
STANISŁAW:	*(Harshly)* They're entirely reasonable …
JULJA:	You're like one of the family …
STANISŁAW:	Why should I treat a strange family with respect when they showed none to me …
KORZECKI:	It's paranoia, clearly!
STANISŁAW:	I am a cast off!
JULJA:	Who has judged you? I don't want to judge, or condemn. No one, ever, anywhere!
STANISŁAW:	I am my own judge. I am guilty.
JULJA:	Don't mention guilt …
STANISŁAW:	I must. Filth is filth, guilt is guilt, and a stain is still itself, even if it's hidden …
JULJA:	Have you no generosity, no sympathy at all?
STANISŁAW:	Why do you need it?
JULJA:	If only you knew!
KORZECKI:	Don't be so naïve.
JULJA:	You no longer wish me well?
STANISŁAW:	It's precisely because I honour and respect you …
JULJA:	No, no, just be kind. Don't hold it against me, don't condemn me …
STANISŁAW:	Why would I dare, me, why would I …
JULJA:	Do you wish me joy?
STANISŁAW:	*(Quietly)* Yes …
JULJA:	I know what you felt for me …
STANISŁAW:	Best left unsaid.
JULJA:	If you feel offended …
STANISŁAW:	No. I'm perfectly aware I had no right …
JULJA:	It's not about rights … If you'd seen me happy …
STANISŁAW:	Go ahead.
JULJA:	Swear you'll never think ill of me …

STANISŁAW:	You can be sure of that …
JULJA:	You won't think ill of me, whatever happens … Whatever may occur?
STANISŁAW:	Whatever may occur?
JULJA:	You'll soon find out.
STANISŁAW:	I entertained no hopes. I knew that at some point you'd be someone's wife …
JULJA:	I know what you're thinking. I won't be a wife … I cannot be his wife, and yet …
STANISŁAW:	Julja!
JULJA:	Remember what you swore. Whatever happens.
STANISŁAW:	You're upset. Tears in your eyes. Tell me.
JULJA:	It's nothing, really. I can't now. You'll find out … *(Runs to her room)*

Scene Nine

KORZECKI, STANISŁAW

STANISŁAW:	*(Runs after her, wants to open the door)* She's locked herself in. What's going on? I don't understand.
KORZECKI:	Not everyone is made to be a confidant, dear boy.
STANISŁAW:	I won't be a wife … I cannot be … And yet … Is it possible … NO! Listen, sir – no!
KORZECKI:	Why are you shaking me like a fruit tree!
STANISŁAW:	She can't have said that. I misunderstood.
KORZECKI:	She said what she said. You heard.
STANISŁAW:	Whatever happens! What's going to happen? What has happened! I don't know anything.
KORZECKI:	You think someone's going to raise an alarm?
STANISŁAW:	That wasn't her talking! It was you speaking through her! Your whispering!
KORZECKI:	Stop yelling! You're off again?
STANISŁAW:	It can't be true! Him! Him!
KORZECKI:	Well not the pope.
STANISŁAW:	Him … 'whatever happens' … Tell me, you know …
KORZECKI:	Know what? Domestic tragedy. To understand, you need a heart, knowledge of the world, of life …
STANISŁAW:	She loves him?
KORZECKI:	It's mutual.

All the Same (1912)

STANISŁAW:	No, no! She has succumbed to you, your persuasion! Whispering! She's doing it for you, a sacrifice!
KORZECKI:	Stop it or I'll leave!
STANISŁAW:	You will stay. Not one step. Unhappy girl!
KORZECKI:	Believe me, she loves him and she is happy.
STANISŁAW:	It's eminently clear.
KORZECKI:	You have to know women, dear boy. Different beings. More idealistic. They don't need much. They're content with feeling. They survive on misty mornings, rainbows, fantasy, in all areas …
STANISŁAW:	Nonsense. I can't comprehend. 'You won't think ill of me.'
KORZECKI:	Because there's nothing to think ill of.
STANISŁAW:	Julja does not have her head in the clouds …
KORZECKI:	Platonic love, you see? There's your solution. My wife, for instance? I'm understanding. Years have passed, she became a mother, and still she nurtures a former love. Inner life. Different world.
STANISŁAW:	Don't compare Julja …
KORZECKI:	Why not? Mother and daughter! Heredity.
STANISŁAW:	The rubbish in your head.
KORZECKI:	What do you know about my head …
STANISŁAW:	It's good at forward-planning.
KORZECKI:	Don't rub my nose in it! I know what I think. I look at things clearly, as they are …
STANISŁAW:	*(Slowly)* Isn't your forward-planning …
KORZECKI:	What?
STANISŁAW:	… in evidence here as well?
KORZECKI:	God save us! You heard. She said. Not remotely.
STANISŁAW:	Look me in the eye, old man!
KORZECKI:	What is this? An enquiry?
STANISŁAW:	Supposing it is?
KORZECKI:	And here's the judge!
STANISŁAW:	Summoned by the devil, maybe, but yes!
KORZECKI:	Go back to him then!
STANISŁAW:	Don't insult him, old man! I wasn't born yesterday. I can see and hear.
KORZECKI:	You've made your own bed.
STANISŁAW:	Frankly I think we've shared one.
KORZECKI:	Don't test my patience.
STANISŁAW:	A light has finally come on – in *my* head.
KORZECKI:	Thank God, you numbskull.
STANISŁAW:	Enough! I think you were looking for a woman to keep things in order, but a man would do just as well.

KORZECKI:	Meaning?
STANISŁAW:	With a great big key.
KORZECKI:	Are you joking?
STANISŁAW:	You might find yourself under lock and key.
KORZECKI:	How funny. Ha ha.
STANISŁAW:	Don't make light of it, there's no room for humour. Listen and take note. Don't play the hunter; you may miss your mark. That would be dangerous. It's gross! Completely gross! I won't allow it!
KORZECKI:	I don't care what you think!
STANISŁAW:	You're mine. One word, you're behind bars.
KORZECKI:	You're ridiculous!
STANISŁAW:	Really?
KORZECKI:	Yes, yes, yes! Stupid little threats. Think you're special? You fool. Look here! *(Pulls out the cheque)*
STANISŁAW:	What's that?
KORZECKI:	You see? Order prevails.
STANISŁAW:	His signature!
KORZECKI:	Order prevails.
STANISŁAW:	She knows about this?
KORZECKI:	It's between him and me. Nobody else
STANISŁAW:	An arrangement, she knows nothing?
KORZECKI:	Man to man.
STANISŁAW:	Your schemes! Show me! *(He reaches towards him)*
KORZECKI:	Stay away! Don't touch!
STANISŁAW:	Give it here.
KORZECKI:	I will not.
STANISŁAW:	*(Grabs him around the waist with one arm and with the other reaches in his pocket)* Give it to me or I'll take it by force!
KORZECKI:	Let go!
STANISŁAW:	*(Pulling papers out of his pocket)* Look, here it is.
KORZECKI:	Give me that.
STANISŁAW:	*(Looking through)* Wait.
KORZECKI:	Don't touch it. *(Wanting to tear it from him)*
STANISŁAW:	Your letter! Ha! Ha! A treasure! We've reached the source!
KORZECKI:	Take this but give that back!
STANISŁAW:	Never! Never! A treasure! Now I understand! A trade-off!
KORZECKI:	Have you gone mad! Give it back!
STANISŁAW:	No, no, no!
KORZECKI:	Surely you don't want a fight.
STANISŁAW:	Have a go!

All the Same (1912)

KORZECKI:	It's mine!
STANISŁAW:	It's ours!
KORZECKI:	Day light robbery!
STANISŁAW:	Hands up! A trade-off, filth, shit, you criminal! Now I know!
KORZECKI:	Give it back!
STANISŁAW:	Disgusting! Impossible! This can't happen! It won't. At any cost!
KORZECKI:	For the last time …
STANISŁAW:	I'll save her! Now it's my turn! *(Grabs his hat and runs out)*
KORZECKI:	He's gone mad! Give it back! *(Also grabs his hat and runs out)*

Act 3

The same room. Late evening. It is dark in the room.

Scene One

KORZECKI, KORZECKA

KORZECKI:	*(Enters quickly, in a hat and coat. He lights a match. He opens the door to* STANISŁAW'*s room. Returns. He lights a lamp. Goes to his wife's room. Opens the door carefully)* You asleep?
KORZECKA:	*(From behind the door)* Not yet.
KORZECKI:	Stach hasn't been?
KORZECKI:	Haven't seen him.
KORZECKI:	Where's he got to!
KORZECKA:	Probably back soon.
KORZECKI:	I looked everywhere …
KORZECKA:	Why bother at this hour?
KORZECKI:	Never mind, never mind … Jula in her room?
KORZECKA:	Yes
KORZECKI:	Sleeping?
KORZECKA:	Doubt it. Only just gone ten.
KORZECKI:	Yes, ten. Good night.
KORZECKA:	Goodnight.
KORZECKI:	*(Paces uneasily about the room. He looks for a few moments at the entrance door, listening. Glances at his watch. Sits by the table, lights a cigar. Rises, paces feverishly once more, now and again clenching his fists)* Damn that lunatic! *(Stops short, all ears. Enter* STANISŁAW, *drunk)*

Scene Two

KORZECKI, STANISŁAW

KORZECKI:	At last.
STANISŁAW:	Here I am.
KORZECKI:	Lost your reason?
STANISŁAW:	More or less.
KORZECKI:	I went to all the drinking dens looking for you.
STANISŁAW:	Completely unnecessary.
KORZECKI:	Oh it was necessary. Give it back right now.
STANISŁAW:	What?
KORZECKI:	Spare me. You know exactly what.
STANISŁAW:	No.
KORZECKI:	I'll be forced …
STANISŁAW:	No you won't – can't force anyone to do anything. You'll choose to back down.
KORZECKI:	I will not!
STANISŁAW:	I said – gently and quietly.
KORZECKI:	You're winding me up.
STANISŁAW:	I have something that'll bring you round, tame you, like a wild bird. You'll eat from my hand.
KORZECKI:	Enough!
STANISŁAW:	Temper temper? I have sugar, sweet as can be.
KORZECKI:	I'll tear it from you.
STANISŁAW:	No. I'll give it myself, but slowly.
KORZECKI:	I'll take it by force *(He grabs him by the lapels)*
STANISŁAW:	*(Threateningly)* Lay off, old man! Not so rough. I don't like old men. I might do something bad; catch your ankle.
KORZECKI:	Where is it? What have you done with it?
STANISŁAW:	Whatever pleased me.
KORZECKI:	I'll go mad.
STANISŁAW:	You're welcome.
KORZECKI:	You didn't destroy it, surely.
STANISŁAW:	I surely did not.
KORZECKI:	Tore it up?
STANISŁAW:	Unlikely.
KORZECKI:	You're drunk!
STANISŁAW:	Could be.
KORZECKI:	You stink. You've been drinking.
STANISŁAW:	I paid for it.

All the Same (1912)

KORZECKI:	I don't give a damn who paid …
STANISŁAW:	Precisely.
KORZECKI:	But you are drunk. Maybe you lost it, drinking, or on the way.
STANISŁAW:	I did not.
KORZECKI:	Where is it then?
STANISŁAW:	In a certain pair of hands – more certain than yours.
KORZECKI:	Of course, you didn't give it to him, Stefan.
STANISŁAW:	No.
KORZECKI:	Or cash it. No one pays out at this time of night.
STANISŁAW:	I can.
KORZECKI:	It wasn't payment in kind, was it? You were drinking with empty pockets.
STANISŁAW:	I have credit, I said, I'll pay.
KORZECKI:	You and your stupid credit.
STANISŁAW:	Not stupid and not drunk. I drank but I'm not drunk. I drank, out of bitterness, for Dutch courage.
KORZECKI:	You'll confess, immediately.
STANISŁAW:	One step at a time.
KORZECKI:	In this state who knows what you may have done.
STANISŁAW:	No drama. All arranged. Best possible taste.
KORZECKI:	Then at least give back my letter. I must have my letter at least!
STANISŁAW:	*(Takes out the paper and shows it from a distance)* Wait, wait … Ah, there … You see? Leave it, stay back … Sweet little scrap. Pure white, like a dove, but covered in shit. Rustles gently, like a love letter, but it's pornography. And your other little slip won't fund it … I won't allow it …
KORZECKI:	*(Reaching out)* I hardly need permission …
STANISŁAW:	All arranged, I said.
KORZECKI:	Return the letter at least!
STANISŁAW:	I will.
KORZECKI:	Now … none of this hilarity.
STANISŁAW:	I will … but not to you …
KORZECKI:	Who then?
STANISŁAW:	The proper addressee.
KORZECKI:	Stop confusing the issue.
STANISŁAW:	Where's Julja?
KORZECKI:	What's she got to do with it?
STANISŁAW:	Where's Julja?
KORZECKI:	You should be ashamed of yourself.
STANISŁAW:	I want her to see me. She must.
KORZECKI:	She won't deign to speak with you.

STANISŁAW:	I can bet she will. I'll go, let her see, who I am, what I'm worth.
KORZECKI:	She'll chase you off.
STANISŁAW:	She'll chase someone.
KORZECKI:	Sleep it off first …
STANISŁAW:	Later.
KORZECKI:	Have some sense. Surely you wouldn't want to show her that piece of paper!
STANISŁAW:	Why not? I do in fact – both.
KORZECKI:	You're being stubborn because you're drunk.
STANISŁAW:	Because I'm responsible. I'll say a few words, that's all. I'll stand before her, hand her this paper, keep the other in reserve – as proof.
KORZECKI:	You won't do it.
STANISŁAW:	I will. I'll stand there and say the following – Here is your honour …
KORZECKI:	It's a measly scrap of paper …
STANISŁAW:	Not 'paper'. I will say – honour. A symbol. You see? She will, for sure. I'll say – here is your honour. It is in my hands … I give you back your honour …
KORZECKI:	You've no idea. You stole those papers. Stole them!
STANISŁAW:	I said it's been sorted. Don't worry. You won't lose one filthy grosz. I said I'd pay and I will.
KORZECKI:	You're a tramp, a layabout.
STANISŁAW:	Everything will become clear. Come here. I bought this piece of paper. I can do what the hell I like with it. All paid for. *(He empties in turn the pockets of his overcoat, waistcoat and trousers, pulling banknotes, gold and silver coins from them and tipping everything onto the table)* There you go … here … here …
KORZECKI:	Where? Where's this money from?
STANISŁAW:	That's my business … Take what's yours … This paper belongs to me … And the other … They've cost me very dear … very dear …
KORZECKI:	You were … You raided the safe!
STANISŁAW:	Whatever. Doesn't matter … She's been released, now she's free, she can return this bond.
KORZECKI:	I don't want this money. I want nothing to do with it. Take it, give me back my property.
STANISŁAW:	All gone. Take what you see.
KORZECKI:	Don't want to.
STANISŁAW:	Grab it while you can.
KORZECKI:	They'll think I …

STANISŁAW:	No they won't … I took … I'll say nothing … It's done …
KORZECKI:	But it's …
STANISŁAW:	I imbibed Dutch courage. No regrets. I do pity her. And won't let her be sold, oh no. She doesn't want that, she can't. You seduce, force, oppress her. You dress things up, gild them, mislead her … And she knows nothing about this scrap, or this one … Julja … who in my heart I … hold pure … She knows nothing of the price, its monetary form …
KORZECKI:	Oh be quiet!
STANISŁAW:	A housekeeper. 'It's honest work', she thinks, 'I'll resist him, his desire, even in his home' … But it doesn't ring true, she knows … She's afraid … 'You won't think ill of me, whatever happens …' You heard? She's afraid. She's succumbed, because she's ignorant … of this. She can't see what's been hidden …
KORZECKI:	The presumption!
STANISŁAW:	You've hidden it … Money! But I … nothing, just two words: your honour. I give you back your honour. Let her know what I'm worth. Let her see I'm not in your pocket …
KORZECKI:	You won't go in there!
STANISŁAW:	Let go!
KORZECKI:	Over my dead body!
STANISŁAW:	*(Struggling)* Get away!
KORZECKI:	I'll teach you, drunkard!
STANISŁAW:	Out of my way, granddad! Julja!
KORZECKI:	Shut your mouth!
STANISŁAW:	*(Tangled together in their struggle they bash into the door)* Julja! *(Enter JULJA)*

Scene Three

KORZECKI, STANISŁAW, JULJA

JULJA:	What's all the shouting?
KORZECKI:	*(Blocking STANISŁAW's way and trying to prevent him from reaching JULJA)* He's gone mad. Gone mad, I say.
STANISŁAW:	I was calling you. I want to talk, urgently.
JULJA:	Now?
KORZECKI:	Now's clearly not the time.
STANISŁAW:	No time like the present, if it's not too late.
KORZECKI:	And it is in fact too late.

STANISŁAW:	There's still time, luckily still time.
KORZECKI:	*(To JULJA)* He's drunk.
JULJA:	*(Accusatively)* Stach!
STANISŁAW:	I've been drinking, it's true. I had to. But I'm not drunk. I know what I'm doing. I'm fully aware …
JULJA:	How could you …
STANISŁAW:	I am completely sober. Absolutely.
JULJA:	I'm not accusing you …
STANISŁAW:	I need to talk to you now.
KORZECKI:	Child, don't let him, please, you can see …
STANISŁAW:	She sees nothing. Don't fool yourselves.
JULJA:	Alright, let's talk. But only when you've calmed down.
STANISŁAW:	*(Stopping her)* It has to be now, this minute. It's about you.
JULJA:	Me?
KORZECKI:	No, don't listen!
JULJA:	Why the intrusion, so sudden, so urgent?
STANISŁAW:	*(Commandingly)* I have to find out. Tell me, what you know, everything you know … The whole truth …
JULJA:	I don't understand …
STANISŁAW:	You must own up, about you and him …
JULJA:	Confess?
STANISŁAW:	Call it what you like. I must know, I need to know …
JULJA:	It's not what I want … under duress? I'm very surprised …
STANISŁAW:	Hold back. There's always room for more …
KORZECKI:	*(To JULJA)* I told you.
STANISŁAW:	I insist. Listen. I insist, I demand!
JULJA:	By what right!
STANISŁAW:	For your own good. My fear and concern, to counter filthy lies …
JULJA:	You came here to shout me down?
STANISŁAW:	They are my reasons and I won't back down, until I know.
JULJA:	I won't be forced.
STANISŁAW:	Exactly so … You are being forced.
JULJA:	You're wrong.
STANISŁAW:	It's about your honour.
JULJA:	It's about my honour and you're its defender?
STANISŁAW:	Yes, I am … tell me everything. You must.
JULJA:	*(With dignity)* I don't need defending. I know what I'm doing. Of my own free will and after my own thought. Accordingly, I can speak when I choose, not because of your over-stimulation and yelling in the middle of the night.

All the Same (1912)

STANISŁAW:	Don't you worry about my over-stimulation. It's evaporated. I can't let this happen.
JULJA:	I make decisions and take responsibility.
STANISŁAW:	You don't know what's happening!
JULJA:	I'm not being harmed.
STANISŁAW:	That's how it seems. You've succumbed to persuasion. But it's dirty. Believe me, dirty and disgusting. Maybe it's not true. Tell me it's not true.
JULJA:	I can't when you choose words like that.
STANISŁAW:	So prove me wrong.
JULJA:	I'm not involved in anything dirty.
STANISŁAW:	Let's speak clearly and openly … Have you and he … Stefan, why hide it?
KORZECKI:	It's jealousy! Petty revenge!
STANISŁAW:	No, no! The thought of you, clean, and sacred to me, it's …
JULJA:	I regard it as clean and it is … Nothing stands in the way of my self-respect.
STANISŁAW:	Now, when they're brainwashing you, lying, rubbing soap in your eye, gilding the shit, all innocence … But later. You don't know how you'll behave … They're deceiving you and you're deceiving yourself – you think filth and purity can be reconciled, that you'll resist, stand firm …
JULJA:	I act alone. We differ in our seeing and our naming. Life and love call to me, I follow, my honour is a personal thing. I remain faithful when life beckons, face the truth within me. My honour prevents me from fooling myself, hiding from my own feelings and the world. It instructs me not to be small-minded – I can't please everyone all of the time.
STANISŁAW:	Don't do it, step back! You'll regret it … Listen to me, I can't let it happen, I want to open your eyes … It'll only come to light later. I'm trying to create an obstacle. One day you'll thank me.
JULJA:	Thank you. But I don't act rashly. I've thought it through. It's good you're talking openly – no need for ambiguity. I want, I've chosen it. I didn't succumb to temptation or whispered persuasion. I succumbed to my own will.
STANISŁAW:	Or to a rush of blood. But the magic, satisfaction, will dissipate. Then, all the rest.
JULJA:	I know what's in store!
STANISŁAW:	You really want to be …
JULJA:	Go on …
STANISŁAW:	You do know what it's called?

JULJA:	I know, what it is, the name doesn't bother me. Say it ...
STANISŁAW:	You want to be his ...
JULJA:	Go on!
STANISŁAW:	Lover?
JULJA:	A dirty word on dirty lips.
STANISŁAW:	Commonly known as a concubine, mistress, and whore!
JULJA:	Quite horrible! I feel nothing but contempt for verbal abuse.
STANISŁAW:	Julja, you don't know. I knew a woman, just like you ...
JULJA:	Like me?
STANISŁAW:	I once had a mother I was ashamed of ... I don't know what it means to honour your mother, but I know shame and disgrace ... My mother was what you wish to become!
JULJA:	In that case, I don't know what your mother was.
STANISŁAW:	She sold herself!
JULJA:	I love!
STANISŁAW:	For exactly the same price.
JULJA:	That's not true! Love is all I know. It lifts me above this stupid name calling, your pathetic judgements.
STANISŁAW:	You think that today, you think it now ... Julja, I beg you, turn away! There's still time!
JULJA:	Absolutely not. The time has come. *(She runs towards the door of her parents' room, opens it and calls)* Mother, please join us, witness my words. *(Enter KORZECKA)*

Scene Four

KORZECKI, STANISŁAW, JULJA, KORZECKA

JULJA:	Listen mother, you as well. You should know. I am Stefan's lover.
KORZECKA:	What are you saying? What does it mean? Impossible ...
KORZECKI:	Julja, have you abandoned all reason ...
STANISŁAW:	It's not true!
KORZECKI:	Unconventional use of language. 'Lover' and 'lover'. Two meanings, two words.
JULJA:	I gave myself to him, yesterday, freely. I am his and will be so fully, without restriction, while the world looks on. You should know. That's all.
STANISŁAW:	Julja ... you ... you ... you ... could ...
JULJA:	You heard.

All the Same (1912)

KORZECKA:	Daughter, this is shocking, I can't believe it! You've sullied the name of love!
KORZECKI:	Don't you start moaning as well!
STANISŁAW:	You've given yourself, already. *(He succumbs to wild laughter)* Ha-ha-ha! What a fool I've been!
JULJA:	Your laughter is evil, grotesque. I will not be shamed. Look. I've owned up and I'm not blushing …
STANISŁAW:	All the same! And I … I didn't dare come near you. Thinking my touch would sully you. Pure, white, sacred. Unworthy, I thought. But we deserve each other. Brother and sister in filth. Let's shake on it, here's my hand.
JULJA:	Keep back. We've nothing in common. Let's go our separate ways.
STANISŁAW:	*(Laughing)* Because I can't afford you!
JULJA:	That's sick!
STANISŁAW:	I thought you were innocent, but this little mouse in its trap is just as cunning as the cats. All the same …
JULJA:	Silence!
STANISŁAW:	I was sacrificing myself for you, like a fool … my life and honour in exchange for your good name … Here's your bond. You were cheap, cheap. *(Passing the paper)*
KORZECKI:	Give it here!
STANISŁAW:	*(Pushing him away)* Like a fool I thought you were ignorant. You knew the score … Take it.
KORZECKI:	*(To JULJA)* Don't touch that.
STANISŁAW:	A father sold his daughter with her agreement … Here …
JULJA:	What's this? *(Takes the paper)*
KORZECKI:	Go to hell …
STANISŁAW:	And here's daddy's letter. *(Handing her the letter)* Who's nasty now!
KORZECKA:	Are you all mad?
JULJA:	For God's sake what is this!
STANISŁAW:	*(Laughing)* Your free will. At a discount price. Along with your beauty. Thought I didn't know? It wouldn't come out? Where's your pride now and your big words?
JULJA:	Father's letter! His signature!
KORZECKI:	*(Attempting to take back the papers)* Of course not, something else entirely.
JULJA:	*(Defending the papers)* No, no, they belong to me … They're mine … *(Hides them in the bodice of her dress)*
STANISŁAW:	That's it, defend your disgrace. Hide strips of paper next to your heart. Your father closed his eyes …

KORZECKI:	I wish you were struck dumb!
STANISŁAW:	… and your daughter consented.
ORZECKA:	What does it mean! What does it all mean!
STANISŁAW:	Proof, concrete proof.
JULJA:	Stop it! Enough, that's enough …
STANISŁAW:	It is – at last, consensus.
JULJA:	Where am I, what's happening, I can't see properly …
KORZECKI:	*(To JULJA, trying to pacify her)* It's his anger, revenge!
JULJA:	Don't touch me, don't touch me!
STANISŁAW:	God bless the family! And the auction!
KORZECKI:	*(To STANISŁAW)* Thief!
STANISŁAW:	Liar, pimp! You've treated her like chattel and debased me, you old criminal, my whole life. *(Throws himself at him and hits him in the face)*
KORZECKA:	*(Throws herself between them)* Don't hit him, for God's sake!
KORZECKI:	Don't ever raise your hand again!
JULJA:	Jesus Christ!

(STANISŁAW comes to his senses, takes a step back, covers his face with his hands)

KORZECKI:	He hit me …
KORZECKA:	Don't you have God in your heart? You struck an old man, a husband, father …
STANISŁAW:	*(With a startled cry)* Ah! *(Slowly, in shock)* Someone, somewhere, might treat my father like this … *(Seizing his head in his hands)* Have mercy! *(Runs out)*

Scene Five

KORZECKI, KORZECKA, JULJA

JULJA stands as if turned to stone.

KORZECKA:	Did he hit you hard?
KORZECKI:	Not really … It's nothing … *(To JULJA)* Give me those papers.
JULJA:	*(Reviving)* No, no, no! … He's gone! … This is terrible! It's monstrous! Ah!
KORZECKI:	Calm down! It's out of proportion … Was it really necessary?
JULJA:	Father, do you recognise this paper …
KORZECKI:	Yes, I do … but …
JULJA:	And you could do this!

All the Same (1912)

KORZECKI:	Child, don't take the tragic view. One day I'll explain everything …
JULJA:	No need, there's no need … I know too much already …
KORZECKI:	Best to forget this foolishness. I assure you, it's nothing.
JULJA:	Enough! Enough! Enough!
KORZECKI:	And collect yourself. Calm down …
KORZECKA:	What have I lived to witness!
KORZECKI:	*(To JULJA)* Things will look different tomorrow!
JULJA:	You could do this … and he … *(Suddenly)* He should be here … he must surely have his say … surely … Yes … *(She moves towards the exit)*
KORZECKI:	What's the rush?
JULJA:	I'll fetch him *(She runs out)*

Scene Six

KORZECKI, KORZECKA

KORZECKA:	Heavy day … my mind is swimming … it's all falling apart!
KORZECKI:	The trouble-maker – raised hell! Bloody fool! What's the use? Preacher, moralist, idiot! Turned the world upside down …
KORZECKA:	And in our family! Our good name! …
KORZECKI:	We don't need all this grief … It's over … We must think how to fix things … One stupid piece of paper and chaos. I could break his bones … He can …
KORZECKA:	Why now, just before bed, when we try to escape our daily woes …
KORZECKI:	Shut up woman. No one wants to listen. *(JULJA runs in, behind her STEFAN)*

Scene Seven

KORZECKI, KORZECKA, JULJA, STEFAN

STEFAN:	For God's sake, what's happened, why did you come? Don't speak. You look so confused. Is someone sick? An accident? You all look helpless … Julja … Julja … say something …
JULJA:	*(Fighting her breathlessness)* Wait, wait …
STEFAN:	You're out of breath …
KORZECKA:	Some water. *(She brings a glass of water)*

STEFAN:	*(To JULJA)* Speak, you're so pale … Don't prolong this. *(To KORZECKI)* What's happened?
KORZECKI:	Oh, the lunatic …
STEFAN:	Who?
KORZECKI:	Stanisław. I don't know any more, I'm losing my head …
KORZECKA:	Oh God! Oh God!
STEFAN:	Julja …
JULJA:	Don't call me Julja sir. I can't believe it. Yet still, here in my mind …
STEFAN:	I don't understand …
KORZECKI:	That sorry piece of paper …
JULJA:	*(Trying to stay calm)* Sir, one word. Do you recognise this?
STEFAN:	I do.
JULJA:	You signed it?
STEFAN:	Yes.
JULJA:	You knew what you were signing for?
STEFAN:	But …
JULJA:	You read this letter?
STEFAN:	Yes.
JULJA:	That'll do …
STEFAN:	Julja! Listen …
JULJA:	That's enough for me …
STEFAN:	These papers indicate nothing about you.
JULJA:	Yes, it's meaningless, whether you pay by cheque or cash. Of course it's all the same!
STEFAN:	None of this has any bearing on your person …
JULJA:	Of course. I've been bought already. It shouldn't matter …
STEFAN:	What are you saying! What's happening to you!
JULJA:	You can see I'm perfectly collected.
KORZECKI:	Yes, child. Keep calm. It will all come right …
JULJA:	Even without me. *(To STEFAN)* Did you both arrange that day as well, our day? A set up?
STEFAN:	Julja! What a thought! I beg you …
JULJA:	You must've had a discussion that focused on buying and selling, including details of time and place …
STEFAN:	You're really hurting me Julja. I don't recognize you.
JULJA:	You never asked of course if I wanted to sell myself … that might have been decent …
KORZECKI:	But child …
JULJA:	*(With a weak smile through her tears)* Naturally, I wanted to give myself …

All the Same (1912)

STEFAN: Julja! You're hurting me. How can I speak with you? If I'm guilty of something, it certainly doesn't merit being spoken to in this way.

JULJA: Oh, I forgot, my words offend decency – you respect that so much, you wanted to spare me, make me your housekeeper – have your cake and eat it … I now understand what I couldn't believe …

KORZECKI: Explain it to her please …

JULJA: I also understand, father that you were happy to look on through your fingers, if I insured against loss. Things would have come right, without any fuss … All stitched up on my behalf … Only I did want to give myself freely …

STEFAN: That's what happened, Julja.

KORZECKI: It did, child. Hard to accept. It goes that way sometimes. You must come to terms. His ravings change nothing … It did happen. That's that.

JULJA: They have. Everything has changed, though how I'm not sure …

STEFAN: You gave yourself freely …

JULJA: Really? You'd like us both to believe that? How good of you. I should be grateful. I was sold as a package, after all.

STEFAN: Julja, perhaps I made mistakes, but not in the way you suggest. If I'd known you'd judge …

JULJA: You would have been more careful. But you were anyway. It happened without me, right, cloak and dagger …

STEFAN: I hesitated more than once, believe me …

JULJA: About whether to buy me?

STEFAN: *(Accusatively)* Don't use that word …

JULJA: There are others. What's one little word? And what's the problem? These things happen … It's hardly a disgrace … *(Laughing)* I believed in my strength, rebellion, sacrifice, struggle! … How straightforward. Together in secret, you wove a web. And all the while the fly believed it was her heart at work. I was proud, to be free and bold, I went against the grain … And here, a pact … behind my back …

STEFAN: *(With pain)* You wrongly accuse me of playing a part!

KORZECKI: Stop this. What's done is done.

JULJA: Never mind … All the same … I gave myself to you … That's the thing … All the same, but not quite …

STEFAN: What can I say in my defense?

JULJA: Self-defense becomes handy when things are just as they appear … one shouldn't really play dirty and then own up. Appearances must be defended. Damage limitation … But this paper! *(In an*

	outburst of despairing anger) You've disgraced me, deceived me! Spat on my purest thoughts, toyed with me! What's it to you, sir – one lover more, or less! And cheap at the price! All eventualities fully covered.
STEFAN:	I accept all possible consequences!
JULJA:	(*Shaking the letter*) And here's the proof … Money! Shame! Filth! I felt proud, clean and pure …
STEFAN:	Julja, listen to my love …
KORZECKI:	Exactly …
STEFAN:	Have your feelings changed?
JULJA:	(*In a muffled voice*) It's only now that I feel shame, or guilt. The price of physical love …
STEFAN:	You denigrate our love and yourself.
KORZECKA:	Love is untouchable.
KORZECKI:	Shut up!
KORZECKA:	I cannot remain impartial. You are guilty!
KORZECKI:	Me?
KORZECKA:	Didn't you treat her like a whore? And didn't I warn you?
JULJA:	You warned him?
KORZECKA:	I live with this man! (*She weeps*)
JULJA:	(*Numbly*) Increasingly bleak. Like my own thoughts. Love is so much more than sacrifice and freedom … Yesterday, I didn't feel this way. (*In a whisper*) Today for the first time nakedness is impure. Alongside wonder and pleasure, there is lust – hot, hungry, breathless – and the rest is lies!
STEFAN:	Julja, you unjustly accuse me of deception.
JULJA:	Very good. (*With a bitter smile*) As a respectable man, you had to secure your own delusion. That way you're more likely to get a better class of whore. As for a young girl, you have to build bridges – it's her first time – ha! Ha!
STEFAN:	Julja! I feel terrible but if you could see my heart, you'd spare these bitter words.
KORZECKI:	Stop, child. Control yourself.
JULJA:	(*With sad mockery*) Father, with his soft heart. I was surprised, you didn't rage, scold, condemn me, curse your wayward daughter. It suited you to forgive … (*Losing control*) How disgusting! I'm choking, choking on this shit! (*She runs to the window, opens it rapidly*)
STEFAN:	Julja, how to convince you, explain?
JULJA:	Why bother? You've made your purchase.
STEFAN:	That word was never uttered.

All the Same (1912)

JULJA:	Keep it down. Even whispered, it's shameful. Best to say nothing. A few gestures, in the dark, hand to hand, like a bribe.
STEFAN:	I didn't set out to trick anyone!
JULJA:	And how did you phrase it? *(With disgust)* Chattel! A piece of meat!
STEFAN:	For God's sake listen. I curse the moment I signed that miserable paper. This morning.
JULJA:	It may as well have been yesterday! No! I do believe you didn't want to spoil that.
STEFAN:	Julja, your view of me! I swear …
JULJA:	Only today? It might be best! Goods should be examined prior to payment! You can't buy a cat in a bag! *(She throws the paper under KORZECKI's feet with disgust)* Take it, take it! It's yours! Yours! *(STEFAN a gesture of helplessness; KORZECKI takes an automatic step forward, but stops himself, uncertain; JULJA involuntarily grabs KORZECKI by the hand and holds him)* Don't be afraid, father … Let's leave it … I'll strike a bargain … No need for any housekeeping … We'll be so good, no one will ever know … Cash only, just to be safe … And no paper trail! … The first time was the hardest … Now I can sell myself … *(She bursts into spasmodic laughter)*
STEFAN:	Julja!
KORZECKI:	Be reasonable! *(He grasps her by the shoulders)*
JULJA:	*(Tears herself away)* Let go of me! *(She runs towards the door)*
KORZECKI:	*(Following her)* Where are you going? Where?
JULJA:	*(In the doorway)* Onto the street! Onto the street! *(She runs out)*
KORZECKI:	*(To STEFAN)* Go after her! *(STEFAN seizes his coat and runs out; KORZECKI follows him. Shouting beyond the door)*
KORZECKA:	*(Opens the door, turns suddenly, shields her eyes)* Oh Jesus! Through the window! Oh! *(Curtain falls)*

www.ingramcontent.com/pod-product-compliance
Ingram Content Group UK Ltd.
Pitfield, Milton Keynes, MK11 3LW, UK
UKHW050522150426
5217IPUK00026B/1758